A More Merciful God

Truth is Older than Tradition

Scott S. McAliley

Crickets Publishing LLC

Scott McAliley / Crickets Publishing LLC

www.cricketspublishing.com

scott@cricketspublishing.com

www.amoremercifulgod.com

A More Merciful God: Truth is Older than Tradition/Scott McAliley -- 1st ed.
ISBN 978-1-7323429-0-3

For my wife and children, praying you always grow in the knowledge of how merciful the Lord is and how very much He loves you.

Interior artwork courtesy of my wife and children. Thank You!

Special thanks to Scott Smith for help with the websites related to this study, help with the cover art, and overall encouraging me to finish something.

Thank you to my wife and family for bearing with me during the last decade as I agonized over whether to pursue the writing of this study, and for your patience during the times I was tunnel-visioned on it.

And thank you to the many people who let me talk their ears off about this matter as I was working out my own position on it in those early years of discovery.

Bible Versions used and their abbreviations

(WEB) World English Bible
(ESV) English Standard Version
(LITV) Literal Translation of the Holy Bible
(NIV) The 2011 New International Version
(KJV) 1769 King James Version
(BBE) 1965 Bible in Basic English
(DRB) 1899 Douay-Rheims Bible
(Darby) 1889 Darby Bible
(ALT) Analytical Literal Translation
(Webster) Webster Common Version
(YLT) 1898 Young's Literal Translation
1587 Geneva Bible
The New English Bible with Apocrypha - Oxford/Cambridge

Table of Contents

Preface

If God isn't good, there's no hope; and if we need anything, it's hope. Without it we're lost. And most of us have probably at times placed our hopes in the things of this world more than we should, to ultimately end up feeling somewhat empty. We need to hope in something bigger than and beyond this life.

For those of us who have accepted the Bible as truth, and whose hope is in the God of Scripture, just exactly Who the God of Scripture is becomes very important. Jesus said to love God with all our heart, mind, soul, and strength. I've found this difficult at times, for many reasons, and it's often my own issues that interfere with following Jesus's command. But another major hindrance to an all-out heavenward love is simply some of the attributes and concepts of God which have become part of Christian tradition, with virtually no Scriptural support. For me personally, believing that God is wholly merciful to all His creation is an integral part of loving Him. Yet some of the doctrines which have become part of mainstream Christianity make believing in a merciful God almost impossible, unless we push these teachings someplace out of mind, as I suspect many Christians do.

The traditional Christian doctrine of judgment tells us that all who reject Christ will suffer conscious punishment in Hell for all eternity. This is, and for centuries has been the predominant stance of mainstream Christianity. But should it be? I'm a

Christian, and yet found myself struggling with the ramifications of the doctrine for years, as much in terms of the light it paints our Merciful Creator in, as in what it means for individuals. As I suspect so many others do, I found my own ways to handle the doctrine, inadequate as they were, and generally put as little thought into it as I could. But a number of years ago, while trying to answer a question about hell for a friend, I dug in a little deeper, and some promising finds pushed me into an intense months-long study of the subject. It was quite revealing, and has continued for well over a decade now, as I've turned my study into the book you're holding. I was relieved and surprised to find that serious Bible study on the matter reveals a quite different fate than we're most often taught for those who never find salvation, and most importantly, reveals a far more merciful God, hence the title.

Rather than being tormented for all eternity, the lost will instead be taken out of existence altogether – not a soft punishment, or a fate to pursue, especially when an eternity at peace with your Maker is the alternative. But considering we were nothing before God brought us into being, I found it relieving to learn that the ultimate punishment for those who reject the pull of God is to be returned to what and where we were (or weren't, technically) before we were created. This is in stark contrast to the traditional idea of those who reject God burning "alive" for all eternity, with the first billion years not being even a drop in the bucket of timelessness.

In the pages that follow, I'll offer substantial scriptural evidence against the traditional position. There are about ten verses in the Bible which have been used to build and maintain the doctrine of the eternal conscious suffering of the lost, and I'll show alternative ways to understand those verses, without violating other themes and concepts from Scripture. But before we get to those, we'll find some serious scriptural problems with the idea that all humans, even without salvation, already possess an immortal soul that cannot be fully destroyed. This belief is really at the core of what appears to be error in final judgment doctrine. And we'll also see that from Genesis to Revelation, death, not eternal torment, has been the stated punishment for failing in faith by rejecting God.

This study did not convert me into an "annihilationist," not in the strictest sense at least. Let me be clear that physical death is not the final end of being for those without salvation, and yes, I do "believe in Hell."   However, with multiple Greek and Hebrew words all being translated into the same English word "hell," the question "Do you believe in Hell?" isn't as simple to answer as it might seem. But the lost will be raised to stand judgment prior to their destruction. And contrary to even many other non-traditionalists who believe in full soul sleep between the time of physical death and final judgment, there's a great deal of evidence this phase could be a conscious one, at least for some portion of that time period. So, while I consider myself a "conditionalist," in the sense that I believe immortality in any form is *conditional* upon whether or not one puts their faith in the one true living God, I have some differences with other conditionalists, especially with any who believe physical death is the final end of consciousness for the lost.

I've been greatly encouraged and enlightened by conditionalist writers like Edward Fudge and others, but have also at times felt like some of the more common conditionalist answers to the traditionalist arguments aren't the most sound or Scriptural. In the end however, I hope to take very little away from these who have gone before me in the fight against what appears to be a false doctrine within mainstream Christianity, and hope to add much more evidence to the non-traditional position. I wouldn't be writing at all if I didn't believe I had something to offer the conversation, and I hope you find this volume valuable in your search for truth on the matter.

I also cannot address the topic of judgment and ignore the growing movement toward Universalism. There are many names for this belief, but ultimately those who call themselves "Christian universalists" (CU) and similar designations all believe that at some point, after a time of initial judgment and punishment on those who do not accept God's salvation in this first physical life, there will be another opportunity for salvation and that none will be judged eternally - either with true death and cessation of being - or with eternal conscious punishment. I've read Rob Bell's book *Love Wins* promoting this universal redemption idea as well as Julie Ferwerda's more in-depth and very well written universalist book *Raising Hell*, which is the best modern attempt I've seen at promoting this doctrine.

While I believe that both of these authors are probably Christians who believe in the stance they take on this, I still find their doctrine wishful and their evidence lacking. In the end, I'm going to settle where the bulk of evidence is on our doctrines. For me personally, I found it in the middle ground, in between those who claim all mankind will be saved one day, and those who state that most of human creation will exist in conscious torment throughout eternity. And even though I could hold out a little hope that the universalists are correct, it's a dangerous doctrine to teach, in light of so much evidence that final judgment is in fact *final*.

Is this book for you?

If you've ever wondered how a God so loving that He would take the punishment for sin on our behalf could also be the same Person who causes or allows the eternal torment of billions who never find and accept His grace, then yes!

If you're not yet a believer, having never put your faith in Jesus Christ for salvation, and if your reasons for not taking that step are in any way related to questions you have about the nature and character of God that were raised because of the eternal suffering in Hell issue, then yes!

If you're a Christian teacher or preacher, but you've had your own questions about this issue, and have never been fully convinced by what you were taught in seminary or Bible college, yes!

Do you have a loved one you believe died without salvation, and you're sickened and heartbroken at the prospect that they might be in conscious torment for all eternity, then absolutely, yes. I won't offer you the false hope that a universalist will, but well before you've finished this book, you'll find the biblical truth that no one will be in torment forever, and all suffering will one day end.

And lastly, if you're strongly convinced that the traditional view of Hell is the correct position on what happens at final judgment, even to you I'd say yes!! Please take one look at another viewpoint and see if Scripture doesn't have something quite different to say on the matter than what we've traditionally been told.

Chapter content:

Chapter 1 lays a foundation for why the traditional doctrine needs to be challenged, but it begins with a plea for unity among Christians, even if we disagree on this or many other matters, as Christians always have. Love for God and one another should override all doctrinal differences. As important as I believe it is for this non-traditional view on judgment to be made known, believing correctly or incorrectly about what final judgment entails doesn't make one saved or lost. What we do with the knowledge of Christ does. Salvation is in Him alone, and those who believe this should be able to worship and serve together regardless of peripheral doctrinal differences. Among traditionalists, conditionalists, and Christian universalists, at least two of these groups are wrong about final judgment. But we all have this one thing in common: We believe that Jesus Christ was God with us on earth, and that He suffered and died to provide salvation to eternal life, demonstrating a love beyond compare. This should be enough to unite us regardless of our other views.

Chapter 2 may be the most important chapter. Here we'll deal with a pivotal question. It's become a foregone conclusion – not only by traditional Christians, but by those of many faiths and beliefs – that we are eternal beings from the moment of our conception. This needs to be challenged. This assumption is the basis that leads so many to the ultimate conclusion that the wages for sin is not true death – cessation of being – but some other sort of death that's actually life, only in misery, and separated from one's Maker.   Chapters 2 as well as 6 will strongly challenge this line of thinking with reasonable Biblical arguments.

In Chapter 3 we'll look at the very plain language of Scripture and see that it clearly states what will happen to the lost, and that it's consistent throughout Scripture.

In Chapter 4, we'll analyze the key passages of Scripture that have been misunderstood or misused for centuries to maintain the traditional view of Hell and immortality. Several of these passages, if taken out of context and not viewed in light of all Scripture, can certainly be interpreted to teach that the punishment for unbelief will be conscious and unending. Digging a little past the surface on these and, in some cases going beyond the English to the original languages of Scripture helped me understand these passages in ways that line up more logically with what the entire Bible teaches about final judgment, and add nothing to the traditionalist viewpoint on eternal conscious suffering.

I'm most surprised that I needed to write Chapter 5. It's an argument that death, true death: cessation of life and loss of being, is actually an incredibly severe punishment. But it did seem this chapter was necessary because many of today's teachers and preachers make this out to be almost a non-punishment, claiming that only an eternity of conscious punishment could be severe enough to pay the debt a sinner owes. And often, conditionalists like myself are accused of teaching a soft view of God. We'll find nothing soft about true final judgment.

In Chapter 6 we'll return to the Garden of Eden, and find that universal innate immortality isn't the only false concept that was created there.

In Chapter 7 we'll discuss the time period between physical death and final judgment. We'll look at the ideas of soul sleep, not only for the lost, but also the saved, and consider a number of viewpoints on this. There's a lot of disagreement about the matter, even among those who agree in general about final judgment. We'll take a look at all sides, and perhaps find some middle ground.

Chapter 8 will be a brief look at the universalist doctrine and unbiblical belief that all humanity will one day be saved.

Finally, Chapter 9 will be a look at the statements of several well-known traditionalists on the matter. We'll stretch back as far as 200 AD and analyze some of the early Church fathers' statements on the doctrine, and come forward to modern times as well.

If the reader believes my challenge to the traditional view of Hell and immortality will fall short of truth, or at least not offer any evidence they haven't seen before, then please come to that conclusion only after you read through the evidence I'll present. I've researched this carefully and been very fair to the traditionalist side, but can no longer go along with tradition after taking a careful look at it all. I appreciate your interest in this important subject and I pray this book is a blessing to you.

God Bless,

Scott McAliley

CHAPTER 1

Searching for a Merciful God

Eternal truths predate the traditions of men, and God is far more merciful than we've been traditionally taught. It's been argued that the most important thing about us is what we believe about God, and this would be difficult to dispute. The perception we have of our Creator affects everything else we do and think.

If we believe God is merciful, loving and good, we're far more likely to be merciful and loving ourselves, and more likely to be hopeful in matters of eternity, regardless of the difficulties of this life. And by the same token, if our view of a merciful Creator has become clouded for any reason, that's going to find its way into our thinking and actions as well. Unfortunately, the evidence this has happened is everywhere. If we're confused about the goodness of God, we're on a slippery slope that can lead to an overwhelming sense of hopelessness in this life, and a total loss of focus on eternity. Our concept of a merciful God has come under attack, and it was partially an inside job.

In the Christian faith, we speak a lot about how merciful God is. And absolutely, He is. We see the record of His grace and mercy displayed throughout the old and new testaments of Scripture, most specifically in what He did in His Son Jesus Christ through His atoning death on the cross. Of course, we experience His grace and mercy in our own daily lives as well, but then there's this elephant in the room which few want to talk about; it clouds and confuses something that shouldn't be confusing at all. It's destructive to our concept of a merciful God, and it's had detrimental and far-reaching effects. It's the doctrine of final judgment which states that those who never find or accept God's grace in salvation will be tormented literally and consciously for all eternity.

I've studied this carefully, and have bent over backwards to give the traditionalist side of the argument every benefit of the doubt, and at the end of it all, this is simply not what Scripture maintains. Billions of souls are not going to be in conscious torment for all eternity, yet this is what most Christian ministers and teachers have told us for approximately the last 1800 years. It's a bad doctrine, based on a small handful of misused and misinterpreted verses and a pagan concept that all souls come into existence immortal and indestructible.

Someone suffering with no relief, and for all eternity is a difficult concept to wrap your head around. But just imagine: After billions and billions of years in torment (if there were such a thing as "years" in timeless eternity) the suffering isn't even hours old. The lost soul is just getting started on their torment journey, which will have no end in time or eternity. After ten trillion years (whatever that meaningless number means), one is no closer to the end of their torment than the day it began. It's literally the most disturbing concept I've ever heard in my life, and I don't think we Christians really understand what maniacal horror we're accusing God of when we maintain and teach this doctrine — that a loving Creator is going to allow potentially billions of souls to endure such a thing.

God knows the end from the beginning. While we have the free will to make our decision for or against the Lord during our lifetimes, God knew before He made us what those decisions would be. According to Scripture, many more people are going to be ultimately lost than will be saved. So what's implied in the traditional position, but never stated, is that God brought into existence billions of souls who could not have possibly asked to be created, knowing that their ultimate "end" would be to exist in excruciating torment forever. This brings God's nature and character into question in ways it never should be because this concept is simply never established in Scripture. It's time to clear God's good name. Christians who haven't delved deeply on this subject can't possibly know just how much Scripture has to be violated, ignored, and twisted in order to maintain this tragic doctrine which has done untold damage.

Traditions have their place in our faith, and in life in general. But Jesus and the apostle Paul both warned about the traditions of men, implying that sometimes doctrinal practices begin inching away from truth. In Mark 7:13 Jesus said that man's traditions can even nullify the Word of God. And sometimes a traditional idea just needs to be challenged. That's what we'll do in the following pages.

I'll limit myself to just this one football analogy, but several years ago, the replay system became part of college football. It slows the game down a little, and some people hate it for that reason, but personally I was glad when it was instituted. Let's face it. While referees are critically important to sports, they're also human, and they get it wrong sometimes. And when a coach thinks there's a bad call that's affecting his team's ability to move forward, now he's able to issue a challenge, and the examination of the slow-motion footage begins. But here's the thing about it. The ruling on the field is king, and by rule, the replay evidence must be overwhelming in order to overturn the initial call on the field.

What I'm doing is sort of challenging for a replay in relation to this doctrine. If the evidence I'll offer isn't clear, then by all means, hold onto tradition. But let's rewind, slow it down, take it apart and see if it holds up to scrutiny. I believe you'll find the evidence for a non-traditional view of final judgment to be overwhelming, and the evidence for the traditional view of Eternal Hell almost non-existent.

When carefully examined, the traditional doctrine of Hell and immortality which virtually all mainstream Christian denominations hold to appears to have a number of problematic issues. Most notable, contrary to a consistent theme in Scripture, it maintains that every human, from conception, innately possesses immortality, and is going to exist consciously for all eternity, even those without salvation through Jesus Christ. Scripture on the other hand, maintains that Christ alone has immortality (1 Timothy 6:16) and grants it as a gift to those who place their faith in Him. Scripture tells us the ultimate punishment for rejecting salvation is death. Tradition redefines death to mean "eternal life, only separated from God or anything good." Before you finish Chapter 2, you may be shocked at the number of errors that must be accepted in order to maintain the traditional view.

I hope I haven't misled anyone to think they're about to read a book about a soft fluffy God who doesn't hold His creation accountable for their decisions. That's not where I'm going with this. So please note two things early on. First, I'm not challenging the biblical fact that those who have rejected the pull of God in this life will one day stand judgment. They will. While it stops well short of the sick and twisted idea of eternal conscious torment, what Scripture truly maintains will happen to lost souls is still horrific and sad, and it's more than enough incentive to prompt one to turn from unbelief and to the God who loves us, who is holding His hand out to us all day long. It's also incentive enough for those of us who do know the Lord, to continue sharing the saving knowledge of Christ so others can avoid judgment and the very loss of their soul.

We all have the almost unbelievable opportunity to gain immortality and live in peace for all eternity with our Maker who loves us. Short of suffering consciously forever with no reprieve, I can't imagine anything worse than standing there at final judgment and being rightfully accused of turning down God's offer of salvation, knowing I forfeited eternal life, and that my very existence and any memory of me is about to end. It's a horrible end for a life that had the potential for eternal bliss. Secondly, I'm also not challenging that the judgment God issues is eternal. It is. Once a soul is destroyed in final judgment, it's gone for all eternity. It is truly an everlasting punishment — eternal damnation, as Scripture states clearly, but it's not an ongoing process of conscious punishment that lasts throughout eternity. This concept is *never* established in the Bible.

So this is not another in a growing stack of books that are promoting the increasingly popular idea of Universalism which maintains that eventually everyone will be saved. However, what I'll demonstrate is that there's barely a shred of biblical evidence that a human soul can survive the final Lake of Fire judgment or will exist consciously into eternity. Those are the extremes, and the truth is in the middle ground. I should also note that I didn't take this change in my doctrine lightly as I began discovering the truth on this matter for myself years ago. I'm a don't-rock-the-boat kind of person generally, and it's highly uncomfortable for me to challenge a view held by so many people I respect. I absolutely wouldn't do it if the evidence weren't there.

There's another danger that comes along with the traditional view of conscious eternal suffering in Hell. Most Christians won't admit it, but because a punishment of everlasting torment seems so uncharacteristic of a God who we know in our hearts is a good God, deep down we actually doubt the truth of this doctrine. We teach it and share it because we think we're supposed to. But it's just so unfathomable that there's part of us that just can't believe it. Therefore, the danger is that if we think it's actually stated in Scripture, but we doubt it, then we're doubting Scripture itself. And that's another slippery slope. What parts of the Bible are true then, and what parts aren't? It's all true, the whole thing! But what's missing from Scripture is the concept that God is going to cause or allow the eternal suffering of those who reject Him. He's going to return them where they came from...nothingness. And while it's an incredibly harsh sentence, it also makes sense. This is God's world, and He makes the rules. It's only by faith that we can be saved. He's building a family of faithful believers who love Him because we recognize and appreciate the incredible sacrifice He made in order to give us eternal life.

There was a time we didn't exist. God gives us the first amazing gift by giving us life and being at all. He didn't have to make a single one of us. And then we're offered the immensely greater gift of eternal life if we'll put our faith, hope, and trust in Jesus as Savior. If we reject that, we're returned to the nothingness we were before God initially gave us our life. It's a stiff penalty, but it doesn't bring the nature and character of God into question the way the traditional doctrine of Eternal Hell does because even though the lost soul suffers the great loss of their own soul and the potential of eternal life, the one who rejects salvation is ultimately no worse off than where they began. They were nothingness to begin with.

I've heard it said many times by traditionalist pastors or teachers that "We all deserve Eternal Hell." Often they'll even personalize it and say things such as "I know I deserve to go to Hell for all eternity." I've never believed that or felt that way. I'm just being honest before the Lord and the reader. I do understand why they say this, however. We who are Christians understand that the Lord is holy and perfect and that we fall well short of that standard every moment, and it's only by His grace that there's even a shred of anything good about a single one of us, and it's only by His mercy that we can approach Him in any way. Therefore, those among us who believe in eternal Hell are going to say things like that.

But the truth is, we don't deserve to suffer for all eternity. I can look back on times in my life where I was avoiding God, rejecting the truths of the Christian faith, and living for temporary pleasures, and even if I had died in that state, I couldn't say that I deserved to suffer torment for all eternity. I deserved death. I deserved it then, and I still deserve death now – true and actual cessation of life and existence in any form. We all do. We didn't ask for life. We can't grant ourselves life. We can't earn life. And we therefore don't deserve life, in any form.

That we experience conscious existence at all is a pure act of God's grace. As noted, we were nothing before God dreamed us up and made us, and therefore we, by our own merit, can't deserve anything worse or better that our original state. We were non-existent in eternity past and what we deserve is to be returned to that state of nothingness. Any form of existence above that "is gravy," as they say. This life is a gift. Eternal life is an unimaginably more gracious gift, but those who willingly forfeit it deserve their first estate, nothingness, or "the blackest of darkness forever" as Jude phrased it in Jude 13.

Don't leave your church!

While I feel strongly about this important theological issue, I would never advise anyone to break fellowship with other believers over this, even if you begin to recognize the errors in the traditional position as you read through this study, or other peoples' works on the topic. In one sense this is a really big deal. It concerns the very nature and character of God, and as already noted, our perception of who God is affects us deeply. On the other hand, this is still a peripheral issue, not a salvation issue. As convinced as I am that the mainstream Christian church has misinterpreted a handful of verses and promoted a bad doctrine for centuries, I remain a part of the mainstream Christian church. In fact, during most of the years I studied and wrote on this, I was a Sunday School teacher and regular musician at a local church that constitutionally held to the traditional view of Hell and immortality, the very tradition I challenge. And before choosing to step down, I had served as an elder and a deacon there as well.

When my family and I left that church after over a decade, we didn't go find some cult or even fringe Christian denomination to fellowship with just so we might hear a "lighter" view of Hell and judgment taught from the pulpit. Instead my family began attending and eventually joined another church where the pastor, and I'm assuming, most members hold that same traditional view. And that's alright. In Christian unity, at least in terms of what should or shouldn't cause division, we can overlook all non-foundational doctrinal differences. It's okay to disagree sometimes. However, if there's a traditional doctrine which is disturbing to many, and can also be shown to have little Scriptural support, and if the opposition of it can be strongly supported, then at the very least it deserves a hearing. That's all I'm really asking for. This is not an attempt at a revolution or an attempt to divide believers, but I do hope it causes a little personal reformation and revival in the hearts of those like me, who will find truth and a sense of relief in a non-traditional view of final judgment which paints God in a far more merciful light.

Often during this study and writing project, I was so bothered by the thought of potentially just promoting one more thing for Christians to disagree over that I tried to put this book endeavor down several times. But it would never go away. And of course, that created a new mental struggle I had to deal with: Is this God not letting this go away because it's something He wants me to bring to the attention of others, or is Satan trying to confuse me and then confuse others, through me? You haven't read the evidence yet, so if you're a traditionalist on this matter, I already know which one you believe was happening. But ultimately, I decided that outside of Scripture, I couldn't answer that question with absolute assurance.

Every evidence I see in Scripture points to a non-traditional version of final judgment, while virtually every preacher and Bible teacher I listen to and respect holds the traditional view. This has created a mental battle in my head for years now.

As far as what I personally believe about judgment, I'm going with Scripture and what it appears to say, and not with men, and what they tell me Scripture says. However, whether or not to share my study publicly has been a more complicated internal debate.

I've heard more than one pastor say that in determining what God wants us to be missional about and step out in faith on, we'll never be more than about 80% sure of anything. And that makes sense — I suppose it wouldn't require faith if we were 100% sure on these things. I'm close to 80% sure I should be sharing, so I'm going with my heart, and with what appears to be the bulk of Scriptural evidence, and asking those who will read the material to determine for themselves if it's Bible truth or not. To me, it's clear.

We'll all have to answer to God one day for the things we do. If I've just completely missed the boat on this and looked at it all wrong, I'd rather answer for misinterpretation than for ignoring what has often over the years felt like a prompting from the Lord to challenge what appears to be a bad tradition. And on a personal level, I'll never forget how troubling the doctrine of eternal torment has been to me, and I continue to have people contact me from my website who are similarly troubled, and are thankful for the biblical challenge to tradition I've presented. One sweet woman from Scotland I corresponded with for a while told me that the traditional view of Hell had literally ruined her life. But she has come to peace with God through a new understanding of final judgment. I appreciated her honesty and her sensitivity to the matter.

It's easy to get busy with life and not think about the ramifications of what we teach and believe on this. If tradition is correct, essentially all of human activity and pursuit is to end with the vast majority of people suffering senselessly without relief for all eternity. That's heavy stuff to deal with. People who really sit and think about it instead of pushing it out of mind somewhere are going to be deeply and most likely negatively affected. Thank God the defense of such an idea is so weak, and the evidence for an alternative view is so Scripturally apparent. If this is something that has troubled you, I hope you'll find the same relief I and my friend from Scotland did as you do the research.

The Counterfeit Bill Analogy

Often pastors or Bible teachers will use the following illustration when speaking about recognizing false teachings. They talk about people who are being trained to recognize counterfeit money, and they point out that for long periods of time the students, rather than being exposed to counterfeit bills, are only exposed to original legitimate bills. Then after being entrenched in what is real, counterfeits are easy to recognize. We understand the illustration: Entrench yourself in truth so you can recognize what's false. But it seems that one unmentioned aspect of this analogy is that whatever you're exposed to first and longest (and more importantly, what you're told is right and real by those you trust) is what you will assume is legitimate and correct.   In other words, the students are assuming that the "true" bills they were handed to study are in fact legitimate.

So consider this — If the traditional view of Hell and immortality is wrong, but this is all we've been exposed to, and this is what we, as the Church, have handed down for centuries, then we're going to assume that anything contrary to that tradition is false and that those who oppose tradition are working against Christ.   I've been accused of this, and if the reader is one who currently holds the traditional view of judgment, he or she may be tempted to reject what I'm putting forward, simply because it's contrary to what you've always been told.   But what if someone sneaked in some counterfeit bills for those students to study?   I believe this is what happened, centuries ago.   This is where we've got to come back to the only source of truth, Scripture itself, and see if perhaps it's been twisted a little to support such a doctrine.

What about Universalism?

The traditional view of Hell is at one doctrinal extreme, an extreme that, according to many teachers and pastors, has God causing or allowing billions of people to be literally on fire for all eternity.   Many others have a slightly softer view and teach that there won't be literal fire involved, but the lost will instead be in the throws of mental misery, conscious, but separated from their Maker for all eternity.   Because of the extreme horror of either of these, many who can't accept such a concept escape to the other extreme: Universalism, which maintains that all human souls will ultimately be at peace in heaven for all eternity.

The Christianized versions go by terms such as Universal Reconciliation or Christian Universalism.   These have in common with general Universalism that all souls will ultimately be saved regardless of what they believe about God, but these Christian versions do maintain that it's only because of what

Jesus Christ did in giving His life on the cross that any are saved. However, they remove the individual faith factor – the one thing that Scripture maintains is required for salvation – us placing our faith, hope, and trust in Jesus and His atoning work on the cross of Calvary.

I wish I could tell you my study of Scripture revealed that everyone will be saved in eternity, but that's not what happened. Jesus said that few are taking the narrow path that leads to eternal life and many are taking the broad road that leads to destruction (oh, and notice, He said "destruction"...not eternal conscious suffering). Much like the traditional view of Hell, Universalism is depending on too few verses for support, and being overly creative with them. There's John 12:32 where Christ says that when He is lifted up, He will draw "all men" to Himself, and Colossians 1:20 which says God will reconcile "all things" to Himself. And there are a few other verses like these which on the surface could be taken to mean that all will be saved, but of course they could be understood to mean something very different...and should be.

Universalism has some new allies: Rob Bell is one of them. He, until a few years ago, was the popular pastor of the Mars Hill Church in Michigan, and in 2011 he released a book entitled *Love Wins, a book about heaven, hell, and the fate of every person who ever lived.* I'm not going to an extreme and calling Bell an enemy of the Gospel. I'm assuming he loves God, as he understands Him, and that he believes that it's only through Christ's atoning death that *any* can be saved, something all true Christians agree on. And he probably legitimately believes what he teaches about Universalism. But I have to wonder what drove him to this belief. After reading his position on the matter, I can't help but believe it was the horror of the traditional view.

Bell has an issue with tradition...as I do. But he errs on the other extreme, but by the same method, using too few verses, and even those, out of context, to maintain a doctrine. And at the core of both Traditionalism and Universalism is the idea that every soul created already has the innate ability and right to exist consciously for all eternity.   This assumption is the foundation for both errors, and we'll see strong evidence in chapters 2 and 6 that there's no sound biblical basis for this thinking, and we'll also see how this relates back to Satan's first lie to humanity – that we would not surely die.

Julie Ferwerda took the case for Universalism to another level in her book *Raising Hell*.   I found it well written – so well written in fact that if I had not already been studying this exact issue from a non-traditionalist viewpoint for years, I would have been tempted to buy in, being a person seeking to find answers to the unmerciful God of tradition.   I appreciate any Christian who makes an effort to combat the problematic teachings of eternal conscious torment in Hell.   But I find many errors in the universalist stance, and my plea to those who believe and teach it, is to consider the ramifications of teaching it, if they happen to be wrong.   If you, the universalist are not 100% convinced – if in your mind there's the slightest chance you're wrong, then stop.   You're damaging the concept that faith is the key to salvation, and while you probably mean well, it's potentially leading more people to destruction.

And I don't think any of us in this final judgment conversation, if we're honest, can say we're 100% sure about every aspect.   The Bible was written a long time ago, in various cultures all different from ours today, by multiple inspired (yet human) authors, in multiple languages, with there being some disagreement about and room for discussion over the definitions of many of the original Greek, Hebrew, and Aramaic words that make up the canon of Scripture.   So even as much as I've studied the doctrine of final judgment biblically, I'm not bold enough to believe there's no way I'm incorrect.   I wouldn't be writing if I thought this was likely, but I never rule out that I could've missed something somewhere.

In fact, I hope the universalists are correct.   But based on the research I've done, they're simply not.   Many people will ask a question such as the following: "But what about those who never hear the gospel?"   The universalist answer is the most comforting, although the least verifiable in Scripture. Their answer is that all will ultimately be saved, whether they've heard the gospel in this life or not. Unfortunately, that's not the biblical statement on the matter. But if that's your question, I offer what I believe are satisfying answers to that and similar thoughts in Chapter 8 where we'll address Universalism.

The strongest evidence is on the conditionalist third of this 3-way debate among Christians about how final judgment will play out. And concerning labels, I'd prefer to not identify with any label and instead simply say I'm a Bible believing Christian who has a scriptural understanding of final judgment. Having any label beyond "Christian" almost seems "culty." But it would make writing about this issue difficult if we didn't have terms for the different factions. So if cornered, I'd have to call myself a conditionalist. Both traditionalists and universalists believe all souls are immortal and are going to exist somewhere for all eternity (a view shared by virtually every other religion, which right there maybe should cause one to raise an eyebrow at tradition).

Conditionalists instead believe that being granted the attribute of immortality — the ability to go on living forever — is *conditional* upon putting one's faith in Christ, and this is what the Bible tells us. However this does not mean we believe the lost will simply vanish out of existence at the time of physical death. Some who hold a conditionalist view may believe this, but that would be more of an atheistic belief than any form of Christian position. Traditionalists, most conditionalists, and even many Christian universalists believe there will be judgment and consciousness in the afterlife. However, we vary widely on interpreting how the process will play out, in function and in duration, and certainly concerning what the end result will be.

If the preacher says it, then I believe it!
...almost always

Allow me to share a story from Scripture. One day Paul met with the other apostles and told them that going forward, their primary message to the unbelieving world should be that we all have an immortal soul and are going to live somewhere for all eternity, and that we need to decide where we want to spend our eternity. Okay, NO THAT DID NOT HAPPEN AT ALL! In fact, Paul never said anything like this. Jesus also never said anything of the sort. And no other writer of Scripture stated this either. No, we need to decide if we love the God of the Bible or this quickly degrading world. Do you want to live eternally, or be destroyed? Those are the things we need to decide. But the way I posed my fake bible story is how our eternal prospects are presented all the time in Christianity today.

A few years ago, during a church service, the pastor asked us to turn in our bibles to Hezekiah 3:4. Only a couple people began looking for the passage initially, and then more joined in when he added, "Well, is anyone going to look that up with me?" I'll save you the trouble if you don't already know; no, there's no book of Hezekiah. And his point was this: What *sounds* biblical and right isn't always. He and I disagreed about final judgment, but I appreciated the illustration. It helps my argument, because also notable from his demonstration, even if unintended, was that we assume we can trust what we hear from the pulpit. And the majority of the time, we can.

There are a number of terms and phrases in "Christianese" that sound biblical because many of us heard them all of our lives, but we're going to seriously challenge some of them in this volume.   Here's just a few you've probably heard thrown around: "Your immortal soul," "a Christ-less eternity," and "You've got to decide where you're going to spend your eternity." These force the assumption that we even *get* an eternity to spend somewhere, when, without salvation, we don't. This issue is at the center of this matter, and as often as these types of statements have been made, especially in our modern day, there's nowhere in Scripture where such a proposition is so clearly laid out. Jesus, nor Paul, nor any other writer of Scripture ever said "You're going to live somewhere for all eternity. You need to decide where." Why not? If it's true, and if that's now our primary argument for why people need to make a decision for Christ, why wasn't it phrased so simply when Scripture was being penned? And why didn't it begin with God's warning to Adam? Why did God tell him he would ultimately return to dust instead of warning him that if he disobeyed he was at risk of suffering in fire for all eternity? It's a fair question.

Somehow, against all biblical evidence, it's become a foregone conclusion that from our conception, we *have*, or we *are* an immortal soul and regardless of our faith, will exist consciously somewhere for all eternity, never mind what the Bible says in countless places on this matter. And while many teachers avoid the matter altogether, some bring it right down into the most commonly used terms: "Heaven or Hell. What's it gonna be?"

Please don't misunderstand. In one sense, Heaven and Hell *are* our only two choices. Many words are translated into the English word "hell," and these words sometimes describe the fate of the lost, but the different terms have different meanings, and it's unfortunate that the English language doesn't differentiate among them, but instead lumps them all into one term: "hell." And it's further unfortunate that we've allowed anything other than Scripture itself to define the terms and concepts. Two of the terms translated as "Hell," *Sheol* and *Hades*, refer to either the grave itself, the state of being physically dead, or the place, real or theoretical, where departed souls await their resurrection to life or to judgment. And Scripture is clear that both faithful and faithless souls would await there, at least prior to Christ's death and resurrection; whether that's waiting in a conscious or unconscious state is another debate, and we'll look at that in Chapter 7.

Another term that Jesus used often, *Gehenna*, is also translated as "Hell" in virtually all modern Bible versions, but this was a geographical location adjacent to the city of Jerusalem where refuse was burned. It was a waste dump. And Jesus used it figuratively for the destruction that awaits the faithless. But rather than leave the word which means "Valley of Hinnom" alone, translators and interpreters literally change the words of

Jesus and make it "Hell." It's difficult to believe this is just okay. It was a physical location, and even though He was most likely using it as a figurative type for final judgment, it's inexcusable to plug "Hell" in for a map location, yet almost every modern Bible version does this very thing.

And then concerning the faithful saved, our eternal lives will ultimately be with God in Heaven. So, while the terms can be confusing, Heaven and Hell are our only choices in some sense. But when the "Heaven or Hell" proposition is made, the assumption is that most people hold the traditional impression of "Hell" as a fiery eternal dungeon or fiery lake, and then sensible people are being asked, "Would you rather have this for all eternity, or eternal bliss?" That's a no-brainer, if we believe Scripture is true and if we believe it when we're told that this is what the Bible portrays about Hell. But scaring people into their "salvation" with unbiblical ideas can ultimately backfire. While our Dante's Inferno-like descriptions of a place that will burn forever with fire are the predominant picture people have of judgment, the effect is short-lived — probably because it borders on the unfathomable, and likely, many people simply don't believe it. In fact, many of the great revivals in America's past, at least the one's "fueled" by fiery teaching on eternal hell, ultimately fizzled back out into unbelief.

And what about the state of the church in North America right now? Did those "great awakenings" last? I believe "sick" and "in trouble" were just two of the terms that one of my favorite teaching pastors used to describe today's church, and he may well be correct. And what about all the efforts of traditionalists John Gill, Charles Spurgeon and others in 18th and 19th Century England? Did no one pick up the torch? Genuine Christianity in England has declined steadily since that time, and it's almost non-existent at this point. Without discounting personal sinfulness as a leading cause, is it possible that being taught an unmerciful God of fiery eternal torment has been a major contributing factor in our failure as Christians?

I'm not trying to take anything away from the many positive things these and other well-known past Christians have done, but it seems that everyone who maintains a doctrine that causes people to question God's mercy and goodness is damaging their own efforts to spread the good news of salvation. Wouldn't the truest revival and longest lasting awakening happen when the most merciful and loving God is revealed, assuming what we reveal could be supported with Scripture? We should be teaching a God we can both fear and love at the same time, without having to question His character and nature. And that's Who the Bible actually offers us.

We've seen that the traditional position on judgment has adopted a number of unbiblical phrases that get thrown around constantly in Christian teaching. Let's see what we've done with some common terms that we thought we knew the meaning of, and this will really demonstrate what shaky ground tradition is on. *Die* actually means "live forever in misery," *destruction* and *be destroyed* actually mean "indestructible and unable to be destroyed," and "will perish" means "will never fully perish." Further, the traditionalist position asks us to believe that when God indicated no sinner could endure His wrath, He actually meant they not only *could*, but *would* endure it for all eternity. And this is only the tip of the iceberg when it comes to the contradictions in terms involved in the traditional position.

I appreciate the pastors most who will tell you things like, "Check me on this. I could be wrong," or "Be a good Berean and do your own research" when they're making certain claims from Scripture that aren't blatantly obvious. And truly I appreciate all pastors and preachers who God has called to be His spokespeople for the difficult days we're in...even those I disagree with about this judgment issue. But being called and used of God doesn't mean any are beyond error. Paul called out Peter for error. Barnabas and Paul parted ways because of disagreements.

In our own day, one pastor will tell you that God has a specific plan for your life that you and only you can fulfill, and that if you don't do it, no one will and it will be left undone. Another will tell you that it doesn't work that way at all, and if you don't answer to those nudges from God and fulfill your calling, God has someone else waiting in the wings to take your place. Two of my favorite nationally known pastors are on the two opposite ends of this scenario, and they can't both be right. But I believe they're both wonderful Bible teachers, called by God.

In some ways, the judgment issue is just another peripheral doctrine that we're going to have to agree to disagree over, although in my opinion it's a really important one to get an alternative view of out there, so people can see there's another valid side to the issue – a fact which many people are completely unaware of.

There are many different ways to interpret the non-fundamentals of Scripture, and that's what I hope readers will keep in mind as they're reading this book. I'm not a heretic. Even if I'm wrong, it only comes down to this: I see final judgment taught one way in Scripture, and someone else sees it taught another way. And if I couldn't strongly support the position I'm putting forward, and if I didn't know the same doctrine that troubled me greatly also troubles many Christians and would-be Christians, I wouldn't bother to argue for it publicly. I would simply believe it in my own heart and mind. But I know it's a problem for a lot of people, and it's easy to demonstrate the flaws and holes in the traditional view, so it's impossible for me to hide the answers I've found any longer.

At the end of the day, Mainstream Christianity has portrayed God in a less than merciful light, and then has pointed us to Jesus's command to love this One with all our heart, mind, soul, and strength. This is difficult enough as we battle our own flesh. But it's almost impossible for many of us, when God is made out to be this one who requires the intense and eternal suffering of those who never find His grace.

Adding to the difficulty of conjuring up a love for this god are the Calvinist leanings of many of today's pastors and Bible teachers. If you don't know what I'm referring to, teachers that follow in the Calvinist line of thinking promote the idea that

God only gives the ability to respond to Him with saving faith to the relative few, making faith in God a literal impossibility for most of human creation. So, because He requires faith for salvation, but only gave it to the few, the logical conclusion for Calvinists is that God preordains most to destruction. And making the matter worse is that this "destruction" isn't even a merciful putting away from existence, but is redefined as eternal conscious suffering in a tormenting Hell, by virtually all mainstream Christian preachers and teachers. It is these teachings that disturbed me for years, and made my taking Christ seriously difficult, and my re-approach to Christianity slower than it should have been, after I went away from the faith for several years in my late teens and early 20s.

I began writing a book challenging Calvinism several years ago. I probably won't pursue its completion. Unlike the conditionalist view of final judgment which gets very little attention, Calvinism (Predestination) is often challenged, and there are a number of books already out there that handle the topic fairly well. But in case you're one who has fallen victim to the ideas it encompasses, just a brief defense of the Free Will position here before we center back on the primary topic:

People who hold to the Calvinist line of reasoning (even if they don't technically call themselves "Calvinists") seem to be hung up on a couple of concepts which they can't see past. The first is "predestination." This is a biblical concept, but it has nothing to do with us having free will or not. Romans 8:29 says in part "For those whom he (God) foreknew he also predestined to be conformed to the image of his Son." (ESV) The Calvinist reads this and thinks something like, "see, He planned ahead of time to predestine some of us to salvation and others, not so much." But that's not what the verse says. Unless we want to believe this "foreknowing" means that we somehow pre-existed with God before our conception (an idea which almost all of us would disagree with), then the words themselves explain everything perfectly. And notice that it is not to salvation that any are predestined. Somehow that fact often seems to be missed by the Calvinist.

There's something that God knows – something He "fore" knows. What is it? Leaning back on God's omniscience and foreknowledge answers so many doctrinal questions. God is growing a family of faithful believers to spend eternity with, and our having free will to put our faith in God, or put it in something else, is part of that process. But while we have free will in real time, God already knows what we're going to do with our faith. He knows all future. In that sense, He "foreknows" who are His. And as the verse clearly states, those whom He foreknew (those He knew would be his), He predestined (determined ahead of time) to conform them to the likeness of His Son. God doesn't predestine some to salvation, while others are just "out of luck." No, He knows who are going to be saved by faith, and for those, there's an incredible gift waiting. A common sense biblical understanding of predestination takes nothing away from the concept that we have free will. God simply already knows what we're going to do with our free will. Passages like this are a testament to God's omniscience, and shouldn't be mis-used to damage biblical and common sense concepts.

The other big hang-up for Calvinists is God's sovereignty. I don't understand why this seems to be such an issue with them, but it is. They believe that because God is sovereign, He simply cannot allow humanity to truly have free will, because it would infringe on His sovereignty. Even if unintentional, that's a jab at God's omnipotence. My short answer to this is that if God sovereignly chooses to give mankind free will, then that was His sovereign decision, so it therefore cannot be said that our free will violates His sovereignty. Allowing it was part of His sovereign determination. But even that's a bit of a small picture way of looking at it.

What's truly amazing is that God's plans ultimately go His way even with our free will intact because He is light years worth of chess moves ahead of us. He sees the future and works His plans in and around all of the good and bad things humanity will ever do. Someone will ask, "Why then are we told that most are going down the broad path to destruction and few going down the narrow path to life, since we're also told that God isn't willing that *any* should perish?" The Calvinist answer is that the "any" of that verse only means the relative few that God chose to save. The better understanding is that there are layers to God's will. He isn't willing that any perish, therefore He made a way so that none would have to. But His *ultimate* will and intention is to only grant salvation and eternal life to those who put their faith in Him. There's a distinction between *not being willing that any perish* and *creating a system where none will perish.* The former is biblical. The latter is not.

There are some passages of Scripture which Calvinists believe prove that God overrides our free will and pre-determines who can be saved. First, it needs to be said that pre-knowing who will come to Him for salvation, and pre-determining who is able to are very different things. But let's look specifically at a couple of passages. A common one a Calvinist will take you to is Malachi 3 where we find God pleading with the nation of Israel (Jacob) and stating that He loved Jacob, but hated Esau. First, this "hate" is more the idea of "rejection" than how we may humanly think of "hate." But again, God's foreknowledge solves the dilemma. God knew before these twins were born, and even before creation itself, that one day, the older, who should have been in the line of the Messiah, and the one to receive the birthright, would trade that birthright for a bowl of soup because his stomach was growling. Jacob, the younger (by only seconds most likely) desired the birthright, and valued the promises of God to their family. And this too God knew. God doesn't pick favorites, but His foreknowledge is undeniable, and that's where He operates from. He knows who will value the things of the Lord and knows who will put their hope in this fading world, and He works from that place of knowledge. But everyone, in real time, can choose for or against God.

Except for Pharaoh, right? This is another place a Calvinist will go. When Moses was sent by God to tell Pharaoh to let His people go out from Egypt, we find something interesting. Throughout the various plagues that God sends, sometimes we read that Pharaoh hardened his own heart and wouldn't let the people go, and other times the text says that God hardened Pharaoh's heart. And it's undeniable that back in Exodus 7:3 God says, "I will harden Pharaoh's heart," and in 7:4, "Pharaoh will not listen to you." So does He want Pharaoh to let them go, or doesn't He? If we read on in Chapter 7, we'll see that God's ultimate purpose was not only to free His people from the bondage of slavery, but to demonstrate who the real God of the universe was to the masses of people in Egypt who were lost and headed toward destruction. And this was stated again in Chapter 9. And many Egyptians did in fact leave Egypt with the Israelites; that's who the "mixed multitude" was. And Exodus 9:20-21 tells us that because of the plagues, already some in Egypt, even Pharaoh's servants, were beginning to fear the name of the Lord, while others were still unconvinced.

Ultimately, God was trying to save Gentile souls, and lots of them — not only free His own people from slavery. But what about poor Pharaoh? Isn't he just the victim here? Even though God's ultimate purpose was to demonstrate His power to Egypt so that as many as would, could be saved, Pharaoh was used as the pawn because he wasn't even given a choice — God hardened his heart so he couldn't exercise his "free will" and let the people go, right? Actually, he had already exercised his free will and denied God. There's no way that Pharaoh, the most powerful person in the world at the time wasn't well informed and fully aware of who the Israelites living in Goshen, just outside of Egypt, were. He knew they claimed to know the one true God, and their God wasn't Pharaoh, and he made them slaves and kept them in bondage. So Pharaoh rejected God in this way first. Also, while God did forewarn Moses that He was going to harden Pharaoh's heart, we don't see God actually doing that until Exodus 9:12, well into the series of plagues, and after Pharaoh himself had hardened his own heart multiple times, according to the text.

We could keep looking at these types of places in Scripture that Calvinists believe demonstrate our lack of free will, and keep finding that one has to read information into these passages that isn't there to come away with the conclusion that we don't have free will to accept or reject God. But let's look at it from a different angle. There are so many places where we could get these types of verifications of free will, but let's first go straight to the words of Jesus. In Revelation 2:20-21 where He's dictating to John the letters to the churches, He reprimands the church in Thyatira for tolerating a prophetess named Jezebel who is seducing His people into sexual immorality and eating food offered to idols. But what I find interesting is that in verse 21 Jesus says, "I gave her time to repent, but she refuses..." And then He goes on to tell of the trouble she's about to fall into because of refusing to repent. But wait. Why did He do that, if there was no way for her to repent?

And think about Cain and Abel for a minute. Cain saw that God approved of the offering Abel brought, but did not approve of his own, and was angry about this. We won't get into exactly what all that was about. There are a number of theories on why one was approved and the other not. But what I find interesting is that God came to Cain, even after He had disapproved of his offering, and asked, "If you do right, will you not be accepted?" Either God is practically mocking people, and acting in total futility when He attempts to get them to turn from their faithless acts, or these people truly have the free will to turn or not turn.

Denying we have free will makes a mockery of Scripture and really all of life. What exactly is the point of anything, if God has essentially done nothing more than create a movie in which we're playing a role, but in reality our lines are scripted and we only "feel like" we have free will? The entire Bible is screaming that we have free will, and God is pleading with us to exercise it toward Him, putting all our hope and trust in Him for eternal life. Picking only two of the countless evidences of this seems like a disservice to the topic, and there are so many other facets to the dismantling of Calvinism that we're not even getting into, but we need to move on. This isn't a book about the issues with Calvinism. But before we move on, I must say, regarding God's question to Cain, that "if" is the one word God doesn't need to speak to humanity if we don't have true free will.

Why would God imply that Cain would be just as accepted as Abel "if" he would do right, if in reality, there was no way for him to do right? Now, again, because God knows the whole future, He already knew that ultimately Cain was not going to do right, but was actually going to go totally off the deep end and commit the first murder. But that just proves even more that Cain had free will. Even though God knew what he would do, He still went out of his way to give him the opportunity to do right and be accepted. If Cain had no true ability to make a decision one way or the other, then truly God was doing nothing more than mocking him. I'm going to choose to believe that God doesn't lock people into being unable to act rightly, and then mock them for it. Is that fair enough?

Speaking of "if" being the one word that God shouldn't say if we don't have true free will, that was actually going to be the title of the book I'm probably not going to finish — *If: the one word God shouldn't use if we don't have free will*. Someone should steal that from me. Oh wait, they already did. Not really, but it's sort of a funny story. Years ago, when I was dug in on both my final judgment and anti-Calvinism studies, I was listening to a podcast of one of my favorite teaching pastors, Mark Batterson, and the sermon was about the importance of knowing where we stand on some of the peripheral doctrines of the faith, and he specifically mentioned the Calvinism/Predestination vs. Free Will controversy. But instead of share where he lands on the matter, he chose not to, and instead just emphasized the importance of knowing why you believe as you do, no matter which side you're on. I get that...to some degree. But I really wanted to know where he stood, and I also wished he would take a stand publicly for what he believes, although I think I understand now why he doesn't. These issues can be divisive, and for him to do the things that God has specifically called him to do, it's probably more productive to not publicly get into some of the peripheral issues.

But at the time, I just wanted to know where he was on it. He had indicated in that broadcast that he had been on both sides of that argument at various times in his Christian life. So I emailed him, and shared a lot of what I'd been finding in the way of challenging Calvinism, hoping that if he had swung to the Calvinism side, maybe I could help swing him back. I can't say this with absolute assurance, but I'm 99% sure I mentioned that I was working on a book about it, and about 90% sure that I told him my tentative title was "If." Well I never heard back, and I wasn't surprised. I can only imagine how busy he is, with multiple church locations and all the responsibilities he must have, and all of that on top of having family responsibilities as well. So I wasn't offended or shocked that he didn't respond. But then I'm in a bookstore in the Christian section a couple years ago and I see this black book with a huge white lowercase "if" right there on the cover, and who is it written by? Mark Batterson. Mark Batterson wrote a book called *If* and just a few years prior, I had emailed him and told him I was writing a book called *If*. What are the odds? Now don't get me wrong. First of all, his "if" book isn't even about Calvinism. Secondly, books can have the same title; it's not a violation. Thirdly, it's very likely he never even saw my e-mail, and it's a total coincidence. On the other hand, it's possible he read the e-mail, didn't respond for whatever reason, and the "if as a book title" concept just went into his subconscious. It doesn't matter. I really just find it funny and probably coincidental, and he'll always be one of my favorite pastors and authors. But for some reason, I never read that one. I've read five or six of his books, loved every one of them, but just haven't gotten around to *If* yet. Let's move forward...

While both of these teachings (Calvinism and eternal conscious suffering) are questionable and potentially destructive on their own, together they paint a picture of a god[*] who brings individuals into existence who could not have possibly asked to be born, requires the impossible from them, and then when they of course fail in faith, their punishment is to be tormented for all eternity. Further confusing is that many of those who promote these dual ideas say the reason God does it this way is that it

---

[*] lower case was on purpose, because this is not the One True Living God of Scripture

glorifies Him. What?? How? Yes, this is the elephant in the Sunday School room – the ugly side of our faith, which for the most part is just swept under the rug, but we need to hash these things out.

Us-centric instead of God-centric

God desires people to respond to Him in faith, and in fact it is *only* by faith that we can please Him according to the Bible, yet for centuries, the primary means enlisted by most preachers for drawing people to this loving God is the threat of suffering consciously for all eternity. It doesn't take a lot of faith to make that choice if you believe what you're being told – only a desire to not be on fire forever. And this is one of the detriments of the traditional view. It hinders the act of coming to God in loving faith and appreciation for His expression of love, and replaces it with "You better come to God because you need to decide where you want to spend 'your eternity'...in bliss, or on fire." It becomes more about saving our own neck than falling in love with God.

Jesus, God with us on earth, prayed to God the Father in heaven for those who rejected and mocked Him as He was dying on the cross, yet tradition would have us believe that He requires not the life of the one who rejects him, but rather his or her eternal torment? It just doesn't add up. This is not who God is, but this is the traditional view of Hell and immortality in a nutshell. And this paradoxical view, I believe, while drawing many in to get more answers, repulses many others and keeps them from the God who loves them. The scriptural truth of the divine judgment of those who reject the knowledge of God is scary enough without the threat of having to remain "alive," conscious and tormented throughout timeless eternity to regret the decisions one made against the one true God.

This is not a new teaching!

It might surprise some readers to know that Conditionalism is nothing new. Not only, after years of study, does it appear to be the consistent theme of Scripture, but throughout history many church leaders and even some church "fathers" have held a conditionalist stance. Even in our own day, the often quoted and well-respected Christian author and church planter, the late John Stot announced in 1988 that he was tentatively letting go of his belief in the traditional view of Hell, and stated that he believed the subject needed to be revisited by the mainstream. I hope that's what I'm offering with this book. And Stot is certainly not alone. I could offer a decent list of people who rejected the traditional view of eternal suffering, but even by only mentioning Stot, it's too close to doing something for which I'm critical of traditionalists, which is relying more on the opinions and findings of other humans to strengthen their arguments than on Scripture itself.

One multi-author book I read which set out to defend the traditional view of Hell, *Hell Under Fire*, was difficult to even push through because of the constant footnoting and references back to other men's writings and sayings, especially the other co-authors of that very book. I'd never read a book where on many pages, the footnote section on the lower half of the page was physically larger than the body of "new" content at the top...and the footnotes were even in a smaller font. So I'll spare the reader from much of that at all from this point on, and we'll simply look at what Scripture says on the matter, not what other people believe. But if one finds the philosophical or religious company they're in to be important, then you're not in bad company if you're a conditionalist. But you are in the extreme minority. The traditional view is widely held, and from what I'm seeing, is unfortunately only being combated semi-effectively by Universalism – which seems to be solving one problematic false doctrine with another problematic false doctrine. Today, we who reject the traditional view in favor of the conditionalist position — which should at least be considered an equally acceptable way to understand divine judgment — are spoken of as if we are fools or heretics with no Scripture to back our view. The opposite is true, and if you'll bear with this study, I believe you'll agree there's a better way to interpret final judgment — without violating Scripture.

Debating in Love

I'd like to briefly address the tone this book is written in. I've been putting down and picking up this writing project for over a decade, for reasons already partially explained. I've sat down to study and write in various different moods and modes over the years. Obviously the book has been edited, and the extremes of tone and mood have been eliminated. However, at times the reader may detect that I'm upset with a particular pastor, speaker or author who's made an attempt to defend the traditional view in a less than stellar way. Sometimes the reader may even pick up on some sarcasm, although most of that has been removed. The truth is, the traditional position on hell and immortality not only appears to be doctrinally incorrect, but because it is so disturbing to myself, and so many others, and because the defense of it is generally so poor, if I'm honest, I am upset — and I've let a little of that come through in the writing at times. Sometimes a person's argument is so weak or offensive, to highlight it in a dry, emotionless way seems less than genuine. I certainly could've altered my approach and let this book read like many scholarly works about doctrine - no first-person writing, etc. But this book and this topic are very personal to me. So while I believe you'll find the doctrinal study to be deep and meaningful, I wrote it from the perspective of being a real person, not a stuffed suit that doesn't have personal opinions or get upset when someone is making a weak case that brings the nature and character of God into question. And to be clear, I'm not upset with the general Christian population that holds the traditional view. Most haven't studied the doctrine. If I'm upset with any individuals, it would be those who have been exposed to excellent arguments from the conditionalist position, and instead of admitting it's perhaps at least a viable alternative way to view final judgment, instead it's stubbornly ignored and explained away.

The people I challenge have put their positions out into the public arena, and it's fair game, just as I've now put my own position out there as well, to be assessed, attacked...whatever may come. But what I want the reader to know is that if someone is out there defending the traditional view of hell, that tells me at least one thing: They're a believer in Christ. And I love and respect them as a brother or sister in Christ, and I appreciate that they share the gospel. But that doesn't get them off the hook if they're making other public statements that don't seem to line up with Scripture. If my method for calling someone out seems less than merciful in a book about how much more merciful God is than we've been told, then hold that against me personally, and not against the doctrinal stance on judgment which I'm putting forward. If my personal methods for going about this study and writing project are also less than stellar, then please look beyond my methods to the information itself and know that God is far more merciful than we've been told.

While I'm critical of the traditional view, and at times the people who put forward ideas that don't line up with Scripture (and more their methods than anything personal), in no way do I intend to bring into question any traditionalist individual's ministry as a whole. I've reaped a harvest of biblical knowledge and life-giving words from the numerous Bible teachers I listen to in person, on the radio, Internet, and television. But the vast majority of them hold a traditional view of judgment which I of course disagree with, and I believe they're doing damage to the gospel in this one area. This book is a plea for traditionalists to reconsider the matter, but it is not a slam on a single one of them as a minister of the gospel truth that salvation is in Jesus Christ alone.

I'm also not questioning the intelligence of any person who holds a traditional view. I'm familiar with the proof texts for the doctrine (all of which we'll address in Chapter 4 if not before), and I understand why many people hold this view. But I also understand just how strong tradition can be, and how much we desire to trust everything we hear from our pastors and teachers. And while I don't think this is a matter of intelligence at all, I do believe that many who hold a traditional view have never studied the topic deeply. And even those who do may be overlooking the obvious and simpler message of Scripture in favor of tradition.

Often traditionalists come at the study of judgment with the assumption that all souls are already eternal, and then try to make everything fit into that box, so they begin with a question like "So what will eternal Hell be like?" instead of a fairer question like "What does Scripture say will ultimately happen to those who reject God's offer of salvation?" James MacDonald has consistently been one of my favorite radio/internet/TV Bible teachers over the years, and I continue to listen to, be challenged by, and learn from him all the time. But on a broadcast of *Walk in the Word* a few years ago, he prefaced a short series on Hell by credentialing himself as having spent "an entire week" studying the topic. MacDonald has more Bible knowledge in his little finger than I ever will in my head, but after having been at my study of final judgment for years at that point, I couldn't help but be a little offended at the implication that a week of focused study prepared him to teach solidly on the matter. And it became quickly obvious during the three-message series that he, like most other traditionalists, approached the topic looking for "descriptions of Hell" rather than truly delving into bigger questions such as, "What is the fate of those who reject the pull of the Holy Spirit to come to Christ for salvation?"

And another note: Although MacDonald initially expressed doubt that those who claim to have had glimpses of the afterlife are legitimate, he later seemed to use some of these very accounts as evidence for his own conclusions about Hell. I don't put a lot of stock in peoples' accounts of going to Heaven or Hell and coming back to tell (and write books) about it. I'm not claiming there's no way this could happen. It's at least possible that God has given people in modern times glimpses of what the afterlife will look like, for both the saved and the lost. But there's no way to know who's being honest and who isn't, and they all have varying versions of Heaven and Hell.

I believe I've made this clear, but in case I didn't, I'm not denying that the lost will exist beyond this life. They will. The souls of those who reject salvation will not vaporize at physical death. But they will not exist after final judgment and into timeless eternity. Eternity is for the saved. But the lost will certainly experience *something* after death, and it's possible that some have been given a sneak peek into it. However, while personal accounts of near death experiences make interesting stories, they're impossible to verify. The only thing I'm going to base my doctrinal beliefs on are going to come straight from Scripture or undeniable personal experience.

I realize that asking people to "open their minds" to a new way of looking at a topic which they believe they're familiar enough with can be taken completely wrong. "Opening your mind" has a very "new age" connotation. But the fact is that coming at the topic with a lot of preconceived ideas is the first problem. If you already believe that all souls are eternal, and if you already believe there's a place where the lost will spend eternity, and just can't fathom that anything else could be the case, then you're going to have trouble reconciling actual biblical statements with statements of tradition you've heard from the pulpit.

Tradition tells us the lost will suffer for all eternity. Scripture tells us they will ultimately perish and become non-existent. Scripture tells us the total obliteration of the cities of Sodom and Gomorrah was an example of what will ultimately happen to the ungodly, but tradition tells us that unbelievers will get an asbestos-like body so they are able to survive and suffer in the Lake of Fire for all eternity. While many traditionalists tell us the lost will be on fire for all eternity, the Bible tells us that fire fully destroys all but the faithful. And then in Luke 16, the favorite proof text for traditionalists who believe the lost can and will exist on fire, we read of a lost man in Hades who says he is tormented, but curiously, by a single flame, not the fire that tradition tells us he's in. And when we dig a little, it becomes a fascinating study. Every time that singular flame appears in Scripture it's a reference to the reality and truth of

God Himself, not literal fire. This is expanded on in Chapter 4 where we address every well-known proof text for the traditional position.

I'm in total agreement with traditionalists that those who have rejected God will experience regret and suffering in the afterlife. It's the duration which I'm in disagreement over. Chapter 7 is a study of the intermediate state between physical death and final judgment. And the conscious suffering of the lost may be very brief, or it may be quite lengthy. There's room for debate. But whether it's short or long, that suffering will in fact end.

We could go on and on looking at these diametrically opposed concepts which are not sensibly reconcilable, and the strain to make them all work has created more problems and disagreement among traditionalists than it has solved. Even more unbelievable is that some modern day traditionalists somehow view all the biblical language about the lost being burnt up as chaff, thrown in a furnace of fire, consuming away like smoke, and being thrown into a lake of fire as only figurative language for a spatial separation from God, a separation which most traditionalists maintain was prefigured by Adam and Eve's expulsion from the garden. We'll find many problems with that theory and discover some real treasures as we carefully study through the Garden of Eden scene again in the following chapter. An open-minded and honest look at biblical judgment is sorely needed in Christianity, so yes, I'm asking the reader to open his or her mind. You will not be disappointed by the answers you find.

Christian Unity

Is this worth debating over? Christian unity is a major theme in the New Testament. We need to be very cautious about what we spend time outwardly disagreeing over. I have four children. Nothing makes me happier than when they are getting along and being sweet to one another, and little else bothers me more than when they are arguing or fighting with one another over insignificant matters. I imagine it's not too different with our Heavenly Father. I'm sure the divisions and arguments we have over petty (in the grand scheme) issues hurt the Lord. Mark Batterson (a traditionalist on this judgment matter as far as I can tell, but a wonderful teacher, author, and motivator) calls our wasted efforts and arguments over peripheral doctrines "sideways energy in the kingdom," and I agree with him. Christians often waste a lot of time and energy on issues we shouldn't. And Batterson might even consider this particular topic one to not hash out publicly; everyone has to determine for themselves where they draw the line on whether an issue is worthy of argument or not.

Here's where I personally draw the line: Does it bring into question the nature and character of God in a way that can affect a person's relationship with their Heavenly Father, or for those who have not yet made a decision for Christ, can it affect their comprehension of who God really is? If it doesn't, it should fall into the "let's not waste our time fighting over that" category.

I'm willing to talk about any subject in Scripture, but I'm personally not going to debate someone over certain issues — such as the young earth/old earth issue — not because it isn't important on some level. It is. But because it isn't an issue that concerns the character of God.

I'm also not going to argue with someone over when or if the rapture will occur. Again, not because it isn't an important topic, and not because I don't have my own strong opinion on the matter. I do, and I share it at times, and I'm planning a writing project now where I'll challenge some of our thinking in that area as well. But I'm not going to argue with anyone over it or break fellowship with other believers, because the timing of the rapture, like so many other doctrinal matters, doesn't directly concern our comprehension of our Maker. But the doctrine of judgment does. And Calvinist-like doctrines do as well.

So there are topics to hash out, and times to do such. And there's a precedent of believers bringing other believers back to truth when doctrinal problems arise, especially when it involves falling into the traditions of men. And if I'm wrong on these matters, I pray someone will show me the light and bring me back in line. But if I've found truth, I hope it finds many others. A devotion to unity shouldn't keep us from delving into difficult doctrinal questions, and we can certainly remain unified as believers in Christ even if we disagree over large issues.

Regardless of who's right and who's wrong on these non-essential doctrines, there is one God who loves us and saves us. As already noted, I've continued to attend a local church that maintains the traditional view of Hell, even though I disagree with the doctrine. What would be the alternative? Join an odd sect of Christianity that has a similar view of final judgment, but that adds strange things to Scripture? Stop going to church? We don't need any more separation. We need unity, and while it may appear that there's a form of unity on this issue already, because most mainstream Christians have a traditional view of Hell and immortality, the truth is, there's still no full unity on this topic, even among traditionalists.   There are as many different versions of Eternal Hell as there are people who believe in Eternal Hell.

Truth is older than tradition.

What I'm asking readers to do, especially those who teach, is take this one look into the matter and make sure you are holding the view, not with the most traditional support, but with the most Scriptural evidence, and which most accurately portrays the God of love and mercy we believe in. Tradition can be very strong, but sometimes it can also be a stronghold. We have an Enemy. There is one who does not want individuals to know God as He is, and he's extremely clever. Are we Christians so beyond error that there's no possibility we've been deceived and are perpetuating Satan's very first lie to humanity?   I certainly believe that I was deceived, before delving into this study and re-thinking it. Is it not possible that we have problems in a couple of our major doctrines? Christianity has come a long way doctrinally since the dark and middle ages, but are we there yet? Have we sorted out every major doctrinal issue? Probably not. And certainly every issue doesn't need sorting out to have unity and be effective in the world as Christians, but shouldn't we work toward it?

There's a phrase that's become popular within Christianity over the last several years and it's this: "You need to know *why* you believe *what* you believe." I totally agree, and that concept is foundational to why I'm writing this book. But an equally important, if not more important question would be: Does *why* you believe *what* you believe make the most sense, logically and scripturally? I can believe that every time a bell rings, an angel gets its wings. And I can believe this because teacher says so (or because it's a line in my favorite Christmas movie). But it's based on nothing factual. A number of books have been written defending the traditional view of eternal conscious torment, and these books are filled with the best *why's* humans have come up with to maintain the traditional *what's*. But careful study reveals gaping holes in the logical process behind most of those arguments, and we'll critique some of those as we work through this study.

Tradition appears to be wrong on this matter, and a clearer view of judgment needs to be made available for those who have struggled with tradition. And while I may challenge what certain people believe and teach on this, I don't hold any personal hard feelings toward them — just the opposite. I respect all of the teachers who have spoken life to me through Biblical teaching. And I hope this challenge will be taken in the right spirit. Having disagreement or debate shouldn't ruin us. We're all sinners saved by grace, in need of God's mercy every moment. God bless you as you read on.

CHAPTER 2

Unlearning and Relearning Eden
Are Souls Mortal or Immortal?

Solid factual support for the traditional view of eternal suffering in Hell is not found in Scripture. So where does the idea come from, and why then is it taught? It seems to have three lifelines. One is tradition itself. It's an incredibly strong force, and challenging tradition is difficult, so it often goes undone. The second line of support is created by inappropriate interpretations of approximately 10 verses of Scripture (a few more if you consider repetition of similar themes or duplicate accounts within the gospels). In the case of some of these verses, it's a stretched meaning that causes the error – reading more into the verse than is really there. With other passages, tradition overrides simple logic, and the traditional interpretation is the exact opposite of what a passage seems to be clearly stating. We'll carefully examine all of those mainstay verses in Chapter 4, and find biblically coherent meanings of them which have nothing to do with eternal suffering.

This chapter's focus is the third line of support for the traditional position. It's the erroneous idea that every soul already has immortality. If this were true, it might be a logical conclusion that every soul must then exist somewhere for all eternity — those who've rejected salvation spending it tormented. But this is found nowhere in Scripture, yet it's the common teaching concerning our soul nature, not only in Christianity, but virtually every faith in the world, which should give Christians pause when considering its validity. Instead, this fact that it's an accepted doctrine across many religions has often been presented as evidence of its truth. So we Christians reject every other aspect of some other religion's theology, but their belief that all souls are immortal and eternal is evidence that it's true?

The desire for eternal life is something that God put within mankind. Ecclesiastes 3:11 tells us that God set eternity in our hearts (which is different from creating our souls to be immortal). But the feeling that we almost deserve an eternal life, and the idea that eternal existence is simply a given is not from God. We deserve death, and that's where we're headed without salvation through Jesus Christ.

Others have done the historical research and shown how this idea of innate immortality came from pagan culture. I don't completely agree with every conclusion of conditionalist Edward Fudge regarding final judgment, but I'd recommend reading any of his books about this topic. I haven't read all of his work, but I read *Two Views of Hell* wherein he debated traditionalist Robert Peterson and I found his section on the history of the doctrine of immortality enlightening and informative. But even if we can nail down which pagan philosophers and Church "fathers" made the idea popular, ultimately it's satanic at its core – one of the Enemy's many attempts to create confusion about who God is. Now, in no way am I implying that individuals in the Christian world who teach the traditional view are satanic. Well-meaning people have fallen prey to the doctrine and are only doing what they believe they're supposed to be doing when they share it — Just wanted to clarify that.

Here's an example of how the idea of universal immortality is usually presented in the Christian world:

> "Precious one, what you and I need to know and understand is that once we are born *we are eternal beings. We're going to live for all eternity* in one place or the other. We're either going to live in the presence of God and enjoy eternal life, or we're going to live in the presence of the devil and his angels and

we're going to suffer the torment of eternal punishment"   -
Kay Arthur[1] (italics mine)

This quote is from several years ago when I was in the first year or two of this study. Arthur made this statement during one of her broadcasts of her *Precepts for Life* program. She went on to claim that if we don't believe this, it's because we have not read the Bible, have not read the whole council of God, and have not honored His precepts for life, nor esteemed His Word. I can't speak for anyone except myself, but I love and highly esteem the Bible, yet completely disagree with her premise that all people are already eternal beings. And the word "torment" is never connected with the idea of an "eternal punishment" anywhere in Scripture.

I listen to or watch Kay Arthur on television from time to time, and for the most part she's a fine Bible teacher; I've learned a lot from her, and I certainly don't mean to single her out. They all do this. Another of my favorite preachers, Jack Graham, stated more recently: "That's what Hell is: *To live eternally*, without God."[2] (italics for emphasis). David Jeremiah (and I really like him too, by the way) put it this way on one of his *Turning Points* radio broadcasts: "I got news for ya folks. *Everyone is going to live forever.* It's just a matter of location."[3] Are you noticing a theme? All their statements fall right in line with the common thinking and teaching within Christianity on the matter, and it really is at the core of the problem of teaching the eternal suffering of the lost. Contrary to strong statements in Scripture, our favorite Bible teachers are telling us that everyone is going to live forever. If unbelievers did in fact exist forever as traditionalists claim, then they must be somewhere, and since we know from Scripture a day is coming when they're cast into the Lake of Fire at final judgment, it would be reasonable to assume this would be their eternal home...IF all souls were already immortal and not destined for destruction. But all who reject salvation are in fact destined for destruction, and we'll see in this chapter that Scripture never makes the statement that all souls are immortal from conception.

Arthur offered no Scriptural support for her claim of human immortality, as most who teach this won't — at least not during that particular broadcast, she didn't. The idea of the innate immortality of all souls is such a foregone conclusion, most teachers feel it's unnecessary and throw that idea around freely. So it's stated as fact, but rarely supported. However, a few traditionalists have attempted to give evidence of this, and we'll analyze their arguments later in the chapter. In the quote above, Arthur mentioned "eternal punishment," a biblical phrase which in itself has led some to believe in the immortality of the lost. It sort of sounds like a punishment that continues on for all eternity, doesn't it? The Bible does in fact promise an eternal punishment for the unbeliever.   So this phrase could be stretched by the imagination to mean a form of conscious punishment which lasts forever.   The Greek word being translated as "eternal" is *aionios* and often denotes "permanence" when context is considered. If we take the Word of God at face value, the punishment for sin not covered by faith in Christ is death. This is stated throughout. So, the eternal punishment is in fact a permanent eternal death, rather than all the everlasting perpetual conscious torments that our imaginations could conjure up. It is very simply death which the lost are ultimately headed for, and those who rejected God will remain dead for all eternity...an eternal punishment.

Before we get too deep into this subject, since we'll be discussing the fate of "the soul" throughout this book, we need to know what we mean by that term. It would be easy to get bogged down in all the various definitions.   In fact, a few different Hebrew and Greek words are all translated as "soul" in English bibles. But we don't need a lengthy examination for our purposes in this book. Most Christians agree that the soul is "who" we are. It is the essence of the person. In Genesis 2:7, we see that God breathed into the man and *made him* a living soul, so we don't just *have* a soul. We *are* the soul. The soul is the life that animates our flesh, and the part of us that can outlive the flesh, and which will inhabit a new glorified body one day, for those who have put their faith in Christ. There are places in Scripture where a word translated as "soul" may carry with it the idea of the whole person, the flesh and also the immaterial part that animates it, but our discussion concerns what happens to that immaterial part after the flesh is in the grave. So, when I refer to the "soul" in this discussion, I'm generally not referring to the whole person but the immaterial person.

So, will all human souls, saved or unsaved, go on existing for all eternity? That's the question. The first great evidence that the soul is not immortal from its conception, like so many Biblical truths, can be found early in the book of Genesis. Satan's introduction to mankind was in the Garden of Eden, and while we may have physically misplaced its location on earth, the Garden, doctrinally speaking, is still a stronghold area where the Enemy continues to do his deceptive work. I've found so many of our common teachings about what happened there to be completely backwards. I hear the following phrase applied to many topics these days, so I'm hesitant to use it, but I can't resist: "Almost everything you know about (fill in the blank...in this case, the Garden of Eden) is completely wrong." I was hesitant to use it because it's often sort of a sensational way to draw attention to an individual's "new and better way" to think about or do whatever it is they're wanting you to think about or do. And I'm sure I'll be considered "that guy" by some readers. But I'm not being sensational. We seriously teach the garden scene wrong and therefore come to some backward conclusions which are antithetical to the gospel.

Tradition has redefined the concept of *eternal death* and turned it into *eternal life, but separated from God,* and traditionalists believe they have evidence for this right from the beginning in the Garden of Eden. The common teaching would go something like this:

> God told Adam there was a tree in the midst of the garden
> which he was not to eat from, the tree of the knowledge of
> good and evil. Adam is told that in the day he eats of it, he
> would surely die. Eventually he and Eve did both eat from it,
> but they didn't drop dead on that day, so death must mean

something else. They were expelled from the garden in what appears to be that same day, apparently separating them from God in some sense. So death must not mean death as we commonly understand it: loss of life, existence, and being, but rather separation, leaving God's presence, so in that way, they "died spiritually."

That's probably similar to how you've heard it explained before. On the surface, it sounds reasonable enough. But when you dig a little deeper, it falls apart.

In the original language of Scripture, the phrase being translated as "You will surely die," is simply two words, and it's actually only one word, "death," repeated twice in two different tenses. Literally, it says, "Dying, Die." It's called an "infinitive absolute," and this Hebrew verbal technique indicates an emphatic statement concerning whatever verb it's being applied to. So, what we have is an emphatic statement about death being a result of eating from the one forbidden tree. If I can put it this casually...Death wasn't a thing yet, prior to sin. The warning from God wasn't that if they sinned, they would drop dead physically, or immediately die in any other form – spiritually, etc. The emphatic warning rather was that on the day they chose to sin, death itself would change from only a potential, and into reality.

Remember that the original Hebrew only says "dying, die." It's not a stretch at all to take what has been interpreted as "you will surely die" and express it more accurately as "death will become sure," especially since the "you" part of "you will surely die" which appears in English bibles isn't even in the Hebrew original. On the very day they ate of the tree of the knowledge of good and evil, death (their future death) became a sure reality. But wait, they were expelled from the garden, right? So couldn't that separation still be part of what God meant by death? Absolutely Not. That theory is dead on arrival because God tells us specifically why they were expelled from the garden, and we'll get there shortly. But let it be noted that God's presence didn't stay confined back in the Garden, and God continued to have encounters with mankind, and still does...all outside of Eden.

So with a grammatically equally acceptable, but alternative rendering, we'd have something like, "In the day you eat of it, death will become an absolute certainty for you." Remember that prior to sin, Adam and Eve still had the theoretical capability of eating of the Tree of Life, which the Bible says will make them go on living forever (Genesis 3:22), i.e. eternal life, eternality, immortality — at least for the soul. And most likely the dusty body would have been transformed at that point as well, thereby even avoiding a death of the physical body. So, while God always knew from eternity past that they would *not* eat from the Tree of Life before first eating from the forbidden tree, sin had not yet occurred in the course of time, so there was still the potential for death not to take hold of Adam and Eve as long as they had access to the Tree of Life, at least in theory. We don't need to try to support the idea that their own death in some way occurred on that day they first sinned, even though this idea has a couple of interesting defenses. It's unnecessary. As God promised, death became a sure reality in the very day they ate of the tree of the knowledge of good and evil, but no part of them died yet, nor was it prefigured or foreshadowed in their expulsion, nor did any part of them need to die on that very day for God's warning to come true.

In fact, in the day they ate of it, they brought the reality into effect that they would ultimately, surely, and unavoidably die, and it is the expulsion that made this sure because the Tree of Life was back in the garden. It's a bit of a fine line, but the expulsion did not represent their death by separation. Their expulsion however would result in death because they lost access to the thing that could make them go on living forever. Scripture confirms this when, after Adam's sin, God tells him that he is dust, and now because he has sinned, to dust he will return (one day...not *that* day). He was confirming to them that, just as He had warned, they had now, on that day, brought death into reality.

As noted, the general line of thinking from traditionalists is that Adam and Eve's banishment from the garden and the Tree of Life figuratively represents eternal conscious separation of the soul from God, or what traditionalists commonly call "spiritual death." We'll find multiple flaws in this theory as we work through this topic of mortality and immortality in this chapter and Chapter 6 when we return to the Garden. But the answer to the "in the day" question is much simpler. We only need to understand that Adam and Eve were created mortal and could only become immortal by eating of the Tree of Life, a fact for which we will see much evidence, perhaps the most obvious being that otherwise, eating of the Tree of Life would offer them nothing they didn't already possess — ever think of that?

Please don't miss it. Countless traditionalist pastors and teachers will tell you that Adam and Eve were perfect and immortal prior to sinning, but not one will be able to give a sensible answer for what value the Tree of Life would have to perfect immortal beings who we're told were in perfect relationship and harmony with God (another idea we'll challenge). Why was it even planted there? We'll see later in this chapter that its presence in the garden helps lay down a fundamental aspect of the gospel, but this seems to have gone completely unnoticed.

> If Adam had immortality even without eating from the Tree of Life, what then is the significance of this tree which the Bible says eating from would make him go on living forever?

Getting back to the immortality issue, Genesis 3:22 tells us that eating of the Tree of Life will make one go on living forever. The only logical conclusion is that they didn't naturally possess the ability to go on living forever. Therefore, they were mortals. Is this a stretch?

Prior to eating from the tree of knowledge of good and evil, they had not yet disobeyed God and were therefore at a crossroads, mortal, having not yet eaten from the Tree of Life, but still with the potential to do so, and therefore having the theoretical potential to avoid death, body and soul. It seems to explain itself sufficiently if we won't deny the obvious, that Adam and Eve were created mortal, with mortal souls. I'm defining a "mortal soul" as one that can die, and now that sin has occurred, *will* die, come to an end, and no longer exist, if God does not intervene.

Eat from them all, or freely eat from any?

So, the Tree of Life was in the garden, but it was never eaten from. Remember that God had told them they could eat from *every* tree in the garden except the tree of the knowledge of good and evil. But here again, the English translations may not be giving the most accurate rendering of the Hebrew when they read something like, "you may *freely eat* from every other tree..." In the Hebrew, it seems likely that this is more of an emphatic command to *make sure to eat* from all the other trees except the forbidden one, more than simply an allowance that they *could* if they so chose — not that there was any time limit imposed in which to do this, but it seems most likely that there was a command to make sure and get this done. We have another infinitive absolute here with the word "eat": "eating, eat," creating an emphatic statement about eating from "every" tree, and the common interpretation that there was simply a free allowance to eat from "any" of the trees may likely not fully represent the meaning. Also, the word "command" is used in the same statement in Genesis 2:16-17 which adds some weight to the argument.

> Genesis 2:16-17: And the LORD God *commanded the man*, saying, Of every tree of the garden thou mayest freely eat: But of the tree of the knowledge of good and evil, thou shalt not eat of it: for in the day that thou eatest of it thou shalt surely die. (italics for emphasis — 1833 Webster Bible)

It doesn't make sense that a person is "commanded" that they "may" do something. If one is commanded to do something, the assumption is that there is something to do — not that there is a free choice. "I command you to be free and do whatever you so choose..." That doesn't really work does it? There was a command, and it was to eat from all the other trees except the tree of knowledge. We have the phrase "every tree," not simply "any tree," and we have the word "command," and we have the Hebrew infinitive absolute creating an emphatic statement about eating. In every way, there seems to be a command to eat from every tree in the garden.   Yet, it's commonly only translated as "may freely eat." This just doesn't add up. Now, someone might argue that the command was only referencing the second part of the phrase about what *not* to do, and that it had nothing to do with the freely eating part. I suppose that's possible. But it seems like the statement of the free allowance to choose which trees to eat from would have then come *before* the "God commanded" part - or even after the entire statement of what not to do.

It's open to interpretation, but I see two commands – one of what *to* do, and one of what *not* to do, both of which follow the statement, "The Lord God commanded the man." Also, if there were not a command to eat from all the trees, since we don't see God specifically telling Adam or Eve about the Tree of Life anywhere in the garden account, it could be claimed that the Lord never told them to eat of the Tree of Life – only that they could if they so chose. This seems highly unlikely that the Lord would take such a dispassionate position on whether or not they ate of the Tree of Life and gained immortality. But it does make sense that He would veil the specific command to eat of the tree which would give eternal life inside of the greater command to eat from all of the trees, and we'll see why in Chapter 6.

As we already noted, the Tree of Life was there for the taking yet remained untouched, and this is highly significant in the discussion of whether souls are created eternal or not. Even more significant is the fact that God drove them out of the garden after they sinned for the sole purpose of making sure they did not reach out their hand and eat of the Tree of Life. Genesis 3:22-24 states,

> "And the Lord God said, Now the man has become like one of us, having knowledge of good and evil; and now if he puts out his hand and takes of the fruit of the Tree of Life, he will go on

living for ever. So the Lord God sent him out of the garden of Eden to be a worker on the earth from which he was taken. So he sent the man out; and at the east of the garden of Eden he put winged ones and a flaming sword turning every way to guard the way to the Tree of Life."

This seems very clear. Now, due to the banishment, we find there is no way mankind can "go on living forever," at least not by his own effort, and it just so happens that this matter of whose effort is behind the gaining of or granting of eternal life is at the core of understanding the banishment (and the gospel, for that matter). Genesis 2:7 says that God breathed into man, who we know was only earthly dust, and he became a "living soul." I don't think any of us would deny that we are living souls. But our disagreement, if we have one, is over whether or not being a living soul is the same thing as having a soul that will live consciously for all eternity, without God granting it by some condition. It seems very reasonable to assume that in the same way that our flesh is living and dying simultaneously, so the soul without redemption is as well (not that the body and soul must die together at the same time, but that they are both on a course that leads to death). One is the outward picture of the other.

Not only does it seem that the Lord has provided us this perishing body as an object lesson indicating the fate of our soul without redemption, I'll ask my question one more time: If Adam had immortality prior to eating from the Tree of Life, what then is the significance of the tree which the Bible says that eating from would make him go on living forever? There was no promise that eating of it would allow Adam to live in God's garden paradise forever, or would make him wealthy and happy, or lock in any other blessing — only that eating of it would make Him "go on living forever" generally, as the Bible clearly states. There is nothing about "going on living forever" which would bind God into allowing them to stay in the Garden. In fact, God does *not* say, "Since man has an eternal soul and will go on living forever, we certainly can't allow him to live here in the garden now that he has sinned." But unfortunately, this is how the banishment is generally taught, but it's an obvious distortion of Scripture.

Adam was mortal and already prone to death even before he sinned. As I phrased it above, he was at a crossroads, and whether he sinned or not would determine whether he would go on living forever or continue on a path of mortality. Please don't miss the following. Notice that after Adam sinned, God took no new action against his flesh or soul to make his death certain. He only banned him from the one thing that Scripture says would have made his life continue eternally — another clear indication that he was mortal, even prior to sinning. And it all happened "in the day he ate from the forbidden tree." As promised, death became a sure reality that day.

Let's see if following the timeline of actions helps solidify the thesis. God creates man and causes him to become a living soul when he was still *outside* of the garden. So it stands to reason that this Tree of Life which was *inside* the garden offers something more than what the man already possessed after God first breathed into him. This is significant. When Adam was created, he had no access to this Tree of Life, even though God had already made him as a "living soul," until God later put him in the garden. How much later he was put there is irrelevant. It could have been seconds or weeks, or even longer. It doesn't matter in the discussion of whether or not souls are unconditionally eternal. It's the order of events that's critical to recognize and which will create sound doctrine.

Genesis 3:22 plainly tells us that eating of the Tree of Life is what will make them "go on living forever." And Adam did not have access to that tree when he first became a living soul. So being a living soul, in and of itself, is not the same thing as his having the capability of going on living forever – possessing immortality, if we accept the simplicity of God's Word. Now, is it possible that this passage has nothing to do with the immaterial soul, and that God only meant that their *flesh* would somehow go on living forever if they ate from the Tree of Life after sinning, and is it that He simply didn't want that to happen since they had sinned in their flesh? No, because no human flesh can be animated without the soul (James 2:26). It is nothing more than dust, earthy chemicals, and it never was.

The Genesis warnings of impending death concern the whole man, body and soul. And by the same token, eating of the Tree of Life, were it possible after they sinned, would have given their souls eternal life, and likely would have transformed their mortal bodies as well (however, this is only my own speculation regarding their bodies). But God, knowing the end from the beginning, knew He wasn't going to let them gain immortality by their own efforts. This is the same problem we have in the world still – people trying to attain eternal life (or earn their place in Heaven) by their own efforts and works, which was never God's plan. We have to remember that God is omniscient. He knew they would sin and that Adam and Eve by their own free will were going to find and take the forbidden fruit which held so much "promise" before finding and taking the other fruit that would give eternal life.

The Ancient Gospel

In Genesis 3:24, God drives them from the garden and blocks access to the Tree of Life, specifically, the Bible tells us, so humanity cannot eat of this fruit and live forever. But we can't assume that eternal life is no longer available for them because of this. They and all of us are created with the potential to live forever (our soul, that is, in a new body that we will receive after this life), and it is God's will that we all become eternal (2 Peter 3:9). The following is important, and I think it is *the* most important thing we can take from the garden account: Being driven from the Garden and the Tree of Life only represented that Adam and Eve had no ability *on their own* to gain immortality, just as we do not.

The banishment in and of itself was not, nor did it represent, their spiritual death. It couldn't be, and we'll see the obvious reason why shortly. Banning them from the Tree of Life was nothing more than a clear statement that mankind cannot attain eternal life by his own efforts. Don't miss the key phrase: The only reason they are banned according to Scripture is *"lest they reach out their hand and take also of the Tree of Life and eat, and live forever."* This is simply a clear expression that God alone saves, and that we cannot save ourselves by our own hand. It's the same principal that we see in Judges 7 when God is whittling down Gideon's army so that when God delivers them, the Israelites will not think they did it by their own power. In fact, even this idea of it happening by their own "hand" is expressed in Judges chapter 7:

> **Judges 7:2** "The LORD said to Gideon, 'The people with you are too many for me to give the Midianites into their hand, lest Israel boast over me, saying, *'My own hand* has saved me.'" (ESV — italics for emphasis)

And this is a common theme throughout the Bible, and it's what we teach all the time when it comes to salvation: It's not by our power but by God's, not by our good works, but by God's good work. But we fail to see it in the garden, instead taking valuable symbolism, and turning it on its head to teach something entirely unscriptural — that we are immortal beings, which lays the groundwork for the false doctrine of eternal torment.

It's only by accepting God's work and sacrifice that we are saved from death — not physical death — God never relented from His statement that we are dust, would return to it, and that death would become a certainty. But the saved are saved from the very destruction of the soul in the Lake of Fire, which is the destiny we were headed toward from birth, as enemies of God (Romans 5:10). It's the second death which we are saved from, not the first one.

So specifically, how can a person gain immortality? How can we avoid the death of the soul and "go on living forever"? It's certainly not by merely having been created as Kay Arthur and countless others imply, and then our faith or lack thereof determining our eternal location. No, it requires more than merely coming into existence to become eternal. It required a sacrifice from God Himself. We now know that God's work and sacrifice was fulfilled in Jesus's death on the cross, and this is the means to eternal life. The Bible tells us this act atoned for the sinful condition of mankind, for any who will accept it and confess it, and that we are saved from eternal death when we, by faith, accept Christ's work as necessary and sufficient to right our relationship with God.

But this does not mean that salvation was not available for those who lived prior to Christ. Revelation 13:8 calls Jesus "the lamb slain before the foundation of the world," meaning that while His sacrifice had not yet occurred in the course of time, it was as sure as God Himself, and no one could ever have been saved at any time, before or after Christ, if this sacrifice was not certain. Jesus said Himself that none could come to the Father but by Him - by the actions He took on our behalf. Shortly before Jesus was to die on the cross, He prayed to the Father that if there was any other way, to let that cup pass from Him (Matthew 26:39). But it didn't pass. It's safe to conclude then that there was no other way.

So while no one could be saved at all were it not for what Jesus did on the cross, people have always been saved by faith in the one true God, even prior to specific knowledge of Christ, and their faith was always exhibited by their actions. We're told that when Abraham put his faith in God, it was counted to him as righteousness, and he exhibited his faith by following God's instructions to move to a new land, and ultimately by offering his own son Isaac as a sacrifice (which God did not require him to go through with). In the Old Testament story of Rahab, the non-Israelite harlot who hid the Israelite spies, we find that she expressed little knowledge of God, yet she acted on what she knew and she earned a mention in what is commonly called the "Hall of Faith" in chapter 11 of the New Testament book of Hebrews, and I believe we safely assume she is saved eternally.

So how were Adam and Eve saved from the death of their souls, if they were? What action did they exhibit that indicated faith in God's work and sacrifice? The answer to this is so important because it's the primary thing that negates the argument that the banishment indicated "eternal separation from God," or so-called "spiritual death." After they sinned and became aware of good and evil, they realized they were naked and needed a covering. They tried to provide their own, but apparently God found their attempts to cover themselves to be insufficient. The symbolism is overwhelming. We're sort of touching on the same theme we saw before – that people innately try to do things for themselves, including covering their own sin and shame in an effort to show they are without need of God's involvement. But this is not God's way.

We're told in the New Testament to "put on Christ." He is our covering. We have no sufficient covering for our shame except in Christ. It was similar for Adam and Eve. Their own attempts at coverings were not sufficient. And so we're told that the Lord Himself provided skins for them as coverings, indicating that He apparently slew an animal to do so. Hebrews 9:22 tells us that without the shedding of blood there is no forgiveness of sins, speaking of Jesus on the cross, and it was no different in their case as God shed the blood of an animal to provide for them. So it is commonly accepted (and I'm in total agreement with the idea) that this covering provided for them was a foreshadowing of Christ's sacrificial death. And for Adam and Eve, this was, in a primitive form, the very offer of salvation, which they could have rejected, had they been so prideful. But they didn't, and therefore I believe they were saved and reserved for the inheritance of eternal life.

So how does this fit with the theory that their expulsion from the garden foreshadowed eternal conscious separation from God or "spiritual death"? It doesn't, nor should it. The Bible plainly indicated why they were expelled and we've covered it sufficiently. Following the timeline of events will again give us a sound doctrine. Their covering preceded their expulsion, so either the covering did not represent salvation, or the expulsion did not represent eternal separation from God because Adam and Eve's "salvation" could not precede their "damnation," as would be indicated if we took the traditional stance on the meaning of the banishment. And isn't it strange that most of the same people who tell us the banishment is symbolic of eternal separation from God also believe Adam and Eve are saved? Thank the Lord that He gave us an order of events because it really does clear up the matter. Because the symbolism for the covering representing salvation is so strong, and since Genesis 3:22-23 tells us precisely why they were expelled, I'm forced to view these aspects of the garden in a light not commonly expressed in Christian circles.

Now, a traditionalist might challenge what I've written and say to me, "If you believe the covering represented their gaining eternal life, then the banishment from the life-giving tree has no meaning. They already had eternal life." I would have to agree with this if the covering had literally and immediately caused them to become immortal. But it didn't. That's why I said the covering "reserved" them for eternal life, just as when we put our faith in Christ today we are reserved for eternal life. We "have" eternal life in the sense that it is a sure guarantee, a promise from God, but we are not literally immortal yet. We, nor any believer while still in their flesh, ever "attained the prize" or "received the inheritance" (as Paul referred to it) prior to physical death. Read Ephesians 1:13-14:

> "In Him (Christ) you also, when you heard the word of truth, the gospel of your salvation, and believed in him, were sealed with the promised Holy Spirit, who is the guarantee of our inheritance until we acquire possession of it, to the praise of his glory." (ESV)

Even those of us who are "saved" have not yet actually eaten of the Tree of Life that causes one to go on living forever, but we will after we have endured to the end. The Tree of Life makes another appearance in Scripture and we'll come back and examine this toward the end of the chapter.

I need to clarify something in case I've been unclear. I'm not claiming there's no such thing as "spiritual death." I'm only claiming that the expulsion from the garden did not represent it or cause it, and I'm claiming that an unbelieving soul is temporarily alive, yet spiritually dead in the sense that it is headed for death. Only after Adam and Eve sinned did God come to them and lovingly make a sacrifice for them and begin open two-way communication; only after sinning did they recognize their weakness and God's strength; only after they accepted God's covering and His authority did they become spiritually alive. Before, they were spiritually dead. I know this statement creates some cognitive dissonance because it's so contrary to what we're inundated with, but we'll see more and more evidence as we move forward. And I'm still waiting for anyone to show me in Scripture this awesome relationship Adam and Eve had with God or each other prior to sin. You won't find it in Scripture, even though we teach it all the time. And again, our bodies, alive yet wasting away, seem the perfect object lesson for what's happening at the immaterial soul level, and since they had not eaten from the Tree of Life, they were prone to decay as well. They had not obeyed the other command to eat from all the other trees, which would include the Tree of Life, so they were as much on a road to perishing as any of us.

And while there's now no hope for our flesh, in that there is no avoiding the first death, God has graciously made a way of escape from the second death (Rev 20:6), the one that would take our souls. And Adam and Eve were not the exception. They were the foreshadowing example of the state in which we all come into existence.

John Gill, an influential 18th century theologian, in his extensive, verse-by-verse study notes begins his analysis of this portion of Scripture by claiming that Adam and Eve were at first unwilling to go out of the garden upon orders.[4] I suppose this is possible, but it's never stated in the Bible, and it's hard to believe they would be arguing with God much at that point. We know they were ashamed and hiding from God after they sinned, and they had just been inundated with judgments but then graciously covered in skins the Lord Himself made. I just can't picture them putting up much of a fight as Gill states. He then indicates that Adam and Eve were only forbidden from eating of the Tree of Life because they might flatter themselves by eating it, thinking that they could live forever. Gill goes on to theorize that "very probably" the devil planted that idea in their minds. I only mention all this because it epitomizes how theologians and Bible teachers read so much into the Garden account (and Scripture in general) which isn't there, and isn't even implied there.

God says in His Word that eating the fruit from the Tree of Life would give them eternal life, but noted theologian John Gill implies that this is not so, and that Satan planted the idea in their minds. The Bible plainly states that eating the fruit of the Tree of Life would cause them to live forever, so rather than say, as Gill does, that eating the fruit could *not* cause eternal life, it's far safer to say that they were simply not going to eat of the Tree of Life before eating the forbidden fruit, and God surely knew it, although the potential was certainly there. In fact, He did not say to Adam, "*If* you eat of it (the tree of the knowledge of good and evil). Rather, He essentially said "*When* you eat of it," when He said "In the day you eat of it." We can't get away from God's omniscience. He knew the plan of Salvation before time began, and knew that we would not resist sin. God also knew that humanity, with a nature which leaves us unable to fully obey, would succumb to what was forbidden before choosing obedience that would lead to eternal life. In their case, obedience would mean avoiding the one forbidden tree, and then obeying the other command to at some point eat from *all* the other trees in the garden — again, not only "freely eating" from the ones they chose.

Summarizing what we've covered so far, many traditionalists claim that verses referring to man as a living soul prove innate immortality. Here in Genesis we have the first clear proof to the contrary. Adam is first created to be a living soul, then *later*, God gives access to a Tree of Life that according to His own Word, has the potential to cause Adam to become immortal. But Adam never eats of the tree God said would make him live forever, and his access to it is then blocked by an angel with a flaming sword, and we aren't even left to wonder why this was done. God's Word tells us that it is so he cannot reach out *his hand* and take of its fruit and live forever. But prior to this, God took an action that in every way appears to indicate the preservation of Adam's soul until the Tree of Life is one day available again. The angels weren't told to cut the tree down after sin occurred – only to block access to it.

The Garden account so plainly teaches that even living souls are mortal and dying without God's taking further action in salvation, and then us, the living/dying soul, accepting and trusting God's action. As we've noted, God's action was slaying an innocent animal and covering them with its skin, and this foreshadowed Christ's then future sacrifice for sin. I was discussing this with a Hebrew scholar who was helping me with some word studies, and he advised that I not make too much of this provision of skins in this book, since it is never confirmed in Scripture that this was a foreshadowing of Christ's death to cover our sins. But many of the actions and stories in the Bible that we commonly accept as precursors or typing of later events are not necessarily called so within Scripture.

Some might say that this provision of skins was only demonstrating that God cares about the little things too. I can personally testify that God does in fact care about the little things of life, and this is one of the aspects of God that is so amazing. But I hope that anyone who claims this as the meaning of the provision of skins isn't also in the theological camp that claims the banishment from the garden is representative of eternal separation from God in Hell, because then we essentially would have God saying, "Here's a nice new outfit for you because I care about the little things...HOPE YOU ENJOY IT ON YOUR WAY TO ETERNAL HELL!!"

Obviously I write that in jest and believe no such thing was intended. We have the hindsight of knowing from Scripture that all of the sacrifices of animals for sin in the Old Testament were a picture of what Christ would later come and do. And we also know from Scripture that it was the Father's will to show His love for and forgiveness of mankind through the sacrifice of His Son. It falls right in line then to see this action of God providing skins to cover their shame immediately after sin, as a foreshadowing of Christ. The Bible doesn't need to come right out and say it. It is apparent. It further seems that God could have easily instructed Adam to make his own skins, if there were no significance in God's doing it for them and if the only reason was to provide a more durable outfit than fig leaves.

It seems that not only was this act evidence that God provides a more sufficient covering of shame and sin than we ever could, but that He does it Himself, and without our even asking (while we were yet sinners, according to Romans 5:8), and it's up to us only to accept it or not. Adam and Eve accepted the provision, and I believe they are with the Lord and will inherit eternal life, just as all believers will. How appropriate that God gave such a clear and complete picture of the entire gospel story and the two potential fates of the soul, all in the first three chapters of the Bible.

Before we leave the garden topic, let's look at 1 Corinthians 15:45-54:

> "45 So also it is written, 'The first man, Adam, became a living soul.' The last Adam became a life-giving spirit. 46 However that which is spiritual isn't first, but that which is natural, then that which is spiritual. 47 The first man is of the earth, made of dust. The second man is the Lord from heaven. 48 As is the one made of dust, such are those who are also made of dust; and as is the heavenly, such are they also that are heavenly. 49 As we have borne the image of those made of dust, let's also bear the image of the heavenly. 50 Now I say this, brothers, that flesh and blood can't inherit God's Kingdom; neither does the perishable inherit imperishable. 51 Behold, I tell you a mystery. We will not all sleep, but we will all be changed, 52 in a moment, in the twinkling of an eye, at the last trumpet. For the trumpet will sound, and the dead will be raised incorruptible, and we will be changed. 53 For this perishable body must become imperishable, and this mortal must put on immortality. 54 But when this perishable body will have become imperishable, and this mortal will have put on immortality, then what is written will happen: 'Death is swallowed up in victory.'" (WEB)

This is very plain. Look at verse 45. It supports the claim I've made that being a living soul and having eternal life are not the same thing. It plainly confirms that Adam was in fact a living soul, but that the last Adam, Christ, gives life. Why did Christ need to give life if Adam was already a living soul that would live eternally? Because a living soul without Christ's salvation is also a dying soul, headed for death, just as our living flesh is headed for death. I once heard one of my favorite pastors claim that the *eternal* suffering of the soul is the "logical extension" of the picture of death that we have in the body. With all due respect, I could not disagree more. The most logical extension of the finite dying body would most certainly be a finite dying soul. In what way could the death of the body, due to our sin, be the foreshadowing of eternal torment in Hell? It just couldn't.

Regarding our bodies, dying is temporary, yet death is eternal. Why would we assume anything different for our soul?

Moving on with this passage, in verse 46, that living souls do not yet have eternal life is further supported when we see that the natural came first, and the spiritual later through Christ's death. And then in verses 53 and 54 we see that immortality is something for the future as we've noted, not something we already have, and not for all souls, but for believers only.

We've seen that God, early on, wanted people to know that their eternal fate would be death if they didn't accept His free gift and grace. Why would He veil such a thing as eternal conscious suffering? Would you not tell your children the consequences for their potential actions or inactions? Of course you would. Knowing our potential punishments is the deterrent to sin.

I've heard it theorized that the truth of eternal torment in Hell is something that God intentionally built up to gradually, progressively, and that He dispensed a little more information here and there, until now, with the full Word of God in our hands, we can finally understand just how horrible Hell is. Well, if this could even be supported, I guess that would be fine for those of us who have lived since the New Testament was completed, but what about all those before then? Why didn't God fully warn them? Why don't we see God warn Adam and Eve about the potential to live in conscious torment for all eternity if they disobeyed or even failed to accept the covering He offered? That would have been a great place to implant that warning into humanity so it would get passed down.

The reason we don't see that warning is obvious. Eternal conscious torment is not the fate of unbelieving people. God laid out the potentials for the soul over and over: Life or Death. And He started early, back in Genesis. God also shows us clearly in nature, the life and death cycle. It's simply understood that things die. That's why immortality is such an amazing gift – It goes against everything we naturally observe. It's normal to assume that what is living today will someday cease to live. That's the case with everything we could observe scientifically. It's the law of Entropy. And it's the law laid down in Scripture as well, but with one loophole: faith in the one true living God saves us from death, and we who believe will, instead, *go on living forever.*

Modern Teaching

I said we would address a couple of fellow-Christians who have attempted to defend the idea that all souls, saved or lost, are immortal and eternal and will exist consciously into timeless eternity. I considered trying to do this without naming names. It's certainly not my intention to potentially damage any well-known Christian's ministry by causing people to doubt their doctrinal judgment or interpretation skills. But because I needed to quote them, I couldn't do this without giving their names. I believe both of the people I'm about to challenge are Godly Bible teachers and I've learned a lot from them both. None of us are beyond error, and I certainly don't have everything figured out yet. So I hope my challenging the method of someone's doctrinal judgment isn't taken in the wrong spirit by the reader. But the intention of this book is to demonstrate where we've erred on this doctrine, and it would be less effective without pointing to some of the specific instances and examples of exactly where we've gone wrong. I hope this doesn't come across as in-fighting or back biting. It's just part of the process if we're going to challenge a traditional take on a particular doctrine which appears to be in error.

If a line-by-line analysis of someone's statements on soul immortality isn't your cup of tea, I don't blame you. It was tedious work to do on my end, and it will make for somewhat tedious reading, to some. The following two chapters are where we'll take a close look at what Scripture actually says about final judgment, and also analyze the top ten most used verses to defend eternal conscious suffering, and I don't fault anyone who wants to jump forward to that. But if you want to see just how poor the arguments for lost souls being immortal are, I'd recommend pushing on through this chapter. To me it's enlightening to find that some of the most respected Christian teachers have no better defense for the doctrine than they do.

Several years ago, I was listening to a former president of Moody Bible Institute on the radio and wasn't surprised to hear that he, like the majority of Christians, holds the view that all souls are eternal, even without salvation. But like everyone else I've heard attempt to give some reason for this belief, he failed to make the case. But before we go through what he said, I must say that otherwise I hold him in high regard. His name is Michael Easley. When Joe Stowell stepped down from that position in 2005, I was disappointed. I had enjoyed his radio teaching for years. It was my Sunday morning routine to get up and listen to him on Moody Presents while making breakfast before church. But when Easley began being broadcast in Stowell's place, I was relieved to hear that he was another down-to-earth Godly man like his predecessor, and I was fed many times through his teaching before he too stepped down a few years later.

The broadcast I want to address was one in a short series on doctrine, and the primary intention was to make believing listeners see the importance of knowing *why* they believe *what* they believe. I couldn't agree more about the importance of that. That's one of the reasons I'm challenging people in this book to answer some hard questions about why they believe as they do regarding the immortality of souls and the nature and duration of suffering in Hell. He and the announcer were conversing about the various areas in which the thinking of the world has crept into the church, and how that has done great damage. Again, I couldn't agree more. But then Easley made reference to "annihilation" and my ears perked up because I had been on this track and study for a while at that point. He had just given a list of various different lies that are creeping into the Church and then says that there are even some theologians now who are saying there is no Hell, and we're just annihilated, and go into nothingness.

Let me first confirm with him that there are in fact those who believe that, and that's not what I'm putting forward. The Bible plainly teaches that the unsaved soul, after physical death, and after suffering consciously, for at least some portion of time in Hell (*Sheol* in Hebrew/*Hades* in Greek) while their physical body lies in the grave, will then be resurrected after the 1000-year reign of Christ, judged, and cast into the Lake of Fire, or what Jesus called Gehenna (also translated "Hell" in English in the New Testament).   There is a conscious afterlife for unbelievers in Hell (*Hades*) and at judgment. Although I believe Scripture teaches the ultimate annihilation of the lost soul, in no way do I think those without Christ just disappear without conscious judgment. There's no argument with Easley's initial statement that some theologians do not "believe in Hell" and that this is in error. But there needs to be a distinction between those like myself who believe in *ultimate* annihilation of the unsaved only after suffering, resurrection, and judgment, and those who believe that all souls or at least unsaved souls *immediately* go out of existence upon physical death.

Let's move on to Easley's argument. This is where he begins a line of logic that would work if the second building block in his argument had any Biblical foundation. He reasons that...

"if we are made in the image of God, if we are image bearers, there is what Augustine called a 'spark of divinity,' a fair illustration. God is not going to eradicate that part of his divinity. It is therefore eternal. So if all human beings are eternal, the difference is location, with Him or apart from Him."[5]

That ends his statement about the eternality of souls, but he went on to say that what we believe "better be grounded in the truth."[6] I'm not sure his reasoning holds up to that standard on this particular issue. He begins with the truth that we are all image bearers of God, but then relies on the uninspired writing of Augustine which claims we all have a spark of divinity in us. It really doesn't matter if Augustine says we have a spark of divinity in us. I've searched for any Biblical reference that would indicate that we, prior to salvation, share or possess divinity in any form or amount, and I can't find it.

So what *does* God mean when He says He created us in His image? This statement that we're created in the image of God is used, it seems, more than any other to defend the idea that we are already immortal beings, so it's important to look to the Bible, not our imagination, for an answer to this. I won't pretend to know everything this might mean, but there are a number of ways we are like Him. In the Bible, we're told that God loves. We love. God gets angry. We get angry. God is jealous for that which is His. We get jealous for what we believe is ours. God is Merciful. We can be merciful. God feels pity. We feel pity. God creates. We create. And, ever since mankind's first sin, we now know good from evil and are like Him in that respect according to His Word. I could go on and on. As sinful as we are, and far short of divine, we are like God in many ways, in our actions and emotions.

Thankfully, God hasn't left us to wonder or speculate about what He means by "in God's image." He hasn't required Augustine or anyone else to attempt to define this outside of what the Bible maintains. Perhaps I shouldn't have even pointed out my own ideas on ways we're like God. In Genesis 1:26, which is the first verse that says we are made in God's image, we're told we are made that way *so* we can rule over the fish in the sea, the birds of the air, the cattle, all wild animals on earth, and all reptiles that crawl upon the earth. The *Oxford Cambridge New English Bible* translates the Hebrew as "Let us make man in our image and likeness *to rule* the fish in the sea, the birds of..." (italics mine). So "to rule" means "for the purpose of ruling." According to Genesis Chapter 1, we are in His image in the sense that we have been put in control of the earth and been commanded to rule over it.

That makes sense. God rules over the entire universe and we are in His image, or like Him, on a much smaller scale, in that He gave us the task of ruling over the earth. But there is no call, Biblically, for us to connect anything having to do with immortality of souls with this fact that we are made in God's likeness and image. In fact, there's no call for us to attach *any* meaning with it other than what the Bible plainly gives us. So does this Biblical understanding of the concept make sense with later mentions of us being in His image? I think we could say it does. We find the statement that we are in God's image again in Genesis 9:4-7. God is blessing Noah and his sons and giving them instructions and warnings.

> "4 But flesh with its life, that is, its blood, you shall not eat. 5 I will surely require accounting for your life's blood. At the hand of every animal I will require it. At the hand of man, even at the hand of every man's brother, I will require the life of man. 6 Whoever sheds man's blood, his blood will be shed by man, for God made man in his own image. 7 Be fruitful and multiply. Increase abundantly in the earth, and multiply in it." (WEB)

Here God confirms what He means by "in His image." Just as there is nothing over God, he makes it clear here that nothing on earth should be over us. No man is permitted to murderously take the life of another man, and if one of the animals, of which we are to rule over, takes a man's life, then God requires its blood. The point is then driven home again when God says, "Whoever sheds man's blood, his blood shall be shed by man; *for God made man in his own image.*" (italics for emphasis) There's nothing about eternal souls here. The concept is about ruling over the earth and the sanctity of life.

Continuing with Easley's statements, after concurring with Augustine that being in the image of God equals possessing some of His divinity, he then says, "God is not going to eradicate that part of His divinity." This statement might be true if we, before salvation, were divine in some way, but this portion of his statement relies on the Biblically unproven assumption that being in his image equals possession of divinity in some measure. Claiming innate divinity might be offensive to a Holy God, Who Isaiah couldn't even bear to look up at, and Who throughout the entire Bible, repeatedly reminds us just how "not God" we are. There is nothing good in us before salvation. Even our righteousness is filthy rags according to Scripture. And does God really have reservations about eradicating things He creates? He had no problem eradicating almost everything on earth in the flood of Noah's day. And He tells us that the whole earth, everything in it, and the heavens will be subject to fire one day, even though when He created it, He called it "very good."

I think God makes it plain in Scripture that He eradicates what offends Him and we, without Christ, the objects of wrath, before acknowledging our need for Him, are on the top of that list — and this includes our souls. We *are* the soul. Further, it makes no logical sense for someone to claim that God will not eradicate a soul because it has a "spark of divinity" within it, but to then assume He would, however, eternally torment that same soul containing that same "spark of divinity." He would be tormenting Himself, by Easley's logic. If one is going to claim that He would not destroy a soul because it has a little piece of Him in it, then how can they any more justify God subjecting those billions of little pieces of Himself to eternal torment? Neither idea really works.

The following is by no means a perfect illustration, but the only one I could come up with that relates to this subject would be a mirror. If I hold a mirror and look into it, it bears my image as long as I hold it up, but if I choose to shatter it and remove my presence from it, it no longer bears my image; yet I have lost none of my own attributes because of destroying it, and likewise

I think Easley is wrong in stating that "God is not going to eradicate that part of His Divinity." It is in fact only an image, not the real thing, not God, and not divine. God loses no part of Himself when He destroys what offends because He was whole and complete before creation. And to take the mirror illustration even further, if I break it, I won't leave it in my house in a shattered state forever. Soon, I'll dispose of it, just as God does the souls He would destroy. It seems clear that Jesus used Gehenna, Jerusalem's burning trash dump, as the illustration for where lost souls would be cast, not because they would be in fires that never end as so many misinterpret it, but because they would in fact be eradicated and consumed just as everything was which was thrown into Gehenna.

Moving on, Easley puts another assertion upon an already faulty one when he says, "It is therefore eternal," "it" being that Augustinian part of us which is supposedly divine. He then goes on to say, "So if all human beings are eternal, the difference is location, with Him or apart from Him." There is no proof Biblically that all human beings are eternal, and it was not proved here in this argument either. And the Bible certainly doesn't come right out and say that we, before salvation, have anything divine in our nature. Why would God not make such a thing obvious? Doesn't it seem strange that, if it were true, in the entire Bible there is not one clear statement that all souls are immortal or divine in some way. Would it not be stated clearly at least once if that were the truth?

Easley's conclusion can only be arrived at through the projection of non-Biblical concepts. Easley began building his argument with a truth misused, then used a human, non-Biblical assumption for his next building block, and then everything else on top of that crumbles. Not surprisingly, he ends up at the same wrong conclusion about the immortality of souls and duration of Hell that all Christians do who rely on the early church fathers instead of the plain text of the Bible as it relates to this issue. In fact, our core problem is the very mistake of trusting uninspired man to give us our doctrine of judgment instead of the plain teaching of God's Word. And maybe that's why Christianity has been turned over to the captivity of a false doctrine for so long.

What we have here is a faulty line of logic from an otherwise astute Godly man, all in the interest of trying to find some reason to "know why he believes what he believes" about Hell, while being unwilling to accept the fact that orthodox tradition isn't always the pinnacle of truth. Faulty logic or reliance on extra-Biblical writings and teachings is really the only way one can come to the conclusions which mainstream Christianity has on these matters. But if the question of "Why we believe what we believe" is important, then even more so is the question "Do my reasons for what I believe hold up to Scripture?" If not, then we need to believe something that will. It's that simple.

I've already said it, but I think it bears repeating here. I don't mean any of this criticism personally. I respect Michael Easley as a sound Christian teacher, generally. I continued listening to his teaching until he left Moody. Both of these faulty doctrines, the "eternal suffering in Hell" doctrine and the inseparable "innate immortality of all souls" doctrine are deeply entrenched in Christianity, and common to most Christians' beliefs, and I don't completely fault anyone who hasn't researched them for following the mainstream. In fact, I respect them for trying to find some way to justify it since it is so vital that we know why we believe what we believe, but we should go to the Bible for our answers and not Augustine or anyone else. The Bible does not tell us that we have some divine piece somewhere in us that keeps us eternal. It says the opposite over and over. It is a false notion that cannot be proven.

Modern-day misinterpretations about our immortality are plentiful, and John MacArthur is another teacher who I've learned a lot from, but who also has been very vocal about innate immortality, but with little evidence. As I said of Michael Easley, I have a lot of respect for his teaching and I generally believe his ministry to be of God, although with MacArthur, the subject of immortality isn't the only strong disagreement I have with him — but that would be a different book, and I'm not writing that book. If I were, it would be entitled *If*, as I mentioned in Chapter 1. Regarding innate immortality, he too tries in vain to hold on to traditional views that won't hold up scripturally. During a radio sermon series on the subject of the afterlife which was broadcast several years ago, before getting into the topic of heaven, MacArthur first wanted to establish that all souls are immortal — that essential doctrine for trying to prove eternal suffering in Hell. No less than twelve times in the first ten minutes of the broadcast he stated in one form or another that every soul was eternal. So did he prove it? Let's first look at what he claimed and then we'll look at the scriptures and even extra-Biblical sources he used to attempt to support his claims.

After giving a definition of the soul or spirit, similar to what most, I believe, understand the soul to be, he next states that "it is that living spirit that lives forever."[7] He gives no scripture to support that, and then, like Easley and so many others, says that having or being a living spirit is "part of what it means to be created in the image of God, who is that eternal Spirit."[8] God is indeed the Eternal Spirit, but I think we've covered the "image of God" topic sufficiently already. There's nothing Biblical to support the assertion that being created in His image means we're immortal.

Consider this: If being created in His image enabled us to claim the immortality which belongs only to God according to 1 Timothy 6:16, then we could just as well claim any other attribute of God that doesn't actually belong to us. It would make no less sense logically to claim that all humans, saved or unsaved, are omniscient, and omnipresent, or at least have a "spark" of omniscience or omnipresence. After all, God is omniscient and omnipresent, and we were made in His image according to Scripture, so therefore we must be as well. I hope you see the absurdity of this and therefore the absurdity of claiming divinity or immortality when Scripture does not attribute those to us, and I don't think *divinity* is ever attributed to us anyway, even after salvation, only the promise of future immortality, eternal life. We will not become God. And I also hope you see that we could no more be partially omniscient or omnipresent than we could be partially divine. Next MacArthur says, "Every living person is an eternal soul. Every living person is an eternal spirit."[9] Again, no scripture is given to support these statements. He then says,

> "Everyone who has ever lived will always live. No one goes out of existence. Everyone whom God has created is eternal. We are all designed to live forever and will indeed."[10]

Here again we have the common teaching that we will all, saved or lost, live forever, which completely opposes Scripture. And again, we have more repetition of the traditional view without any solid Biblical basis or defense for his statements. And far from being "designed to live forever," we're told in Romans 9:22 that we are vessels of wrath, fitted for destruction. If we trust Scripture and not man, we will find that we, the whole person – body and soul, were "designed" to perish, as all of this initial creation was. This design is why the gift of eternal life is so amazing.

For his first attempt at evidence, MacArthur uses Zechariah 12:1 which says toward the end of the verse that "it is God who forms the spirit of man within him" and then, with no indication to the listening audience that he has stopped quoting scripture, MacArthur continues, "and that spirit of man is an everlasting spirit."[11] To the radio listener who doesn't go behind MacArthur and check the Bible, it portrays the Bible as saying that this "spirit of man" is everlasting. But it doesn't say this in the Bible. He added that statement without informing the listener that he had stopped quoting the Zechariah passage.

MacArthur continues to make claims with no evidence when he says this everlasting spirit of man is "everlastingly self-conscious, everlastingly able to reason and think and feel and understand, everlastingly alive."[12] Continuing on, MacArthur next quotes Job 32:8: "But there is a spirit in man, and the breath of the Almighty giveth them understanding." This is repeating what we learned in Genesis. God breathed into man and made him a living spirit or soul. We've covered this extensively. It offers no evidence of souls being eternal. And then we see in this same verse, Elihu, Job's younger friend who is speaking, go on to say that because God did this, we have the ability to understand, not that because of this we will go on living forever. It seems that this latter portion of the verse exhibits the purpose of the former. If the point here in Job were that all souls are immortal, then it seems he would have stated that. The verse is about understanding, not immortality. We should also note that this is Elihu speaking, not God. And God chastises Job and all his friends for their assumptions in the book of Job. This doesn't mean that nothing they stated was true. Much of it was. But we need to be careful when drawing doctrine from someone God chastises.

John MacArthur goes on to talk about humans having self-consciousness after death. I have no argument there. I too believe that consciousness extends beyond physical death, but not beyond the end of time for those without salvation. MacArthur continues:

> "None of us will ever go into an unconscious state. None of us will ever go into some kind of condition of soul sleep in which we feel nothing, think nothing, reason nothing, have no idea what is reality around us."[13]

I disagree with his overall statement. After a lost human soul is cast into the Lake of Fire, they're finished, destroyed, and no longer consciously existing. But I partially agree with him here regarding soul sleep. Many Conditionalists who hold a similar view to mine regarding final judgment believe that when we die, whether we're saved or lost, we enter into a sleep state that we only awake from at resurrection. I'm going to address this more in depth in Chapter 7 where we'll take a look at the intermediate state between physical death and resurrection, but I've personally found biblical evidence for both consciousness and sleep, for the saved and for the lost, during that intermediate state, and what I'll propose is that perhaps both happen, for varying lengths of time and various reasons. It's a gray area, and I can't offer many 100% conclusions but I do disagree with many other conditionalists, such as those of the Seventh Day

Adventists, who believe all souls are in a sleep state for the entire time between physical death and resurrection. I've looked into all the verses that cause people to believe this way, and I can see how the case could be made, but there are excellent explanations for those verses, and we'll get into it later in Chapter 7 where we discuss Hades, where souls await judgment.

MacArthur continues, stating that we are souls and that we are self-conscious, both of which are very Biblically verifiable, but again, as he does so often, he concludes with the unbiblical statement that, "We are eternal spirits. Every one of us will live consciously forever."[14] This would be true if he were referring only to Christians, but clearly he is not. He's trying, but failing, to establish that all souls are eternal regardless of salvation. Next MacArthur refers to the book of Job where Job asks, "If a man dies, shall he live again?" MacArthur says the answer is a "Resounding Yes."[15] Again, I agree with him and with the clear teaching in the Bible that all souls will exist consciously after physical death. The Bible is conclusive on this point, but this verse in Job does not confirm anything having to do with eternity for those who do not know God, only that the soul will not *immediately* go out of existence upon physical death, and certainly Job and other believers *will* go on living forever. But MacArthur somehow finds support for his theory in this verse from Job, and again states, "*Everyone* will live forever."[16]

Next, he references a former president of Yale University who wrote that there had to be an afterlife because there is the "tug of the afterlife in the human spirit."[17] The president likened it to a blind boy flying a kite who, though he couldn't see the kite, could feel it pulling. No offense to the Yale president, but we need to believe in the afterlife because God's Word tells us about it, not because of a feeling that we may or may not feel. Again, I regret being so repetitive, but the reality of an afterlife for the saved and unsaved still does not prove that unsaved souls are not ultimately annihilated as the Bible appears to say they will be.

Next, MacArthur references some of the practices of pagan cultures which reveal they too believe in an afterlife. I don't really see the relevance there. I've studied some of the extra-Biblical interpretations of the afterlife, and I can find nothing that even deserves comment, at least nothing that supports Scripture; however, I do see from these studies where many of our myths about the sufferings in Hell and the immortality of souls derive from, but pagan belief in universal immortality should cause us to question the doctrine, not give us a reason to believe it.

After detouring from Scriptural proof, MacArthur then comes back to the Bible and says that we have "the testimony of the Word of the Living God."[18] I couldn't agree more that this is what's needed, but let's see where he goes with this. He reads from John Chapter 5, verse 28 and part of 29:

> "Do not marvel at this; for an hour is coming in which all those
> in the tombs will hear His voice, and come forth, those who
> have done good, to the resurrection of life; and those who have
> done evil, to the resurrection of judgment."

This is the Word of God and there's no problem with it. Still, there is no mention of eternal existence of the souls of the unsaved, however. The Greek word being translated as "judgment" which is also sometimes translated 'damnation' is *krisis*, and *The New Strong's Exhaustive Concordance of the Bible* (referred to as *Strong's* from here on) has among its possible meanings: a tribunal, divine justice, and accusation. I think it's fair to assume that this judgment referred to is the Day of Judgment, or the actual act of God accusing the unsaved of their sin and failure to receive the only acceptable pardon. The unsaved's *sentence* could possibly be implied here, but the *accusation* is the only thing we can know is indicated here, by definition of the words "damnation" or "judgment." This is the judgment that precedes being cast into the Lake of Fire, which is the sentence. And even if the ultimate sentence (not only the momentary act of judgment) was implied by the verse, we're only told that the lost will be resurrected to receive it, not that the Lake of Fire will torment human souls eternally. But

MacArthur again concludes from this verse that every soul is eternal, when this is not in the text at all. Only the assumption, first of all, that this verse is telling of the sentence and not only the accusation, and then by the unfounded, preconceived notion that the Lake of Fire does not ultimately destroy lost humans as Jesus said it would, can he come to the conclusion that every soul is eternal. This is a lot of assuming. MacArthur makes reference to the truth that believers will be fitted with a new body to go into eternity, but then he says that the unbeliever will "receive a body fitted for the eternal Lake of Fire, which is the final form of Hell into which they will be cast at that time in the future."[19] MacArthur again seems to be reading information into a passage when it cannot be supported with other scripture.

Jesus asked, "What does it profit a man if he gains the whole world but loses his soul?" The man *is* the soul according to Genesis Chapter 3, so the answer to Jesus's question is: It profits him nothing at all, and it can't. The loss of your soul means that you *are no more* because you are your soul, and this lines up with concepts established in the Psalms which we'll look at in Chapter 3 where we'll see language used for the lost that indicates "non-entity" and "non-existence." The soul is who you are. One can't lose it and still exist. The Bible tells us the unsaved are going to be cast into a lake of fire. We have every Biblical reason to believe this fire, figurative or literal (more likely literal), is the end of unrepentant human souls. So it is entirely out of line—and arguing in a circle—for MacArthur to go on from this last quote of his to this conclusion:

> "We will live forever. We will all live forever. We will all live forever, consciously, self-consciously, aware of our surroundings and aware of our response to those surroundings. And we will all live forever with a body suited for our surroundings; in the case of those raised to life, there will be a body like the resurrection body of Jesus Christ that can absorb all the glories of eternity, and manifest our eternal spirit through that glorified body, in praise and in service and in communion with God and all the redeemed. For those who are

given a body fit for Hell, it will be a body suited to feel the agonies of that eternal judgment."[20]

I'm in total agreement regarding the saved souls, however, there's nothing in Scripture that indicates the unsaved will "feel the agonies" for all eternity, nor that the unsaved are given a new body "fit for Hell." These are assumptions based on faulty doctrine about what follows judgment. There are indications that the unsaved will feel agonies in the intermediate state as they await judgment, for at least some period of time, and there is evidence they will be in agony again on judgment day, but as Scripture will show us more and more as we continue to explore deeper, no human soul will survive the Lake of Fire. None can endure it. As noted, Jesus figuratively used *Gehenna*, the Valley of Hinnom, Jerusalem's burning landfill, as the term associated with final judgment, which gets translated to the word "Hell." If He had wanted to indicate unending and eternal agony, misery, or torment, then He could have figuratively referenced any form of these in a way his audience of the day would understand it. But to represent final judgment, He chose Gehenna, a burning trash pile, a place they were familiar with, where nothing thrown in continues to exist in any form because it is consumed. And how many times does God tell us He will consume His enemies? Quite a few. It all adds up when we read and trust Scripture. We have no reason to believe that this reference to the Valley of Hinnom (Gehenna) indicates eternal existence. Just the opposite is true.

There's a very good reason why even two Godly men like Michael Easley and John MacArthur, both greatly used by the Lord to impact many souls for Christ I'm sure, have no better defense than this for the concept that all souls are eternal. The concept is not Biblical, plain and simple, and they are grasping for something that isn't there.

To sum up, there is no Biblical connection between being made in His image, and being divine or eternal. The Bible says we are desperately wicked (Jeremiah 17:9), far below God (Isaiah 6:1 and 55:9), spiritually dead (John 11:25, Romans 4:17, Ephesians 2:1), separated from God (Ephesians 2:12 and 4:18), insufficient (2 Corinthians 3:5-6), that He alone has immortality (1 Timothy 6:16), and that eternal life is the gift of God (Romans 6:23) and that even those of us who believe have not yet become immortal (1 Corinthians 15:54). The notion that we are partially divine and therefore wholly eternal without salvation is completely foreign to scripture, but all too common, unfortunately, in Christian teaching.

As just noted, Paul in Romans 9:22 and 23 indicates that God has endured with longsuffering "the vessels of wrath fitted to destruction." This Greek word for destruction, *apoleia*, is strikingly similar to the English word "abolish" which means "abolish, to make no more." *Strong's* has among its definitions waste, destruction, perish, die, ruin, and loss, none of which in any way give even a hint that these "vessels of wrath," these unsaved souls, will survive in any form after judgment. It also doesn't say they are given a new body, fitted for continued existence in the Lake of Fire, only that they are "fitted for destruction." The Bible is clear that souls are innately mortal, not immortal, and therefore are fitted for destruction at the point of their creation. This is not something that happens right before they are cast into the Lake of Fire. Unsaved people have not eaten and will never eat from the Tree of Life that would make them go on living forever, anywhere. In fact, just make a careful reading of Romans 9:22 and I think you'll see that this "fitted to destruction" was past tense. The 1965 *Bible in Basic English* translates it this way:

> "What if God, desiring to let his wrath and his power be seen, for a long time put up with the vessels of wrath *which were ready for destruction*" (italics for emphasis)

And the Literal Translation reads:

> "But if God, desiring to demonstrate His wrath, and to make His power known, endured in much long-suffering vessels of wrath *having been fitted out for destruction, . . .*" (italics for emphasis)

It seems clear that whatever it is about the unsaved that makes them fit for destruction was already in place from the point of their creation. So what is it? Is it the "asbestos-like" body that some defenders of the traditional Hell doctrine claim the unsaved souls are fitted with? Not likely. No, it's the mortal soul that our Merciful God created just that way for the express purpose of being able to rid Himself of human offense, but without there being eternal agony for those souls. "Fitted for destruction" essentially means "created mortal, and headed for a date with destruction by fire."

Let's look at another passage of Scripture that tells us all souls are not eternal. In Matthew Chapter 10, Jesus is forewarning his disciples that they are going to be hated for His Name's sake, and that they will be persecuted. Then He tells them in Matthew 10:28:

> "Don't be afraid of those who kill the body, but are not able to kill the soul. Rather, fear him who is able to destroy both soul and body in Gehenna." (WEB)

Here's another passage of Scripture that is undeniable. Do we really have innate immortality? 1 Timothy 6:15 and 16 say,

> "15b...who is the blessed and only Ruler, the King of kings, and Lord of lords; 16 *who alone has immortality*, dwelling in unapproachable light; whom no man has seen, nor can see: to whom be honor and eternal power. Amen." (WEB — italics for emphasis)

This is quite a list of divine attributes that Paul gives us here, and one of them is immortality. And it specifically says that He alone possesses it. That makes sense, since we are not divine, according to Scripture. So how do we get this immortality? The same way it would have happened in the Garden of Eden, were Adam and Eve capable of obedience – eating from the Tree of Life. We've come full circle now. Matthew 10:28 concerns persevering through trial to reach the goal, and this chapter of Timothy follows suit. Paul tells Timothy in 1 Timothy 6:11-12,

> "But you, man of God, flee these things, and follow after righteousness, godliness, faith, love, perseverance, and

gentleness. Fight the good fight of faith. *Take hold of the eternal life* to which you were called, and you confessed the good confession in the sight of many witnesses." (WEB — italics for emphasis)

So we have Jesus advising them to fear God because He can destroy (*apollumi*/abolish) the soul, thereby not giving it eternal life, and then Paul tells Timothy (and us) to pursue righteousness so as to "take hold of eternal life." We began this chapter in the Garden of Eden with the Tree of Life representing the availability of immortality but with Adam and Eve being driven away from it, representing man's inability to attain it by our own efforts. And now we've been promised this eternal life if we endure. So where in Scripture do we see our receiving this eternal life? Appropriately, it's in the very last book of the Bible, in Chapter 2 of Revelation and then finally in Chapter 22, the very last chapter in the very last book of the Bible. That Tree of Life makes another appearance. God is the first and the last, the beginning and the end and He alone has immortality. It's more than coincidental and it's quite significant that this Tree of Life is found in the first and last books of the Bible. We begin with it, the entire Bible is the story of God's love and how *He* wants to give eternal life to us, not let us gain it on our own, and then we end with Jesus's own words, saying in Revelation 2:7:

> "He who has an ear, let him hear what the Spirit says to the assemblies. To him who overcomes *I will give to eat* from the Tree of Life, which is in the Paradise of my God." (italics for emphasis — WEB)

In Revelation 22:2, we're told that the Tree of Life is for the healing of the nations. "The nations" means it is offered to those from all people groups of earth who persevered in the faith, and the condition that all nations need to be healed from is our perishing souls.

The only other mentions of the Tree of Life outside of Genesis and Revelation are in Proverbs, most notably 11:30 which says, "The fruit of the righteous is a Tree of Life." The

Hebrew word translated "fruit" is *periy* and *Strong's* defines it as "reward." And that fits exactly with the other teachings about it. Yes, immortality belongs only to God, and He rewards it to those who overcome. Paul called it a prize. So how do we overcome? Jesus tells us we will have trouble in this world, but to take heart because He has already overcome the world. We only need to put our faith in what He has done, put on Christ, and when our faith is there, He will empower us to overcome, and one day receive eternal life, which we even now have the surety of because of the indwelling of the Holy Spirit.

There's one more thing that we should not miss about this life-giving tree. Remember that it is eating of its fruit that leads to eternal life. It's no coincidence that the Lord himself hung on a tree when He gave his life for us, or when in Matthew 2:26 He told us to eat of his body. Not only is He the bread of Life come down from heaven (John 6:35), but He is, and offers, the fruit we must "eat of" to gain immortality.

Let's look quickly at a few more verses that seem to tell us that all souls are not immortal.

> 2 Timothy 1:10: "and which now has been manifested through the appearing of our Savior Christ Jesus, who abolished death and brought life and immortality to light through the gospel" (ESV)

According to this verse, Jesus Christ brings about immortality. It is not an innate attribute for humans.

> John 6:50-51: "This is the bread that comes down from heaven, so that one may eat of it and *not die*. I am the living bread that came down from heaven. If anyone eats of this bread, he will *live forever*. And the bread that I will give for the life of the world is my flesh." (ESV – Italics for emphasis)

This seems very clear. If we accept Christ's sacrifice, we will not die. If we do not, the implication is that we *would* die.

> James 5:19-20: "My brothers, if anyone among you wanders from the truth and someone brings him back, let him know

that whoever brings back a sinner from his wandering will save his soul from death and will cover a multitude of sins." (ESV)

Here we have another confirmation that the soul of the sinner is headed for death. He could have easily stated, as so many modern Bible teachers do, that he would save his soul from "an eternity separated from God." But he didn't.

> Jude 6: "And the angels who did not stay within their own position of authority, but left their proper dwelling, he has kept in eternal chains under gloomy darkness until the judgment of the great day—" (ESV)

It's interesting that something was in an "eternal" state *until* a later date, and even more interesting that the later date is the date of the final judgment. This proves, as so many other verses do, that this word "eternal" is not always referring to timeless eternity.

> Psalm 33:18-19: "Behold, the eye of the LORD is on those who fear him, on those who hope in his steadfast love, that he may deliver their soul from death and keep them alive in famine." (ESV)

An Old Testament reminder of the same thing: Souls are headed toward death if they are not delivered.

> John 11:25-26:   " Jesus said unto her, I am the resurrection, and the life: he that believeth in me, though he were dead, yet shall he live: And whosoever liveth and believeth in me shall never die. Believest thou this?" (KJV)

Again the implication here is that if we do not believe this, we *will* die.

> Jude 20-22: "But you, beloved, building yourselves up in your most holy faith and praying in the Holy Spirit, keep yourselves in the love of God, waiting for the mercy of our Lord Jesus Christ *that leads to eternal life*." (ESV — italics for emphasis)

Jude is addressing believers, people who already "have" eternal life we would say, yet he tells them to keep themselves in the love of God, "*waiting* for the mercy of our Lord Jesus

Christ that *leads to* eternal life." Clearly he does not see himself or other believers as technically already literally having eternal life, only the promise of it for those who wait and persevere. This idea of persevering to eternal life is mentioned elsewhere in Scripture such as in Matthew 24:13 where Jesus says, "But the one who endures to the end will be saved" (ESV), in James 1:12 where it says that when one stands "the test he will receive the crown of *life*, which God has promised to those who love him" (ESV), and several other places.

But Jude also advises them to snatch others "out of" the fire. Have they already been cast into the Lake of Fire? Of course not, but they are "in the fire" in the sense that this is their destiny if they do not accept God's offer of salvation from death. They are mortal and fitted for fiery destruction if their turning in faith toward the God who loves them doesn't happen.

> Romans 8:2: "For the law of the Spirit of life in Christ Jesus hath made me free from the law of sin and death." (KJV)

Because all men will die physically, and we know that Paul of course did, this law of death that he claims to be free from could only be referring to the death of the soul.

> Isaiah 10:16-18: "16 Therefore the Lord GOD of hosts will send wasting sickness among his stout warriors, and under his glory a burning will be kindled, like the burning of fire. 17 The light of Israel will become a fire, and his Holy One a flame, and it will burn and devour his thorns and briers in one day. 18 The glory of his forest and of his fruitful land the LORD will destroy, both soul and body, and it will be as when a sick man wastes away." (ESV)

Here we see souls and bodies devoured, and in a single day, and them being compared to a man who wastes away. This could be a reference to how God will deal physically with those being punished, and a simultaneous predictor of the day of judgment when they would be cast in the Lake of Fire.

> 1 Corinthians 15:50: "Now this I say, brethren, that flesh and blood cannot inherit the kingdom of God; neither doth corruption inherit incorruption." (KJV)

This verse really drives home the idea that there is no way the lost can go on existing forever. The Greek word being translated as "incorruption" is *aphtharsia*, and the *Strong's* concordance has as one of its primary meanings "general unending existence." There is nothing in the word itself that denotes a blessed eternal life, only an existence that has no end, the very thing that traditionalists claim even unbelievers possess. Let's look at the context of the verse, and first note that Paul is speaking to "brethren." Then in the very next verse, he tells the brethren that what he is doing is revealing a mystery, the mystery that some would be changed physically at the time of the rapture, and also that those believers who had already died would be raised, but with a body that cannot perish. These are both part of inheriting the general unending existence that Paul spoke of in verse 50, and this is not a promise for the lost, but for the saved. Scripture never anywhere maintains that the lost will go on existing eternally, but clearly maintains that death will be their end.

> Romans 6:23: "For the wages of sin is death, but the free gift of God is eternal life in Christ Jesus our Lord." (ESV)

This free gift of eternal life is contrasted with death in this verse, and because we know that all die physically, we can again reasonably assume that it is the death of the soul that's being referenced. And there's no warning that eternal existence in conscious torment is the wage of sin. The context of the fates however is that the fate will be permanent – either permanent death or permanent life. We can take this at face value and believe it, or we can continue to redefine death and imagine all sorts of things this could mean. It's my hope that we will begin to look at the plain language of the Bible and put our trust in it, and it's also my hope that this chapter has gone a long way toward showing Biblically that there is no reason to believe human souls without God's salvation will go on existing into eternity in any conscious form. But we certainly haven't exhausted the evidence.

CHAPTER 3

The Plain Language of Scripture

One of the things I've found fascinating about Scripture over the years is the vast amount of foreshadowing and symbolism it contains. Often you may hear a Bible teacher say something like, "This event is a 'picture' or 'type' of how when such and such is going to one day do this or that," and things to that effect. For a specific example, we can look to how Abraham was asked to offer his son Isaac as a sacrifice, and how this foreshadowed God the Father offering His Son as a sacrifice. Isaac carried the wood he would have been sacrificed on, just as Jesus carried the wood of His cross — and there are numerous parallels between those two accounts. We looked at some foreshadowing events from the Garden of Eden as well. And things like this are woven throughout Scripture, countless times, many still undiscovered, I'm sure.

With foreshadowing as one of the primary ways God reveals deeper truths to us in His Word, it seems reasonable to understand all the language of the death and destruction of the enemies of God as prefiguring ultimate destruction at final judgment. These actions exemplify how He deals with those He rejects. In this chapter, we'll see this message repeated numerous times in the Old and New Testaments. We'll begin with a simple list of verses to be read with minimal commentary. Then we'll delve in a little deeper with several of them. Some of the following are clearly speaking of final judgment. Others are speaking of the earthly demise or death of the lost or rebellious. And some probably speak to both as perhaps a dual reference. But even an Old Testament verse where an enemy of God is threatened with death seems a clear prediction of a future final death, with prototyping and foreshadowing such a prominent method of establishing truths within God's Word. Most notable is that no story of God's judgment or destruction in Scripture ever seems in any way to type or foreshadow an eternity of torment.

> Matthew 3:11-12 "I indeed baptize you in water for repentance, but he who comes after me is mightier than I, whose shoes I am not worthy to carry. He will baptize you in the Holy Spirit. His winnowing fork is in his hand, and he will thoroughly cleanse his threshing floor. He will gather his wheat into the barn, but the chaff he will burn up with unquenchable fire." (WEB)

We'll look at "unquenchable fire" more closely in Chapter 4. But I'll say briefly here that the connotation it's been given within the traditional Hell doctrine is a fire that burns for eternity. But read it again, and don't read "ever-burning" where it reads "unquenchable." All we can really get out of the word itself is that it won't be quenched. In other words, God or no one else puts it out until it finishes its destructive work. And several verses of Scripture, this one in Matthew chapter 3 for one example, tell us what unquenchable fire will do. It will burn something up — in other words, completely obliterate it. And in this verse, the chaff is a reference to people — souls who do not belong to the Lord.

> Psalm 37:20 "But the wicked will perish; the enemies of the LORD are like the glory of the pastures; they vanish—like smoke they vanish away" (ESV)

No commentary necessary for that one.

> Psalm 68:2b "as wax melts before fire, so the wicked shall perish before God" (ESV)

...or that one.

> Psalm 1;4 "The wicked are not so, but are like chaff that the wind drives away." (ESV)

The lost are again compared to chaff.

Confirming this Old testament idea that the wicked perish in the presence of, and at the appearing of God, we have the commonly misunderstood passage in 2 Thessalonians 1:5-10. I won't comment on it here. We'll dig in pretty deep on it in Chapter 4.

> Isaiah 11:4 "but with righteousness he will judge the poor, and decide with equity for the humble of the earth. He will strike the earth with the rod of his mouth; and with the breath of his lips he will kill the wicked." (WEB)

Killing them and submitting them to torment for all eternity are not the same thing. Different language would be used throughout Scripture if eternal torment were intended.

> Romans 1:32 "...who, knowing the ordinance of God, that those who practice such things are worthy of death, not only do the same, but also approve of those who practice them." (WEB)

"Worthy of death" and "deserving to suffer for all eternity" are vastly different concepts. One is Scriptural, and one is man-made.

> Psalm 73:19 "How suddenly are they destroyed, perished and horribly consumed" (The 1587 *Geneva Bible*)

This is pretty clear. And again, even if this is a passage only referring to the earthly demise of the unrighteous, it's a foreshadowing predictor and example of how God ends those who would oppose Him.

> Isaiah 33:12 "The peoples will be like the burning of lime, like thorns that are cut down and burned in the fire." (WEB)

Another example of being destroyed by fire, not tormented endlessly by it.

> Malachi 4:1 "For behold, the day cometh, that shall burn as an oven; and all the proud, and all that do wickedly, shall be stubble: and the day that cometh shall burn them up, saith the

LORD of hosts, that it shall leave them neither root nor branch." (1833 *Webster Bible*)

This is an end times prophecy and it couldn't be clearer that complete destruction awaits the lost. If this were only a reference to their physical demise, when in actuality what awaits them is an eternity of conscious suffering, wouldn't the latter be the greater threat? Wouldn't that be the warning? But we're told that they will be burned up.

We could list these all day. Perhaps someone has published a more exhaustive list somewhere, but this should be enough for now to establish a precedent in judgment. There must be literally hundreds of verses in the Bible that speak of the death, destruction, and even disintegration of those who reject God, and who He therefore rejects in return. And while not all of these verses were directly speaking to eternal fates, again, the standard for how God punishes is established.

Let's imagine there were story after story in the Old Testament of how God instructed his people in battle to not only take their enemies out, but rather subject them to as lengthy a torment as possible. If that were the case, a traditionalist could argue that God set a foreshadowing standard for conscious eternal torment after judgment. But you won't find this. The most severe punishment, without venturing over into the sick and twisted side, is to lose one's life. And the Bible is filled with this. And it's a picture of how even the immaterial soul will one day be faced with a date with destruction and extinction. There are two deaths spoken of in Scripture. All of us will succumb to the first death (unless we are here in the very last days when the rapture occurs — which is actually possible given world events right now). But those of us who have put our faith in Christ for salvation will not be harmed by the second death which would end the soul.

Let's now go a little deeper on a few verses and passages in Scripture. But I'll warn you up front that it will be a little much. We don't need to disassemble Scripture the way we'll do on a few verses in order to understand the plain meaning. And there's nothing wrong with just trusting the surface meaning of verses such as the ones we've been looking at. God never warns that the punishment for unbelief will be an eternity of torment. That traditional idea has to be painfully extracted from Scripture, first by the false notion that every soul is immortal, and then through poor interpretation of a number of verses we'll address in the following chapter. But the point of taking a few verses apart as we'll do in the following few pages is to demonstrate that even when we dig really deep or go back to the original languages, it still means the same thing. The ultimate punishment for faithlessness toward our Creator is death and annihilation.

Here's one of the foundational verses of our faith. And it has more to say about eternal fates than we may have realized.

John 3:16 "For God so loved the world, that he gave his one and only Son, that whoever believes in him should not perish, but have eternal life." (WEB)

This is probably the most well-known verse in the Bible. Even those who know very little about the Bible or the Christian faith have quite often learned this verse somewhere along the way. This is a cherished verse for Christians because it sums up our salvation in just a few words. But it's a valuable verse in this particular study because it lays out the only two ultimate fates for any human soul. In fact it defines what we non-traditionalists believe and why we are sometimes called conditionalists.

According to this verse, eternal life is *conditional* and dependent upon believing in the Son. It's so easy to miss the obvious because of familiarity with this verse. But listen to what it tells us: We either *perish* or we have *eternal life*. How easy it would have been here and throughout Scripture for those whom God chose to pen His Word to make clear the concept of eternal agony in Hell if that were a possibility. But God, not veiling any warning of punishment, here makes known that the punishment for unbelief is to perish. And we know this perishing isn't simply referring to the physical body because *all* of our bodies will one day perish, whether we're believers or not, and the verse is drawing a clear line of distinction between those who believe on Christ and those who won't. That leaves only the soul to which this verse could be referring.

Every soul that God created will either experience everlasting life or perish. This verse seems to be a clear warning in plain, understandable language. But the traditionalist, because of belief in an everlasting state of conscious torment for lost souls, is forced to redefine the word "perish" to mean a constant state of perishing that never ends—eternal torture. But even a simple definition of the English word "perish" signifies that something perishing will eventually come to an end. The *process* of perishing, in any application, is finite, but the ultimate effect is permanent or everlasting. In fact, there is no precedent in life or in Scripture that something perishing or dying could do so without end. It's a logical impossibility. Something cannot undergo a process of perishing throughout eternity. That would actually mean it was imperishable, since it never finished perishing. Let's look at the Greek word that's being translated to the English word "perish."

It's *apollumi* in the Greek, and the primary *Strong's* concordance definition is "to destroy fully." *Thayer's Greek-English Lexicon of the New Testament* (referred to only as *Thayer's* from here forward) defines *apollumi* as "to destroy, *i.e.*, to put out of the way entirely, to be blotted out, to vanish away, to abolish, put an end to, ruin," and Moulton and Milligan's *The Vocabulary of the Greek New Testament* (referred to only as *Moulton and Milligan's* going forward) has the word as meaning "of destroying life."

Apollumi appears eighty-six times in the Bible, and it is usually translated into English as "destroy" or "perish" and sometimes refers to something being "lost." Regarding the translations into the word "lost," aside from one single usage in a parable when it's used to refer to a coin that a woman lost, it always refers to lost sheep. In parable language, a sheep who was lost, if not found, would surely perish. When Jesus in Matthew 15:24 referred to many in Israel as "lost sheep," He meant that if He didn't "find" them (or more specifically, if they didn't respond when called), they would of course eventually perish, and the analogy involving sheep is used because a sheep lost from the fold and from its shepherd is at the mercy of wolves who aren't merciful to sheep, and also would be exposed to other dangers that it couldn't overcome on its own.

A lost sheep, though alive at the moment, was as good as dead. So the argument could not be made that just because the "apollumi'd" sheep still existed, it could represent something described as fully destroyed, yet remain for eternity. If not found, a lost sheep will die. And the same is true for the soul. An unsaved soul is still a living soul, but it's also a dead or dying soul in the sense that it is ultimately headed for its destruction. The lost soul will outlive the flesh to be sure. But there is an appointment with God, after Christ's 1000-year reign on earth, when every unbeliever will stand before Him to be judged, and will then be cast into the Lake of Fire. The book of Revelation calls this the "second death" (Revelation 20:14). The first thing that died was the body, and now the soul will suffer the same fate. Only by the unfounded presumption that there will be unending misery for lost humanity can the traditionalist support a definition of *apollumi* that means anything other than "to destroy fully" regarding souls.

Jesus used that term again in Matthew 10:28 where He tells us not to fear man who can only kill the body, but to fear God who can destroy (*apollumi*) both body and soul in Hell (*Gehenna* in Greek). This is another great verse supporting the non-traditional position, and we'll also address the word "Hell" and its true meaning and examine the whole verse a little later. But for now, let's look at the words "kill," "destroy," and "body" in this verse. The word "destroy" again is the same word translated "perish" in John 3:16. If it meant eternal misery, it seems that Jesus would not have used it to describe what God would do to the soul *and* to the body because the word *soma* translated as "body" here at the end of the verse is the same word Jesus used at the beginning of the verse referring to that which "man" can kill.   Interestingly, there is however a slight difference in the Greek words Jesus chose to describe how man can "kill" the body and how God can "destroy" body and soul. The *Strong's* concordance defines this word being translated "kill" as a "slaying."   This is significant because a slain body could still exist in the presence of the slayer for a time, but a body, or soul for that matter, fully destroyed (*apollumi*, abolished) is gone, lost, and out of existence as defined by *Strong's, Thayer's,* and *Moulton and Milligan's*.

Further support for this is found in the fact that the multitude that wanted to crucify Jesus was not just calling for Him to be killed in the sense of slaying.   The word translated "slain" was not used there.   They wanted Him slain no doubt, but He was a burden and an offense to them, and they wanted Him utterly out of existence, so the arguably stronger word *apollumi* is used. And the same word is used after Jesus healed on the Sabbath in Matthew 12:14: "Then the Pharisees went out and held council against Him, as to how they might destroy (*apollumi*) Him," not just slay or kill Him.   It is quite possible that, sensing the conviction He put them under, they were, almost subconsciously, knowing who He really was, desiring the government to do the impossible—not only slay this person but, in vain hope, put the very King of Kings and Lord of Lords out of existence as if it could relieve their guilt.   And isn't this what so many false religions are still trying to do with Jesus? Ironically, His death is exactly what would have relieved their guilt, but not because death could keep Him, as they hoped, but because He would live again, and one day keep all those whose trust is in Him.

Psalm 73:27 "For behold, those who are far from you shall perish; you put an end to everyone who is unfaithful to you." (ESV)

Here we have an Old Testament account that claims the same fate for the unsaved that the New Testament verse of John 3:16 did — that they perish and come to an end. In this psalm, Asaph has been confessing that he was jealous over the prosperity of the wicked. And he says that his feet had almost slipped because, although he had made great efforts to maintain a pure heart, he was becoming extremely discouraged with the well-being of the lost in comparison to his troubles. But God didn't leave him in that place. In verse 17 Asaph tells us that it was when he entered into the Sanctuary of God that he came to a realization of the ultimate fate of the wicked who now so often seem to have no problems. The 1901 American Standard Version has that he "considered their latter end," and the English Standard version translates it "then I discerned their end."

So, what was it about entering God's sanctuary that informed him concerning the end of the wicked, and maybe more importantly — that they do in fact have an end? Was it simply being in the presence of the temple? Not likely. Could it have been a special revelation from God? It's possible but still not likely. The most likely reason he came to an understanding of the unsaved's end was simply that the scriptures were opened. God's Word revealed truth to him. So we can know a couple of things from this claim of his. First, we can know that the fate of the wicked is taught clearly enough in the Old Testament writings prior to his, to understand it fully. And we can know what the end of the wicked is. But let's not misinterpret the word "end" to mean "final conscious destination." The fact that the wicked *have an end* as opposed to a continual existence somewhere is the most significant thing we can gain here.

The translations vary but all have the same meaning. This particular rendering is from the English Standard Version, and several other versions also tell us in the latter half of the verse that the unsaved faithless come to an "end." Some versions translate their fate as "destruction" which by any common understanding of the word, would mean the same thing. It's the Hebrew word *tsamath* being translated, and *Strong's* defines it as to extirpate, consume, cut off, or vanish. All of these words describe someone or something that comes to an end. So, does the traditional version of Hell hold up to this scripture? While traditionalists believe the unsaved come to a horrible fate, they maintain that they have no end, that their souls are eternal, and that their torment is perpetual.

But here we see that they do in fact have an end according to God's Word. This is not the only verse for confirmation however. There are countless others, and several more inside this very psalm. Verse 18 says God makes the wicked fall down to ruin or destruction, and the Hebrew word used there is *mashshu'ah* which means "desolation" and "destruction." Verse 19 says they are brought into *shammah* in a moment, which is defined as "waste" and "desolation," among other things. Verse 19 also says that they will be "utterly consumed" which is a combination of Hebrew words, one of which is *suph* and *Strong's* defines it as "terminate, consume, have an end, and perish," and the other word is *tamam* and is defined by *Strong's*, among other things, as "accomplish, cease, consume, have done, come to an end, be all gone, be spent, and be wasted." There is nothing here in this psalm to indicate eternal torment for these souls who do not know the Living God.

Some may try to claim that all of these descriptions of the wicked are referring only to their physical frame, but this can't be reconciled logically. We must first consider that we all die physically, and Asaph is obviously making a clear distinction between himself, a faithful believer, and the unfaithful unbelievers. Also, it would go against his own premise of the entire first half of the psalm. There he is describing the great ease and length of life that many healthy and wealthy unbelievers enjoy.

Clearly, when Asaph says "end" he means "end of being." And doesn't that just make sense? If the punishment for uncovered sin is perpetual and unending, then the sin hasn't and cannot and will not ever truly be paid for, which is contrary to the Word of God, because that essentially maintains that God will not bring the wicked to an end as He promises in multiple places in Scripture. Rather it implies that He will not finish paying the wage for sin. It is God, by the way, who pays the wage, not us. We perform the work of sin, and God pays the wage which we know is death (Romans 6:23), unless we have covered ourselves from His wrath in the blood of Jesus.   Death, and more specifically, the Second Death which we're talking about here is a cessation of life, not just missing out on a blessed life in God's eternal presence as the traditionalist maintains. That's why "life" and "eternal life" are used interchangeably when speaking of the blessing that God offers. There is no form of life for unbelievers, even an awful one in an eternal Hell, after judgment.

We find repeatedly in Scripture that the Lord will eventually accomplish His purposes, and we have numerous verses that tell us He will consume and destroy the unbelieving. So if the traditionalist were correct and the wicked are never consumed and have no true end, but only exist in a conscious state to endure timeless wrath, then we first have to deny the plain language of God's Word to the contrary, and we also have to assume that the Lord will never fully accomplish what he promised the wicked, which was death, to perish, to be destroyed, to be consumed, and to have an end. This is simply not scripturally sound.

Matthew 7:13-14 "Go in through the narrow gate; for wide is the gate and broad is the way that leads to destruction, and many are the ones entering in through it. For narrow is the gate, and constricted is the way that leads away into life, and few are the ones finding it." (LITV)

Much like John 3:16, here, back in the New Testament, we have the very words of Jesus, and very plain understandable words at that. There are two pathways and two gates. Every human soul will walk along and enter through either the broad or the narrow. One path leads to life and one to "destruction," which is the Greek word *apoleia*, a very similar Greek word in sound and meaning to *apollumi*. It has among its definitions: die, destruction, ruin, loss, waste, and perish. Again, we have clear language concerning the ultimate fates of lost and saved souls with no indications that we should presume a state of eternal suffering. And as I've asked before, how easy and appropriate would it have been for the Lord, here and in multiple other places, to warn of eternal suffering if that in fact is the result of unbelief?

Psalm 37:10 "For yet a little while, and the wicked shall not be: yea, thou shalt diligently consider his place, and it shall not be." (KJV)

The Hebrew word being translated as "shall not be" is *ayin* and according to *Strong's*, it means "to be nothing," "not exist," "a non-entity," "none," "nothing," and "to nought," among other definitions. This lines up well with other scripture which claims God's enemies will ultimately perish, be consumed, be destroyed, etc. But interestingly, the psalmist even adds another point. He says that even the wicked's "place" will be non-existent. Why add this? If we're to believe the traditional view of Hell, that there's a place in which human souls will somehow (in spite of all sound Scripture to the contrary) endure to all eternity, then it must be somewhere. Why not say that it will never be found? Why not tell us of the horrors the wicked will face in eternal Hell? It seems the reason is, as the Word of God tells us, the place "shall not be;" it will no longer exist.

And what place is he talking about? Hell, Sheol, Hades, the place of departed spirits. He doesn't say they don't have a place. The Bible makes it most clear that the unsaved do in fact have a place, and that place is Hell (*Sheol* in the Old Testament, *Hades* in the New). And this verse makes it clear that eventually, they and that place will not exist. And when will this happen? The inspired psalmist says in "a little while." Of course, this is speaking relatively. With the Lord, a thousand years is like a day (2 Peter 3:8). And in fact, it will happen at the end of the 1000-year reign of Christ on earth according to Revelation 20:3-7. This is when the heavens, the earth, and everything in it will be consumed with fire. We're told that at that time even Hades will be cast into the Lake of Fire. And we know who will reside in Hades at that time: the unsaved. Also, Revelation 20:11 says that at the time of the great white throne judgment of the lost, the earth and heavens flee away from God's presence. But notice that it also says that there is not even a place for them:

> Rev 20:11 "I saw a great white throne, and him who sat on it, from whose face the earth and the heaven fled away. There was *found no place for them.*" (italics for emphasis — WEB)

This sounds exactly like what the psalmist said about the place of the wicked. And we cannot just claim that the earth and heavens have fled away to some other location. The verse plainly says no place found for them. And we know from elsewhere in scripture that the heavens and the earth will be consumed by fire. Peter claimed this in 2 Peter 3:10 and 3:12 when he talked about how everything we now call home will dissolve in fervent heat. So we have two New Testament references that appear in every way to mirror what the psalmist says in the Old Testament. The old heavens and earth have not fled to somewhere else, simply annexed from the new creation. They flee into nothingness. Having "no place" is equivalent to having been consumed.

So we can take any of the verses that tell us of the ultimate destruction, consumption, and inability to endure of the wicked as stand-alone verses that indicate that they will not always exist, or we can combine them and see the congruence of them all, but then we find a passage like Psalm 37:10 that really sums it up. It makes it so clear that the wicked do have a place, but that in a relatively little while, their place and they themselves will no longer exist. Why do we struggle against Scripture? And why are those of us who wish to take it at face value accused of blasphemy or trying to create a soft, weak view of God in judgment. There's nothing weak about a God who destroys his enemies. One could argue that there's something weak or even bully-like about a god who would allow his enemies to exist in agony for all eternity as the traditionalist claims, but there's nothing weak about the God who destroys, consumes, and from whom the heavens and earth will flee away at the end of time.

"...if by turning the cities of Sodom and Gomorrah to ashes he condemned them to extinction, making them an example of what is going to happen to the ungodly;" (2 Peter 2:6 ESV)

There may not be a clearer statement of what will happen to those who have rejected the pull of God. I intended to reserve this verse for a later chapter, but it is such clear, obvious language that I couldn't exclude it from this chapter on "plain language." First, we see that the wicked's condemnation is extinction. This lines up well with numerous passages referring to the permanent destruction of the wicked. And as I have questioned regarding some verses already and will again, let's ask the question of whether this verse is only describing the earthly demise of the wicked. I don't see how we could claim that. First, this is a verse that seems to be picturing what will become of "the ungodly" as a whole, not only describing what will happen to individuals. And as we know, we will all die physically, and by many sources and in many ways, whether godly or ungodly, so this appears to be speaking of final destinies of souls. Secondly, Scripture is also very clear about the fate of Sodom and Gomorrah in several other books of the Bible. One is Deuteronomy 29:23 where the demise of the land where the Israelites who would turn from God is likened to that of Sodom and Gomorrah:

"...the whole land burned out with brimstone and salt, nothing sown and nothing growing, where no plant can sprout, an overthrow like that of Sodom and Gomorrah, Admah, and Zeboiim, which the LORD overthrew in his anger and wrath" (ESV)

And we have Jeremiah 49:18:

> "As when Sodom and Gomorrah and their neighboring cities were overthrown, says the LORD, no man shall dwell there, no man shall sojourn in her." (ESV)

We see that the land and its inhabitants "burned out" and nothing can live there, not even a plant. This is a picture of total desolation, and a place void of habitation. In fact, it's really no place at all. It ceased to exist. This reinforces Psalm 37:10 that we discussed previously in this chapter where we learned that the wicked's being and even their place of being would cease to exist.

So Peter has claimed that the inhabitants of Sodom and Gomorrah came to extinction, and that this is an example of what will happen to all ungodly people. It doesn't get much plainer than that.

There are many other verses in Scripture that indicate only two ultimate outcomes for every soul, and we could go on analyzing them and the definitions of the words in the original languages for many more pages. But we need to move forward. The following are only a few more verses to consider, if the reader would like to do their own word studies. I'll only briefly comment on these:

> John 6:50-51: "This is the bread which comes down out of heaven, that anyone may eat of it and not die. I am the living bread which came down out of heaven. If anyone eats of this bread, he will live forever. Yes, the bread which I will give for the life of the world is my flesh." (WEB)

If the consequences of not "eating" of the Bread from heaven were eternal conscious torment rather than death, what a perfect place to relate that. But instead the implication is that if one won't live forever, they'll die, and be lifeless forever.

> James 5:20 "Let him know that whoever brings back a sinner from his wandering will save his soul from death and will cover a multitude of sins." (ESV)

From death? Or from eternal torment? "Well, death is eternal torment, as you're separated from God for all eternity," a traditionalist might say. But I would ask them where that's stated in Scripture. And if they had an answer, they'd likely point you to the passages we'll look at in the next chapter. We'll find that those passages do not establish this idea at all.

Many of the verses we looked at in this chapter were speaking of the earthly demise of God's enemies, but they firmly establish how God deals with those He rejects, and who reject Him. And most likely, many are dual in purpose, describing or foreshadowing the ultimate end of being of these as well.

What we *don't* see is notable, too. We don't see after any verse that describes the earthly fall of an unbeliever, something like, "Oh, but after this, it gets even worse, because they will come back to life in a world far different and far more devastating than this one, and there they will suffer torments beyond anything imaginable in this life, and not just for a time, but for all time, and beyond time, into eternity." No, that sort of teaching began a couple hundred years after the penning of God's word was concluded. Nevertheless, this has become the common way we, the Church, represent the afterlife of the unsaved.

Maybe you've heard the old saying, "The road to Hell is paved with good intentions." The idea is that sometimes people mean well, but their efforts are in vain or even destructive to their own good intentions. We could apply that to this doctrine. The road to this doctrine of eternal Hell is kept open and serviced by many people whose intentions truly are good. So many people have simply never studied it. And who can blame them? A deep study on judgment doesn't have the appeal that say, a study on Hope, Healing, or some other positive theme might have. Therefore, most Christians who believe the traditional line of thinking, not wanting lost people to suffer eternally, then share the idea. It's a noble effort, I'm sure, in most cases.

But if we've come to believe that a non-traditional idea of judgment is more Scriptural, desiring people to not be destroyed out of existence is still plenty of motivation to share the good news of salvation through Jesus Christ.   And when we give people the consequences of judgment, and it's something we can easily support with Scripture, we'll be all the more confident and more likely to do it in the first place.   And we won't have to answer a question like, "Why would a loving God make people to be tormented for all eternity?"   There's no good answer for that question because it's not what the Bible maintains will happen to the lost.   However, if you're sharing the true and biblical consequences of denying salvation — that the one without salvation will be destroyed back out of existence, and if the hearer then wants to ask something like, "Well, how could God do such a thing?" — the answer is easy.   You were nothing before God made you, and if you reject the offer of eternal life by rejecting the means to it, you deserve your first estate: non-entity.   And who can argue with that?   Only those who reject the Bible as a whole, because it's undeniable that this is the plain language of Scripture on the matter of judgment.

CHAPTER 4

Traditionalist Proof Texts Examined

As we learned in Chapter 2, the traditional idea of the lost being in conscious torment for all eternity finds its strength first in the mistaken concept that all souls, saved or lost, are immortal and must exist consciously forever. We ruled that out, at least as a concept taught in the Garden. We noted that the expulsion didn't cause or represent eternal separation from God. Rather it proved the inability of gaining immortality by our own hand, at the same time proving we are not immortal but were instead created mortal, with the potential to become immortal. If we were immortal, of what benefit is the Tree of Life that makes one go on living forever? (Just an aside: Keep this in mind as we're coming into days where we may see medical and technological "miracles" which promise immortality. I know this sounds ridiculous to many, but strange things are happening these days, and at some point, the world may offer something that looks too good to be true: It is. It was established in the third chapter of Genesis that mankind cannot by his own hand, go on living forever. There was no exception for "well, unless they gain some new med tech knowledge a few thousand years from now...then they may be able to discover a way to go on living forever." No, it simply cannot happen except at the hand of Jesus Christ.)

I apologize for that detour, but I'm concerned that a heavy deception is at the doorstep.

We are not immortal beings...yet. And unsaved individuals never will be. Therefore, we cannot begin there as a point of support for the traditional doctrine of eternal suffering. So, will the other point of "strength" work? Are there verses or passages in Scripture which tell us lost human souls will suffer for all eternity? I hope you're pleasantly surprised, as I was, to find out these verses don't exist. There are about ten misunderstood and mis-used passages of Scripture that are believed to demonstrate the reality of eternal suffering, but we'll look at them all in this chapter and find they do no such thing.

Over a decade ago, when I began to seriously question the traditional view of eternal Hell and immortality, I purchased a book entitled *Two Views of Hell,* wherein the topic was debated from the traditional position, and a non-traditional conditionalist position. Edward Fudge argued the conditionalist position and Robert Peterson argued for the traditional. As I pursued this study, I found most of Fudge's scriptural logic to be solid, but if I thought he'd got it all correct and addressed the subject from all angles, I wouldn't have pursued writing my own study. Yet I still appreciate his position for the most part, and his knowledge of the history of the immortal soul issue is deep. I found little of value in Peterson's arguments for the traditional position. They were weak for the most part, filled with fallacies, and often he failed to let Scripture interpret Scripture. But I'm not singling him out as "the" problem by any means. While he's probably the most outspoken modern proponent of the issue, and has taken upon himself to write about the subject in numerous articles, and at least three books that I'm aware of, he is simply restating what the Church's position has been on this for centuries. And he's doing so by using the same small handful of proof texts that have always been used, and those either taken out of context, or not considered in light of the overwhelming biblical statement on what is in fact the ultimate wage for the sin of faithless unbelief.

So in the analyses of these 10 passages, which Peterson calls "the footings" of the foundation of the house of Traditionalism, I may occasionally reference or summarize what I believe his commentary on various passages to be, in order to demonstrate where the traditional position may not be the most accurate. But for the most part, we'll simply analyze what the verses themselves have to say.

For those of us who have had the concept of eternal conscious torment deeply ingrained in our minds, it's easy to assume the reality of it, and then see these verses as descriptions or verification of a reality that we already assumed existed. But let's look at what the verses are really telling us, and go at it with as few preconceived notions as possible. We can't first assume a reality of an eternal conscious Hell, and then look to this tiny handful of passages as "descriptions" of something we already "just know" is out there awaiting the lost. If it's truly out there, and if it's a reality, then Scripture should make that crystal clear. Let's see if it does.

Daniel 12:1-2 "And at that time Michael shall stand up, the great ruler who stands for the sons of your people. And there shall be a time of trouble, such as never was since there was a nation; until that time. And at that time your people shall be delivered, every one that shall be found written in the book. And many of those who sleep in the dust of the earth shall awake, some to everlasting life, and some to shame and everlasting contempt."(LITV)

Although there are multiple references to various forms of judgment in the Old Testament, there are only two verses, out of over 23,000, which most traditionalists believe solidly demonstrate eternal conscious suffering, and Daniel 12:2 is one of them.   Actually, this verse neither confirms nor denies eternal conscious suffering. There are two terms in the passage which are defined as "everlasting." The first is the life which believers will be resurrected to. The second is the contempt. But who is feeling that contempt? God is. *Strong's* concordance defines the original word being translated as "contempt" as "abhorring." The eternal loss of those who have rejected the call of God will always be with God in some sense, and they don't need to continue to exist in order for their blasphemous rejection of the Holy Spirit to have an eternal effect. He said he'd forget our sin – the sin of those who have come to Him for forgiveness. But He may never let Himself forget the sin of those who denied Him and wouldn't repent from their unbelief.

And that may be what's meant by this everlasting contempt. But let's look at this even another way. In the following section of this chapter, we'll look closely at the word "everlasting" and find that it often means "of permanent affect" rather than perpetual process. It's at least possible that rather than this everlasting contempt being something that God will always allow himself to feel, the verse could be referring to how God's contempt will cause an everlasting effect on these who rejected Him. And countless verses in Scripture tell us that effect is death and non-existence.

So what about the "shame" mentioned in verse two of Daniel chapter 12? With this there's no question. That's what the lost will feel when they are raised to stand judgment, which is what this passage is all about. While many of these were arrogant in their unbelief in life, there's no room for that now. They know they are fully at fault, and they feel their due shame. There's no place for contempt toward God on their part. So it can't be argued that the "everlasting contempt" mentioned in this verse is what they'll feel. That would be almost the opposite of the shame that the verse clearly says will be theirs. But notice that their shame is *not* described as everlasting. If it was, then I'd have to say this verse at least lends some credibility to the traditional stance. But it doesn't because their shame is the one thing in this verse which is not described as everlasting, and with good reason, since it will end when their very existence ends at the time they are cast into the Lake of Fire, which is in fact called "the second death."

And just a side note which may be irrelevant, at least in this subject — The raising of the saved to life, and the raising of the lost to stand judgment are actually separated by the 1000-year reign of Christ on earth, but Daniel didn't have that revelation yet. That came from John, actually in the book of Revelation, many centuries later.

Overall, because what's described as everlasting in this passage are the life of the saved, and the contempt of God toward the lost (or the everlasting effect that God's contempt will have on the lost), and these are contrasted with the shame of the lost, which is the one thing *not* described as everlasting, I'd say if anything, this verse is a clue that lends weight to the non-traditional argument. However, I don't want to be accused of "arguing from silence." So at the very least, it's fair to say that this verse in no way supports the idea that the lost are going to exist for all eternity.

2 Thessalonians 1:5-10: "5 This is evidence of the righteous judgment of God, that you may be considered worthy of the kingdom of God, for which you are also suffering— 6 since indeed God considers it just to repay with affliction those who afflict you, 7 and to grant relief to you who are afflicted as well as to us, when the Lord Jesus is revealed from heaven with his mighty angels 8 in flaming fire, inflicting vengeance on those who do not know God and on those who do not obey the gospel of our Lord Jesus. 9 They will suffer the punishment of eternal destruction, away from the presence of the Lord and from the glory of his might, 10 when he comes on that day to be glorified in his saints, and to be marveled at among all who have believed, because our testimony to you was believed." (ESV)

Amazingly, this passage, and specifically verse 9, is one of the most relied upon in the defense of the traditional view of eternal torment. And just as amazingly, of all of Paul's writings, it is, as far as I know, the *only* verse he wrote which is claimed by traditionalists to support specifically the theory of eternal conscious punishment. That's not a fact to overlook, with Paul writing so much of the New Testament, and with so much of our Christian theology coming directly from the revelations he received from the Lord. This verse actually verifies nothing that the traditionalist would tell us, but does the very opposite. We'll look briefly at the background of why Paul is writing this second letter to the Thessalonians. We'll also see that there are a number of ways that the Greek word *aionios*, here translated as "eternal," is used in Scripture, sometimes not at all referring to something that will extend into timelessness.

There's also another Greek word in this verse that's being translated poorly and we'll address that as well. And then there's something so obvious, that it's somehow just overlooked by those who force this verse to be a prediction of an eternal process of destruction that never ends, and which occurs "away from" the Lord. So I'll begin there.

This verse is not a picture of eternal destinies at all. It's describing an earthly event, the second coming of Jesus Christ to earth, which will begin His millennial reign. Timeless eternity begins *after* Jesus has reigned on earth for 1000 years. The unsaved lost, those who rejected salvation during their earthly life, are still in Hades (Hell) — whether conscious or unconscious — awaiting final judgment during those one thousand years. Contrary to many other non-traditionalists who believe all souls who have died are in a soul sleep, there's biblical evidence the lost may experience conscious torment during the time between their physical death and the end of that 1000 years. Whether they're conscious for that entire time period is very much up for debate and we'll look more at this question in Chapter 7, but either way, they are still in existence in some form, and this existence precedes final judgment. Think of that intermediate phase as more of a "death row." The fate of the lost has been determined, but they have not been ultimately accused and judged with finality until the end of Christ's reign (Revelation 20:5).

We've seen how the "eternal conscious separation from God" theory has become the bedrock of the traditionalist view on eternal conscious torment, and how Adam and Eve's expulsion from the garden has been erroneously used as the ground zero evidence for that doctrine. And this verse in 2 Thessalonians is another which is misused to teach that same idea. It's the phrase "away from the presence of the Lord" which the verse states is "where" the lost will suffer the punishment of eternal destruction.

But I'm going to come back to that thought, because it's important first to understand the various uses of *aionios* (eternal) in the Bible. There are places in Scripture where the Greek word being translated into English as "eternal" and "everlasting," clearly means "permanent in effect" rather than "perpetual in process." This may seem like the same thing, but it's not.

The word appears 71 times in 69 verses in the New Testament and usually defines the unending life the Christian will experience in God's presence, which will in fact be "everlasting" and "perpetual" in the sense that it has no end. But the word *perpetual* lends itself to being defined as an unending process, and if we limit ourselves to that definition, it simply won't apply properly in every usage of *aionios* in Scripture. Sometimes a word is defined by its context, and the definition which seems to be missing from the sources I've checked is "permanence" and "an unchanging constancy," and at least in one place it seems to mean "wholly effective." So let's go through some verses and see if these are not necessary definitions of *aionios* based on context.

Let's first look at a passage in Hebrews where the word is used three times.

> Hebrew 9:12-15 "12 Neither by the blood of goats and calves, but by his own blood he entered in once into the holy place, having obtained eternal redemption for us. 13 For if the blood of bulls and of goats, and the ashes of an heifer sprinkling the unclean, sanctifieth to the purifying of the flesh: 14 How much more shall the blood of Christ, who through the eternal Spirit offered himself without spot to God, purge your conscience from dead works to serve the living God? 15 And for this cause he is the mediator of the new testament, that by means of

death, for the redemption of the transgressions that were under the first testament, they which are called might receive the promise of eternal inheritance." (KJV)

We see three things here described as being eternal (*aionios*): our redemption, the Spirit of God, and our inheritance. All three of these things are everlasting and permanent, not ongoing processes or a perpetual acts, as people try to claim is meant when the same word is used to describe the punishment of the lost such as in Matthew 25:46 and in the verse we're considering here, 2 Thessalonians 1:9. The traditionalist believes that because it is contrasted with eternal life in Matthew 25:46 that it must indicate something that is ongoing, just as eternal life is ongoing. They miss the point completely. The fact that this life the believer is promised has eternal permanence is what makes it the awesome gift that it is. We had no existence in eternity past, yet we are created and offered eternal life that we cannot lose. The life of the saved is permanent. The death of the unsaved is permanent as well. Death is the punishment. The wages of sin is death. This couldn't be plainer in scripture.

Consider how the same Greek word *aionios* is used here in the passage from Hebrews 9. The clearest example of this is the first of the three usages. We see in verse 12 that Jesus entered once into the holy place and obtained "eternal" (*aionios*) redemption for us. This is not an act He must do perpetually or repeatedly. Once we are redeemed, we are redeemed. There is only one act of redemption and it happened in a moment, yet we will remain in the permanent state of being redeemed forever, just as the unsaved will remain in the permanent state of being dead forever after final judgment. Notice in verse 14 that Jesus did this work "through the eternal (*aionios*) Spirit." Try plugging in "perpetual" in place of eternal and you'll notice it just doesn't work. God is constant and unchanging and is the essence of permanence, and we need to leave room for that definition of *aionios*. Then notice in verse 15 that what we receive because of Christ's death is the promise of an eternal (*aionios*) inheritance. The primary definition of the word being translated "inheritance" is "heirship" according to *Strong's*. And heirship is a state, not a fluid, ongoing process. So when we see this word *aionios*, we need to consider the context and possibly apply a definition of something more static and permanent.

We find the word *aionios* in many places in the Bible, mostly referring to eternal life or God's attributes, but we also find it in Hebrews 6:2 describing judgment. The Greek word translated as "judgment" is *krima* which Strong's defines as "a decision," and this makes perfect sense with the meaning of *aionios* being permanent and everlasting and not an ongoing process. Final judgment is a decision that's permanent and unchanging, not a process that God will undertake for all eternity. This is the most fearful thing about it. The sentence the unsaved are assigned is eternal and that sentence is death. There is no resurrection from the second death. Just as when Christ comes the second time it is permanent and lasting, so is the second death permanent and lasting. And the decision is a one-time, for all-time, permanent decision from which there is no further turning.

The same word *aionios* is used in Jude 7 to describe the punishment of Sodom and Gomorrah. We'll look at it even more closely later in this chapter, but let's briefly consider it here. Verse 7 reads:

> "Even as Sodom and Gomorrah, and the cities about them in like manner, giving themselves over to fornication, and going after strange flesh, are set forth for an example, suffering the vengeance of eternal (*aionios*) fire." (KJV)

If we are to believe, as many traditionalists do, that *aionios* always means "ongoing," then we would have to believe that Sodom and Gomorrah are still burning which clearly they are not. But they are utterly decimated. They suffered the vengeance of a Holy God and were permanently destroyed and were never rebuilt, and we are even told in the verse that this was done to serve as an example to us. Should we assume that it is an example of eternal torment in a permanent Hell? I don't see how. They were destroyed and consumed, and this is our example or sampling of what "eternal fire" will do, according to

Jude. Please don't miss this — The "eternal" fire didn't burn forever but it caused a permanent (*aionios*) forever condition of being utterly destroyed into non-existence, and we're told plainly this is an example or sampling of what will one day happen to the lost who reject salvation. In a singular act in time, it was wholly and eternally effective.

Jude 7 is actually traditionalist Robert Peterson's 7th footing in his "house of Traditionalism,"[21] and it confuses me more than any other how he sees this as evidence for a traditional view of eternal conscious torment.   What happened to Sodom and Gomorrah is past tense, as any example would have to be, yet it is said to be an *example* of what the vengeance of "eternal fire" does.   The people and the cities were consumed down to nothing. We can look at what *is not there*, and know that this is an example of what eternal fire will do.   These places were destroyed into nothingness. Nothing at all remains.

With these two cities that no longer exist as our example, I can't help but see the correlation with what the psalmist said in Psalm 37:10: "For yet a little while, and the wicked shall not be: yea, thou shalt diligently consider his place, and it shall not be." Someone might argue that what is intended is that the souls of those individuals are now in eternal fire. And I would answer that with a simple question: How is that something we can observe? I don't see them being tormented. We see they were decimated. And we're told plainly that what we observed was an example of a future judgment of all unrighteous. So that argument just won't work.

Continuing on with evidence that *aionios* has multiple meanings and applications, depending on context, Luke 16:9 reads:

> "And I tell you, make friends for yourselves by means of unrighteous wealth, so that when it fails they may receive you into the eternal (*aionios*) dwellings." (ESV)

Here again we can see that *aionios* takes on the meaning of "permanence" rather than ongoing process or perpetual.   An "everlasting habitation" implies a *permanent* dwelling.   2 Peter refers to the eternal (*aionios*) kingdom, Hebrews 13:20 refers to the everlasting (*aionios*) covenant, and Hebrews 5:9 refers to our eternal (*aionios*) salvation. These are permanent, not perpetual, ongoing processes.

I could show more examples, but this should be sufficient to prove that "eternal" and "everlasting," when translated from the Greek word *aionios*, do not necessarily refer to continual fluid processes such as a supposed process of destruction, and that they do in fact mean "permanent" and "wholly effective" in many places. In fact, it would be impossible to prove Biblically that destruction and perishing *ever* refer to an unending eternal process. This is in fact what traditionalists claim, but where is the Biblical support? The only state ever described by the adjective *aionios* that could even possibly be referring to an ongoing process would be "life." And even when we consider those cases, it's very awkward, by using the same word *aionios*, to contrast and compare a life that never ends with an ongoing state of perishing or being destroyed. It seems far more likely, in every way, that Scripture is contrasting a life one cannot lose with a death from which there's no return.

Let's look at another Greek word in the 2 Thessalonians 1 passage which seems to be getting a poor translation, at least in modern day bibles. First, it's notable that verse 9 is an awkward way to structure a sentence that's supposed to be telling us where something will happen, where it says they will be "destroyed away from the presence of the Lord...." It's strange to think of someone being destroyed "away from" something. It's grammatically awkward, and if the idea of separation were intended, there's any number of ways this could have been worded more clearly. But there's a reason it doesn't read well, and it's because it's the wrong translation of the Greek. The Greek word being translated as "away from," as well as "shut out from" in other versions, is *apo*, and it can have a number of meanings. But if you'll check your *Strong's* concordance, you'll see that "because of" and "from" (as in 'due to') are also in the list of possible translations. Let's plug that in. Here's 2 Thessalonians 1:9-10:

"They will suffer the punishment of eternal destruction, *because of* the presence of the Lord and the glory of his might, when he comes on that day to be glorified in his saints, and to be marveled at among all who have believed, because our testimony to you was believed."

That makes a lot more sense, and it also lines up with what we noted above where Paul says in chapter 2 verse 8 that the lawless one would be "brought to nothing *by the appearance of his coming.*" There's two more things to note about this poor translation of *apo* in this verse: First, this word appears 649 times in Scripture, and this is literally the only place where that one Greek word alone is translated as "away from." Yes, I looked. And in a search of the *King James* Bible, I found that the places where the phrase "away from" appeared, and where the Greek word *apo* was being translated as "from," the word "away" was being translated from its own Greek word. In those cases it is a 2-word phrase in Greek being translated into a 2-word phrase in English. The one and only time in all of Scripture where the single Greek word *apo* is translated into the 2-word phrase of "away from" is here in 1 Thessalonians, so it is certainly unprecedented, and uncalled for, and it's the result of interpreters and translators forcing their doctrine into the translation rather than translating it most clearly and in congruence with the overall context of the verse. I appreciated the footnote in the *Crossway English Standard Version*. They noted that it could also be translated as a destruction "that *comes from* the presence of the Lord."[22] In other words, it's *because of* His presence they are destroyed. He is a consuming fire after all. And this isn't the only place in Scripture where we're told He is returning in fire to destroy His enemies who are on the earth at the time of His coming. One last thing about *apo* and this whole phrase and its translation — The exact same series of Greek words that make up the phrase "from the presence of the Lord" (*Strong's* coded numbers: 575, 4383, 3588, 2962) is only used in one other place in the entire Bible, and in that instance the Greek word *apo* being translated as "from" clearly means "because of" or "as a result of." It's in Acts 3:19-20a:

"Repent therefore, and turn back, that your sins may be blotted out, that times of refreshing may come *from the presence of the Lord...*" (ESV — italics for emphasis)

If we plugged in "shut out from" or "away from" here, as it was over-interpreted in 2 Thessalonians, it would lose all meaning and be nonsense. We'd have "Repent therefore...that your sins may be blotted out, so that times of refreshing may come shut out from the presence of the Lord." ...or "times of refreshing away from the Lord." What?

Don't lose sight of the fact that this series of words only appears twice in the entire Bible. And this verse in Acts certainly does not imply a separation from His presence, but clearly we do see a contrast between the effect the presence of the Lord has on the faithful and what effect it has on those who persecute the faithful. It's a refreshing comfort to believers, but it consumes the unbelievers. Even just a few verses later in 2 Thessalonians 2:8 Paul writes that the lawless one will be destroyed "by the brightness of His (Christ's) Presence." The idea of "eternal separation from God" has been forced into this passage, and it just won't fit.

Traditionalists believe they have even more evidence for "punishment as separation" in something Jesus said from the cross: "Father, why have you forsaken Me?" What we're often told is that God turned his back on His Son, truly forsaking Him, and that in those moments, Jesus somehow experienced an eternity of suffering and separation in that relatively brief time. Once again we're reading thoughts into the passage that aren't there.

Jesus was fully God, but fully man as well. That's the most amazing thing about the Lord — that He was willing to degrade, condescend, and overall "downgrade" Himself to be like one of us. And what that cry from the cross demonstrates is how He felt. But it wasn't a statement of reality. Here's two things you don't say to One who has just rejected and forsaken you: 1. "Father forgive them, for they know not what they do," and 2. "Into your hands, I commit my Spirit." Both of these Jesus said in those same moments on the cross. Have you ever felt forsaken by God? I'll be honest. I've felt that way a number of times...and I really have no right to. I'm not His One and only sinless son. Jesus had infinitely more grounds than any of us to "feel" forsaken, but in reality, it was only a feeling, just like I know in reality God has never forsaken me either. Jesus, the sinless One, being punished as if He were guilty. He felt forsaken, and because He's real and because He's honest, He voiced that. But He wasn't truly and actually forsaken. He would be in paradise shortly, and after His ascension, be reunited with His Father. If you'll look at John chapter 16, Jesus is telling His disciples that He is about to go back to the Father. He knew where He was headed, but also what was about to happen in the interim, and He was fully willing to suffer in that way, because the Father was willing that it happen in order to redeem mankind, and Jesus knew it was temporary and that He would shortly be back in Heaven. We just can't say that He was in reality forsaken. This account adds nothing to the "separation theory" of eternal punishment.

Let's get back to Peterson's top ten list. The next verse we'll analyze of the traditionalists proof texts is Revelation 14:10, and we'll find it's once again speaking of this earthly event of Christ's second coming, and not giving us a picture of the eternal destiny of the lost.

Revelation 14:9-11 "9 And a third angel followed them, saying in a great voice, If anyone worships the beast and its image, and receives a mark on his forehead, or in his hand, 10 he also shall drink of the wine of the anger of God having been mixed undiluted in the cup of His wrath. And he will be tormented by fire and brimstone before the holy angels and before the Lamb. 11 And the smoke of their torment goes up forever and ever.

> And those worshiping the beast and its image have no rest night and day, even if anyone receives the mark of its name." (LITV)

We just noted that 2 Thessalonians 1:9 could not have been a picture of eternity. And we have the same situation here. This is actually describing the same earthly scene when Christ returns to set up his kingdom. The first thing to note is that this tormenting that occurs happens in the presence of the Lamb and the holy angels. If 14:10-11 is a description of eternity in Hell, then we have a very big problem, because won't the Lamb (Jesus), and the holy angels be with us in heaven during eternity? Secondly, to believe this is a reference to *all* who failed to put their trust in God is to deny the plain language of Scripture that tells us that this is specifically a judgment on those who took the mark of the beast and worshiped him during the tribulation. Thirdly, three verses later in 14:13, it says: "Blessed are the dead, the ones dying in the Lord from now on" (LITV). If 14:9-11 is a description of Eternal Hell, then we've entered eternity at that point in Scripture, and who else could die in the Lord? No one could. These verses are very clearly a description of the judgment coming on the lost that inhabit the earth at the second coming, not a description of eternity in any sense.

As for the smoke of their torment rising day and night, forever and ever, and them having no rest day or night, there are two things to note. First, we need to understand that the "forever and ever" is likely figurative language, for the reason already mentioned – that this process of tormenting is occurring in the presence of Jesus and the holy angels (and this is certain when you look at the Greek) and this is not what they will be doing for all eternity. Also, there are other places in Scripture where the word "forever" and the phrase "forever and ever" indicate something that goes *until completion* or *as long as is possible*, not to eternity. Let's look at a few examples:

> Psalm 145:20-21 "20 Jehovah watches over all who love Him; but He destroys all the wicked. 21 My mouth shall speak the praise of Jehovah; and all flesh shall bless His holy name forever and ever." (LITV)

I appreciate verse 20 because it makes clear what will happen to the wicked, but then in verse 21, David says that it is all "flesh" that will bless the Lord "forever and ever." This argument may not be my strongest, because the word "flesh" (*basar*) could possibly be used to indicate people generally, but its strict definition is the "flesh," and we won't have our present flesh "forever and ever," so it's possible here that again we see "forever and ever" meaning "as long as it is possible" or "as long as the earth endures and we are here" — not that the Lord's praises will not go on in eternity, just that it will not technically be "flesh" that is singing those praises, since we will be like the angels, according to Jesus, and in incorruptible bodies, according to Paul.

Here's a better one:

> Amos 1:10-11 "But I will send a fire against the wall of Tyre, and it shall devour its palaces. 11 So says Jehovah: For three transgressions of Edom, and for four, I will not turn back from it, for he pursued his brother with the sword, and corrupted his compassions, and his anger *tore perpetually*, and he *kept it*, his wrath, *forever*." (LITV — italics for emphasis)

There's something interesting here. We have two things that are past tense, but also being referred to as happening "forever" and "perpetually." His *anger tore* (past tense) "perpetually," and he *kept his wrath* (past tense) "forever." How can this even be possible if the word forever only and always means "into all eternity"? It can't. This is speaking of the wicked Edomites that cannot even exist "forever," yet we are told they did something in the past "forever."

Here's another:

> Isa 34:10 "It shall not be put out night or day; its smoke shall go up forever. From generation to generation, it shall lie waste; no one shall pass through it forever *and* forever." (LITV)

It would seem that with it being said that "no one shall pass through it," we could assume that it would at least exist, but simply never be inhabited or passed through by humans. The phrase "generation to generation" is another key to understanding that we are not talking about eternity, since there will apparently not be reproduction *or* time in eternity, from anything I understand in Scripture. But notice that this will be its condition "forever and forever." But we know that this earth will not even exist forever and forever, so I think we have a fairly good argument here that "forever" can mean "as long as it is possible," given that the earth, and specifically Edom (here meaning Rome according to some theologians) will only exist until it is consumed.

I think a little more weight is added to this when the prophet goes on in the following verses to tell us all of the animals that *will* inhabit that part of the earth after the Lord brings desolation on it. (See verses 13-15) Certainly this will not be its state forever and ever, but only as long as it *can* be its state. And really, in this case at least, it doesn't even mean "as long as it *can* be its state," but rather "until it is burned down," because if this place is literally burning forever and ever, then all of these animals would not be able to take possession of it, as God's word clearly says they will. And one more thing to notice, verse 17 of Isaiah 34 says: "And He has made fall a lot for them, and His hand divided it to them by line. *They shall possess it until forever, from generation to generation they shall live in it.*" One theologian believes the "they" is Israel or the church, and this may be so, but I don't see where Isaiah quit talking about the animals that would inhabit it. Either way, again, this earth will not endure into eternity, so this "forever" cannot mean "to all eternity."

And there's Leviticus 6:18:

> "Every male among the children of Aaron shall eat of it, as their portion forever throughout your generations, from the offerings of Yahweh made by fire. Whoever touches them shall be holy." (WEB)

It says "forever" and "in your generations" in one phrase. This would definitely not be referring to eternity, but only forever in the sense of while you are here and able and while new generations are coming along.

In the second chapter of Jonah we find him praising God for saving him from the belly of the fish and in Jonah 2:6 we read, "I went down to the land whose bars closed upon me *forever...*" It obviously didn't hold him forever, in the same sense that we often think of forever.

It's also notable that the Greek phrase being translated as "forever and ever" can be translated as "to the end of the age." This return of Christ that Revelation 14:10 seems to be referring to happens at the very end of this current age, and the last moments of the destruction of those who rejected God's salvation in this life will be the very last moments of this age. So the smoke of their torment will literally go until the end of the age.

Incidentally, we still use "forever" in lots of ways other than a literal eternity, when we really just mean "a long time," as in, "Man, it's taking forever" or "I'm forever forgetting to...fill in the blank." It seems this has been a common practice to use this word forever in non-literal ways for a long time now.

Regarding the lack of rest "day and night" mentioned in verse 11, if this is a picture of eternity as traditionalists claim, we'd have to assume this is figurative (since there will not be any night in eternity, being that this current heavens and earth will have been destroyed by fire). Or we can take it literally as referring to something that happens while we still have "day and night." I choose to take this literally. I believe, just as the verse says, there will be no rest day or night for those who have taken the mark of the beast, while they are being tormented by fire and brimstone from the heavens. Also, I don't think we should assume that any one *individual* will be able to withstand much of this torment before their physical death occurs. The "those" in verse 11 most likely means that collectively there will be no rest day or night for the masses of people who are being tormented, until they're all ultimately consumed, not that any *individual* is going to be subjected to some sort of lengthy, merciless torture. Overall, this passage has absolutely nothing to do with Hell or eternity, except that any picture of the earthly destruction of the physical bodies of those who reject Christ is ultimately a foreshadowing picture of how one day, at final judgment, their soul will be destroyed in the Lake of Fire as well.

Jude 6-7 "And the angels who did not stay within their own position of authority, but left their proper dwelling, he has kept in eternal chains under gloomy darkness until the judgment of the great day—just as Sodom and Gomorrah and the surrounding cities, which likewise indulged in sexual immorality and pursued unnatural desire, serve as an example by undergoing a punishment of eternal fire." (ESV)

It's so odd that Robert Peterson considers this one of the verses that prove eternal conscious suffering because this verse, maybe more than any of the other nine, does the exact opposite. We just looked at this in the previous section when we analyzed some of Paul's writings and how the word "eternal" has some similar but varying characteristics. Sodom and Gomorrah were completely obliterated – so much so that even among archaeologists, there's a lot of disagreement over where they even were. There is nothing left. And obviously the people who inhabited those cities, other than Lot and his family who were rescued, were obliterated also. And this passage, as well as 2 Peter 2:6 tell us that what happened to these cities is an example of what will ultimately happen to unbelieving sinners who won't put their faith in Christ — another foreshadowing example, and this one is even called such, right there in Scripture. We looked at the following verse in the last chapter but it's worth another look while we're on the topic of Sodom and Gomorrah. Peter wrote:

"....turning the cities of Sodom and Gomorrah to ashes he condemned them to extinction, making them an example of what is going to happen to the ungodly;" (2 Peter 2:6 ESV)

We could probably call game over at this point, and end this book right here. These cities were made to go extinct, and this happened as a result of "eternal fire," and we're even told this is an example of what will happen one day to the lost.

I don't think I can overstate this: If eternal torment were the punishment for unbelief, this would have been clearly stated somewhere in Scripture, (probably even lots of times) and wouldn't be something that has to be painfully dug out, while ignoring clear passages like the ones above which tell us the end game punishment for faithlessness is to lose your very life and existence. Jesus asked in Mark 8:36 "What does it profit a man to gain the whole world and then lose his own soul?" We are our soul. Losing it means losing our very existence. And contrary to many traditionalists who find this to be a soft punishment for unbelief, it's actually the just punishment for denying God, seeing that He is only giving people back to the nothingness they were before He created them.

> These cities were made to go extinct, and this happened as a result of "eternal fire," and we're even told this is an example of what will happen one day to the lost

Let me pose a simple question: What does fire do? It's common knowledge that it burns stuff up, plain and simple. And that's why it's used as the image of what will happen to the unfaithful throughout Scripture. If you'll think about it, the only ones who survive fire in the Bible are the faithful. Shadrach, Meshach, and Abed-nego were cast in a furnace and survived it, while those who cast them in were killed by the same heat. I can't think of any other fire in the Bible that didn't burn something up except for a bush that God inhabited, when He first spoke to Moses. So in Jude 7 and 2 Peter 2:6 we have a fire that causes the permanent condition of extinction, according to the plain language of the passage. God will punish faithlessness, and it will in fact be an "eternal punishment" as the Bible states more than once, an eternal death from which there is no return.

But ultimately God is merciful, and taking people who reject Him out of existence, sad as it is, is far more merciful than letting them exist in torment for all eternity, pointlessly, as if He gains anything from their torment. I've heard and read many weak arguments by traditionalists for why this is "necessary" and they all fall short of biblical accuracy. You may have heard this one: "God is an eternal being, and faithlessness offends Him, so the punishment must last as long as He exists" — Sorry, but that's not in the Bible...Just a weak human argument, trying to justify something that isn't justifiable and isn't in Scripture.

Jude 13 "[They are] wild waves of the sea, foaming out their own shame; wandering stars, for whom the blackness of darkness has been reserved forever" (WEB)

The context of the verse is addressing false teachers and those who blaspheme the things of God which they don't understand. I'm not going to say much about this because I don't think there's much to say. Traditionalist writer Robert Peterson attempts to create meanings for this verse that are much less than apparent, to say the least,[23] but to me, if you had to describe the nothingness of non-existence that false teachers, blasphemers (and other non-believers) are ultimately destined for, the "blackness of darkness forever," as some versions state it, seems like as good a description as anything. And it certainly doesn't line up with the literal traditionalist teaching that the lost will be forever floating and grasping for life in a Lake of Fire.

Traditionalists who believe all of the fire language in Scripture is only figurative for an eternal separation from God could claim that this "description of Hell" is accurate and lines up with the separation theory, but they would first have to prove the Bible even teaches the separation theory – that the lost will be immortal, always in existence, merely without the presence of God; but this will never be found in Scripture. The "blackness of darkness forever" simply means nothingness, and non-existence, the same result predicted in the Jude 7 passage we just looked at. Peterson seemed to make an attempt to legitimize the concept of a figuratively dark Hell by pointing out that Jesus too warned of coming darkness.[24] Here are a couple of those passages:

> Matthew 8:8-12 "8 The centurion answered and said, Lord, I am not worthy that thou shouldest come under my roof: but speak the word only, and my servant shall be healed. 9 For I am a man under authority, having soldiers under me: and I say to this *man,* Go, and he goeth; and to another, Come, and he cometh; and to my servant, Do this, and he doeth *it.* 10 When Jesus heard *it,* he marveled, and said to them that followed, Verily I say unto you, I have not found so great faith, no, not in Israel. 11 And I say unto you, That many shall come from the east and west, and shall sit down with Abraham, and Isaac, and Jacob, in the kingdom of heaven. 12 But the children of the kingdom shall be cast out into outer darkness: there shall be weeping and gnashing of teeth." (KJV)

And...

> Matthew 22:12-13 "12 And he saith unto him, Friend, how camest thou in hither not having a wedding garment? And he was speechless. 13 Then said the king to the servants, Bind him hand and foot, and take him away, and cast *him* into outer darkness; there shall be weeping and gnashing of teeth." (KJV)

From the commentaries I've read, Matthew contains certain portions that are directly tied to Jewish custom, and are written from that perspective, plain and simple. Not that there isn't a lot of information there for the Gentile church as well, but certain parts of Matthew need to be considered in the context of being written specifically to the Jews, or at least considered with the flavor of Jewish tradition, in order to catch the fuller meaning. I was reminded of this as I listened to a pastor recently who commented on a few places in Matthew that have nothing to do with Gentiles at all, according to his study. Adding weight to this argument is the fact that there's no reference in the other three gospels, or actually in the entire Bible to "outer darkness" besides the ones that Jesus makes in the book of Matthew. So that's the first thing to keep in mind regarding these passages.

18th Century theologian John Gill, even though he actually held a traditional view of eternal Hell, didn't believe these verses were a literal description of Hell either, but rather a picture of the rejection of the Jews who wouldn't accept Christ, and I think he makes a lot of sense. Here's what he wrote:

> "The allusion in the text is, to the customs of the ancients at their feasts and entertainments; which were commonly made in the evening, when the hall or dining room, in which they sat down, was very much illuminated with lamps and torches; but without in the streets, were entire darkness: and where were heard nothing but the cries of the poor, for something to be given them, and of the persons that were turned out as unworthy guests;"[25]

If we look at the context of the verses, it seems that Jesus is letting these Jews know that while they very much believe themselves to be justified and right before God, and to be worthy guests, they are the very ones who will be rejected and will not enter the kingdom because they are rejecting the Messiah whom they've been expecting. He even says in 8:12 that it is the children of the kingdom (the Jews) that will be cast out into outer darkness, whereas, in 8:11, He told them that others (Gentiles) from all over would be the ones who enter the kingdom of heaven. And Matthew 22:15 confirms that Jesus was speaking this against the unbelieving Jews, and in their presence.

As far as the weeping and gnashing of teeth is concerned, I used the KJV above because it's one of the few versions that correctly leaves the "where" out of the phrase. Most versions read something like, "...they will be cast into outer darkness, *where* there will be weeping and gnashing of teeth." Some versions go so far as to say, "In that place, there will be weeping..." But that's adding a lot to the Word that isn't there, and even the "where" is not in the original Greek, and dividing this into two separate statements as the KJV does is probably most accurate. It's not totally out of place to phrase it in the way some other versions do, but if we're going to insert something that isn't really there, I think it's more of a "when" than a "where." *When* the unbelieving Jews (and I suppose all others who have rejected God) realize that they have been wrong, that they have rejected their Messiah, and have been rejected from the kingdom of God, they will weep and gnash their teeth. This may happen at that initial moment of realization, or go on constantly or sporadically during the entire time that the lost are in Hades awaiting judgment, or it may happen at final judgment too (or perhaps *only* at final judgment). But there is no reason, based on these verses, to teach that the lost will spend eternity weeping and gnashing their teeth in darkness. In fact, Psalm 112:10 ties the wicked's gnashing of teeth to the next event, their perishing: Here's what it says:

> "The wicked shall see and be vexed; he will gnash his teeth and melt away; the desire of the wicked shall perish." (LITV)

That's a perfect picture of what Jesus taught and how it lines up with the death, destruction, and non-entity judgment. There will come a point when they realize they've been rejected — This is the casting out point. They will weep and gnash their teeth, but not forever. The psalmist says after this they melt away.   Overall, the prior verses do nothing in the way of supporting the idea of eternal suffering, even though they are used for such all the time. I should note that the Jewish people are still God's people. And any Jew that turns to Christ will be saved. These passages do not indicate a sweeping rejection of all Jews...only those who reject their own Jewish Messiah as most of the Jews of Jesus's time did, and that's why Jesus contrasted "all Israel" with this Gentile who demonstrated great faith.

Whether the darkness in these verses is figurative of rejection from the Kingdom, or a description of loss of being and existence, or both, none of these passages add weight to the traditional doctrine of eternal conscious torment of the lost. And it's my hope and prayer that the doctrine will one day be abandoned by the Church and we'll begin teaching the merciful God of Scripture.

Luke 16:19-31 "19 And there was a certain rich man; and he was accustomed to don a purple robe and fine linen, making merry in luxury day by day. 20 And there was a certain poor one named Lazarus who had been laid at his doorway, having been ulcerated, 21 and longing to be filled from the crumbs that were falling from the table of the rich one. But coming, even the dogs licked his sores. 22 And it happened, the poor one died and was carried away by the angels into the bosom of Abraham. And the rich one also died and was buried. 23 And being in torments in Hell, lifting up his eyes, he sees Abraham afar off and Lazarus in his bosom. 24 And calling he said, Father Abraham, have pity on me and send Lazarus that he may dip the tip of his finger in water and cool my tongue, for I am suffering in this flame. 25 But Abraham said, Child, remember that you fully received your good things in your lifetime, and Lazarus likewise the bad things. But now he is comforted, and you are suffering. 26 And besides all these things, a great chasm has been fixed between us and you, so that those desiring to pass from here to you are not able, nor can they pass from there to us. 27 And he said, Then I beg you, father, that you send him to my father's house; 28 (for I have five brothers, so that he may witness to them, that they not also come to this place of torment). 29 Abraham said to him, They have Moses and the Prophets, let them hear them. 30 But he said, No, father Abraham, but if one should go from the dead to them, they will repent. 31 And he said to him, If they will not hear Moses and the Prophets, they will not be persuaded even if one from the dead should rise." (LITV)

This passage is one of the most relied upon by traditionalists as evidence of a conscious afterlife of torment for the lost — and in literal fire at that. It very well may be evidence of a time of consciousness after physical death, and may offer some insight into how, prior to Christ's death and resurrection, both the righteous and unrighteous went to Sheol, but with different experiences. However, many preachers and Bible teachers will use it as evidence of the eternal state of consciousness they believe the unsaved will endure. I've studied this section of Scripture extensively, and while I have a lot of thoughts and opinions on it, I've come to only a couple of absolute conclusions. One of them is that this passage is *not* a picture of a final and eternal conscious state of damnation for those who reject salvation. And the other is that this is not a 100% literal picture, even of the intermediate state between physical death and final judgment. We'll see why.

One Sunday several years ago, one of my daughters brought home from Sunday School her take-home paper and it contained this Luke 16 Lazarus and the rich man story, and right there on the front page is a picture of the rich man up to his elbows in flaming fire. If we're going to send our eight-year-olds home from church with pictures of people writhing in agony, burning alive in flames, and teach them that this (and worse) is what God does to people for all eternity, then we better be able to back that up with evidence which is beyond question.

But let's be realistic. A person in the situation depicted on that take-home paper and in pulpits for centuries, literally on fire, would probably do a number of things differently than what we read of this man, if this were a literal account. He probably would have asked for buckets of water to be cast on him, not a drop of water...and not only for his tongue. If he were really describing himself in a literal flaming inferno, would he not have at least described the fire he's in as "these flames" (plural), or "this fire," or maybe even "this raging hellhole" or even worse? He didn't. He said he is tormented by "this flame" – singular. While some versions of the Bible may read "this fire" or "these flames," that's not how the original Greek reads, and while I'm not a huge fan of the old English of the KJV, on this passage it's probably the most overall accurate translation, and it's clear this is a singular flame this man says he is being tormented by. Its singularity is unquestionable because of the Greek word *taute* used to describe the flame, which *Strong's* concordance states is a singular form. We'll come back and discuss the flame shortly, because not only does its singularity appear to be significant, the Greek word being translated as "flame" is a revealing study in itself.

But before we examine "the flame," let's first look at the different words for "torment," "torments," or "tormented" we find in this passage. Let's first look at the word "torments" Jesus used to describe the man's condition in verse 23. This is where we'll begin to get a reliable picture of his state. The word "torments" is being translated from the Greek word *basanos*. *Moulton and Milligan's* points out that originally the word meant a touchstone or a test. *Thayer's* also has this as their first definition and adds that it is a touchstone by which gold and other metals are tested. There's a similar Greek word that's more clearly defined as torment or torture that it seems would have been used by the Lord if true physical torment had been indicated. It's the same word used in Revelation 14:11 to describe the physical torment of those on earth who took the mark of the beast, when they are physically tormented with fire at Christ's return. We noted earlier in this chapter that this is not a picture of eternal Hell — rather it's an earthly event — the destruction of those rebelling against Christ at His return, but while it adds nothing to the eternal suffering theory traditionalists hold, it does in fact describe true bodily torment.

But Jesus didn't use that word that's being translated as "torment" here, describing Hades. The word He used has to do with the testing of a person, and it reminds me of how in the book of Daniel, the handwriting on the wall said that Belshazzar had been weighed (tested), and found lacking. The souls who await judgment in Hades/Sheol have all been examined, and have, like all, fallen short of the glory of God. However, unlike the saved, they've rejected their one means of redemption from that state and are therefore found wanting or lacking. The other interesting thing about this word is that it speaks of forcing someone to tell the truth. What a great description of Hades. Regardless of how much truth one has denied in this life, it will all come out at the point of death. The truth about who we are, and who God is will be fully known. This formerly rich man certainly knows the truth at this point. There is no more pretending, no more delusion that his worldly wealth would gain him anything after death, and no more denying his need for the Lord although it was too late at that point. In fact, it is truth itself that torments the man, and a study of the singular flame that torments him will prove this out. We've all heard it said, or have said it: "the truth hurts." And that's what is happening here. Truth is literally tormenting this man. But *Strong's* has an interesting note in their definition of *basanos* too.   It acknowledges that the word is perhaps similar to the Greek word *basis*, and can mean "the notion of going to the bottom." That would certainly describe this man accurately. He has reached a low point and cannot go lower. So from the Lord's own testimony, we know that this rich man has been tested and found wanting, and that he has reached the lowest point.

There's another word that's translated into the English word "torment" in this passage, and I think it's significant who is using which words. Jesus, as the one telling the story and describing the initial state of the man used the word for torment that indicates testing. The next time we see "torment" it's the word that Abraham and the rich man both use to describe his circumstances. The word being translated as "tormented" by them is the Greek word *odunao* which *Strong's* defines primarily as "to grieve." Grieving is not exactly the description I would expect of a person who is literally on fire, so this particular "torment" seems much more to indicate a mental anguish, and I think we could argue that it's even a specific type of mental anguish.

The word *odunao* is only used two other times in the New Testament outside of this story and neither one has to do with physical torment or distress. One was in Luke 2:48, when Mary and Joseph accidentally left Jesus in Jerusalem and it describes the anguish they felt as they believed they had lost him. Remember, Joseph and Mary knew exactly Who Jesus was. So imagine, you've been entrusted as the earthly parents of the

Savior of the world, and what did you do? You lost him. You'd think there couldn't be a worse emotion, and that's probably true, but has the rich man not just done a very similar thing? He is now existing with the realization that he has lost any opportunity to see and know his Maker and would-be Savior. Extreme grief, as indicated by the word that's being translated to the English "torment" is a perfect description, but it's not a good description of a person on fire. The only other verse in the Bible where this same term is used is Acts 20:38. Just prior, in verse 25, Paul informed the elders at Ephesus that they would see his face no more. And down in verse 37 and 38 we have this:

> "37 And there was much weeping of all, and falling on the neck of Paul, they ardently kissed him, 38 most of all grieving (*odunao*) for the word which he said, that they were going to see his face no more. And they went with him to the ship." (LITV)

So it seems that *odunao* denotes not only grief but a deep grief that something, rather a person, is lost and may never be seen again, just as they would never again see Paul, who was their spiritual father, and just as Mary and Joseph thought they had lost the twelve-year-old Messiah, and just as this man has lost the opportunity to be saved by God. Many Christians have been burned alive, but they still had Christ. This man is burning with extreme grief because he does not have Christ, and can never attain Christ. What could be worse? ...literal fire? Probably not. But is it possible that God would add insult to injury in the form of literal flames? I suppose it's possible but just unlikely, and it's not indicated in this passage, contrary to what you might have been taught.

Let's look closer at this flame that the rich man says he's tormented by (tested and tried/*basanos* by). I first did some searching to see if the Greek term *phlox* being translated as "flame" in this passage is interchangeable with terms for fire. It really isn't. The English word "fire" appears 83 times in the King James version of the New Testament, and there are several different Greek words that are being translated as fire, and not a single one of these 83 times is it the same Greek word that the rich man uses to describe the "flame" that torments him. Why would anyone engulfed in flames of fire describe their circumstance as being in a singular flame, and not "in fire" or "on fire" or "in these flames"? They wouldn't. This man is not literally on fire. And this would clearly be out of the norm for how the Greek is used to describe fire in the New Testament, and an awkward way to describe his situation, since fire that could do serious physical harm to a person never exists as a single flame.

The Greek word being translated as "flame" (*phlox*) in the account of the rich man is in fact used in conjunction with some of the other Greek words for fire at times in Scripture, and it's probably significant that this passage in Luke is the only place in all of Scripture where it is *not* used in conjunction with another word for literal fire. But this leads to what I mentioned earlier that I found so interesting. The Greek word *phlox* is used in only 7 verses in the entire New Testament (always in the singular), first here in Luke 16, and then in all six of the other passages, it is a direct reference to God Himself or a messenger of the Lord.

Here are those other six references:

The next one is in Acts 7:30, but it's a reference back to the Old Testament where it says an angel of the Lord appeared as a flame of fire to Moses in a bush. The third time is in 2 Thessalonians 1:7-8 where it is Jesus Christ Himself at His second coming. The fourth is in Hebrews 1:7 where we read that God makes his angels and ministers as "a flame of fire." And remember how the Holy Spirit descended at Pentecost? It was as single flames (tongues of fire) over the heads of the believers. This single flame represents God himself, or at least his unveiled reality, and this is what is tormenting this man, not a literal fire, or we'd have seen other words used to describe it, and likely different requests from a man literally burning. The tongue causes a lot of trouble. And this is part of this man's problem. He is asking for one drop of water for his tongue, and he's a man who has probably used his own tongue to speak ill of Lazarus numerous times, as he was laid at his gate. It's his way of saying, "I was wrong, and Lazarus is more righteous than I." But the point of it all, or one of the points, is that it's too late to right the wrongs after physical death. Another contrast could be made between his wicked tongue (which James says can set a whole forest ablaze), and the singular tongue of fire of truth that is tormenting him.

The fifth, sixth, and seventh times we see this singular flame in Scripture is in Revelation 1:14, Revelation 2:18 and Revelation 19:12, and in all three it is the description of the pure eyes of Christ. Not much commentary needed there. Proverbs 15:3-4 says, "The eyes of the LORD are in every place, beholding the evil and the good. A wholesome tongue is a tree of life: but perverseness therein is a breach in the spirit." (KJV) Again, it's about the fact that after this life, all truth will become evident, and everything will become very real, and there will be no excuses, no second chances. It's a powerful lesson which the mainstream church has somehow, against all biblical reason, twisted into a teaching that God is going to torment those who rejected salvation by lighting them on fire for all eternity, and that it begins immediately in Hades at the time of physical death.

In reality, the "flame" this man is in is truth itself and the knowledge that he is under the unwavering scrutiny of a Holy God. John 14:17 speaks of God as being the Spirit of truth. When the Holy Spirit, also referred to as the Spirit of Truth, descended on the believers at Pentecost, a singular flame or tongue of fire appeared over each person. We already noted that one of the definitions for the torment the man is in had to do with truth becoming very evident. So it would appear that the very knowledge and reality of God is the flame that torments this man with all of the truth about who he is, who God is, what he rejected, that he traded eternal life for a vapor, and these realizations are causing him extreme grief (*odunao*). Now the singularity of the flame makes sense because God is One, and God is Truth. To further support this, when Abraham says, "Son, remember that thou in thy lifetime receivedst thy good things, and likewise Lazarus evil things: but now he is comforted, and thou art tormented" (KJV), the word here for tormented is *odunao* which we already noted means extreme grief, not physical pain, torment, or torture. This rich man is in the flame of the Lord's scrutiny, and is painfully aware that his soul is as good as ruined, that he is destined now for destruction, and that there is no possibility of eternal life. He is grasping for some small shred of hope, which he actually knows in non-existent, just as a drop of water would do nothing to extinguish a fire.

Another fact to consider is that even if this were a 100% literal picture of what happens in Hades immediately after death, it would still add no weight to the argument that the lost will suffer throughout eternity. Scripture maintains that one day, even Death and Hades (where this scene is taking place) will be cast into the Lake of Fire, which is called the "second death," the first death being that of the flesh and the second being that of the soul. This Luke 16 passage, even if it were literal, is at most a picture of what happens immediately after physical death, which is *not* the same thing as when those in Hades are one day raised to be judged at the "great white throne," which will end with their being cast into the Lake of Fire, the end of their very existence.

If this passage were picturing eternal Heaven and Hell as many maintain, then we would need to believe a few things that I don't think can be supported Biblically: First, that there is communication between the inhabitants of Heaven and Hell (traditional Eternal Hell), second, that some of those in heaven desire to go to Hell, third, that those in Hell can see heaven and vice versa for all eternity, and lastly, that those who die, saved or unsaved, go immediately into their final eternal state, because Christ is talking about something that has already happened. None of these are true or supported Biblically. In Revelation 20:5 we are told clearly that the unsaved dead will not even be raised to be judged until after the 1000-year reign of Christ on earth, at which point, time ends and eternity begins.

You may be questioning my second point that those in heaven desire to go to Hell. Father Abraham, when he is telling the rich man about the great chasm that separates them, acknowledges that some that are there with him (Abraham) desire to go to where the rich man is. This fact is not totally clear in many English translations, but it seems apparent when we look at the original meanings of the Greek words. In fact, the *Analytical Literal Translation* of verse 26 reads, 'And besides all these [things], between us and you a great chasm has been fixed, *in order that the ones wanting to cross over from here to you are not able,* nor can the [ones] from there cross over to us.' (ALT - italics for emphasis) This could certainly not be referring to the final state of the saved and the unsaved because the Bible makes it clear that in eternity, there will be no more remembrance of former things, and if there were an eternal Hell, who would want to leave eternal heaven to visit there, anyway? And so it also seems unlikely that this would be included even in a parable referring to eternal states. However, it's far more likely that if this is referring to the intermediate states the lost and saved go into, that even people who are in Abraham's bosom (a Hebraism for paradise according to scholars) wish they could see their lost friends and relatives once more for various reasons.

So again, we have clear evidence that at the very least, this is not a picture of the final end of unsaved souls. If you take nothing else from this section, hold onto that fact. And in this passage, even considering that it's a picture of what may happen immediately at the time of physical death, it's more likely we're seeing what *would* be said, if anything *could* be said at that point of death, and not a literal account.

I've personally questioned whether or not all of the communication that we see in this story between Abraham and the rich man could actually take place between those who are divided by the impassable chasm, or if the Lord is using an imaginary conversation to describe their very real intermediate circumstances. It does seem a little unbelievable that Abraham is the assigned spokesperson, or go-between, for those who find themselves on either side of the chasm, although it's possible.

But why would we see Abraham speaking, and not Lazarus? They were both just sinners saved by the grace of God. They may have been very different positionally in their earthly lives, but after this life, both are redeemed sinners, both either able to speak or not. So it seems more likely that the Lord is figuratively using Abraham as the spokesperson because "Abraham's Bosom" had become what Jews called the place where they would go and await redemption, and it seems very likely that every detail of this story is not intended to be taken literally.

God can certainly make the intermediate state after death function however He so chooses, but not only does it seem unlikely that Abraham has been or will be the go-between who is communicating for those who end up on one side of the chasm or the other, consider this – The only people who would have called him Father Abraham would be Jews or Christians. Christians have Abraham as our father in the sense that he's the father of the faith. And Jews have him as their father in terms of genealogy. So where does that leave the unsaved Gentile who is reading this passage? They don't even see themselves represented here. Jesus was in the business of condemning His own Jewish people who were ignoring the visitation of their Messiah, and that's most likely why we see Abraham, the father of their genealogical race and faith, as the spokesperson in this story. But again, it's most likely not literal, but rather intended to lay down a number of principles.

Some traditionalists argue that this passage in Luke 16 couldn't be a figurative parable because Jesus never used a personal name in a parable, and therefore this must be a literal story, because the beggar's name is given to us. That's not a bad argument, but let's look closer at the beggar's name. According to the *Thayer's* lexicon, it means "whom God helps." Here's a man being laid daily at a wealthy Jew's gate, desperately in need, while the wealthy man lives in luxury, probably with little concern for the man, and maybe even hating that he "dirties up" the entrance to his home. There's someone with a need right there, and he's blowing the opportunity. But although he won't help him, God will. And that's the point of the story, or maybe only one of many points — that success in this life is no indicator of what things will look like after this life. God will help that man, and it says so in his very name.

I think what's *not* given to us is important as well. The story/parable doesn't give us the name of the wealthy man, and the contrast between the named one and the unnamed one may be significant. It's obviously my belief that one day the lost will, instead of being tormented throughout eternity, lose their very soul and being, and no longer be an entity of any sort. And Scripture backs up the non-entity idea in many ways as we've seen. Perhaps this is why the other main character is given no name — because he's on a path to becoming a nameless, faceless, non-entity. It's at least a possibility. Proverbs 10:7 says "The memory of the righteous is blessed, but the name of the wicked will rot." Isaiah 14:20 says "the offspring of evildoers will not be named forever." — more evidence that the namelessness of the man indicates his judgment, and perhaps his future non-existence, but it is certainly contrasted with the named one, and that name meaning "the one God helps."

Names are vital in the Bible. The study of all of the names of God is a fascinating study that gives us a fuller picture of who He really is. And many times in the Bible, we see God change someone's name to represent a change in their life or a promise that God will fulfill. For example, Abram to Abraham, Sarai to Sarah, Jacob to Israel, Simon to Peter, Saul to Paul. And often when we're told someone's name in a Biblical account, it's followed by an explanation of the always relevant meaning of the name. So what are we to make of this rich man being given no name? It seems apparent in light of other scriptures. Psalm 9:5 states: "You warn the nations and destroy evil people; you wipe out their names forever and ever." The 1898 Young's Literal Version has it, "Thou hast rebuked nations, Thou hast destroyed the wicked, Their name Thou hast blotted out to the age and for ever." (YLT) It seems that a nameless soul is ultimately no soul at all, gone forever. If this formerly rich man were a soul that was eternal, he would still have a name, even if he were suffering for all eternity as the traditionalist claims. He would be no less the person and soul he always was and worthy of at least an identity. But that's not the case. He has no name because he will not even exist soon. He is as good as a non-entity. He will have no being, as David stated of the wicked in Psalm 37:10 that we looked at previously. In God's economy, his soul is as good as dead already, as all of us are prior to salvation.

We cannot Biblically support the teaching that we are getting a glimpse of eternity here in this story, whether or not it is a parable or an actual account because, among many other reasons, the story is told in the past tense, and eternity has not begun yet. And let me pose this question: If this were eternal heaven, why would we not see Lazarus with Christ? After all, Jesus told the believing thief on the cross, that he would be *with Him* that very day, in paradise, not simply comforted in "Abraham's bosom." Well the answer is obvious. Christ is telling this story. He had not finished his earthly ministry. He had not entered the Holy of Holies. And he had not yet ascended to heaven. And no dead person that He refers to, saved or unsaved, is yet in their final state. We're told in 1 Thessalonians 4:17 that when we meet the Lord in the air, "so we will ever be with the Lord," but that doesn't mean we will be "in the air" with Him forever, only that we will always be with him. We are told we will first come back to earth and rule with him and then a thousand years later the earth and heavens will be destroyed and replaced with new ones. There's a lot that has to happen before we enter timeless eternity, so Jesus telling a past tense story could not be giving us a representation of eternity, even if, beyond all likelihood, this is a literal account.

As I noted earlier, I've studied this passage inside and out. I've written extensively on it, and I've analyzed Robert Peterson's interpretation of it, and I've also written extensively about that. In some ways I feel like I'm shorting the reader by not including it all, but if I did, this already long book would be far longer, so I've had to cut a lot of it. Read this passage for yourself. Ask God to speak to you. Ask Him if this is a story about how people who die without salvation are set on fire to be tormented for all eternity. I found it interesting that faith and salvation weren't even mentioned in the passage.

Overall, I confess I don't have every answer in the interpretation of this part of Scripture. But I'm sure this passage is not a literal picture of eternal suffering in Hell. At most, it's a literal picture of the intermediate state, but even that theory has lots of issues. But what I want the reader to really take away from this brief study is that the man is not on fire, or in fire, but is "tormented in this (singular) flame" as Jesus tells us, and if we look at the original use of the Greek language, it is a mental anguish, not a physical torture. And this flame which is causing his anguish, in every way appears to be the Holy Spirit of Truth Himself, which this man cannot rid himself of. After this earthly life, there will likely be a time of regret for those who only lived for this life, didn't give of themselves to help others, and ignored the pull of God on their hearts. I would never argue that this passage couldn't be an indicator of that. But there's nothing here to tell us this is the man's eternal state, and that's the main thing I want to drive home. As already noted, we're told they are in Hades, and Hades, whatever and wherever it is, is not the permanent estate of anyone. Its inhabitants will one day be cast into the Lake of Fire according to Revelation 20:14, and this casting in is the second death, the death believers will be saved from.

Matthew 18: 7-9 "7 Woe to the world for temptations to sin! For it is necessary that temptations come, but woe to the one by whom the temptation comes! 8 And if your hand or your foot causes you to sin, cut it off and throw it away. It is better for you to enter life crippled or lame than with two hands or two feet to be thrown into the eternal fire. 9 And if your eye causes you to sin, tear it out and throw it away. It is better for you to enter life with one eye than with two eyes to be thrown into the hell (Gehenna) of fire." (ESV)

The traditionalist, with the preconceived notion that all human souls are immortal and indestructible from conception, will naturally assume that since the lost are cast into a fire, they must therefore exist in that fire for all eternity. If the Bible anywhere confirmed that we're immortal without salvation, then I'd have to agree (and I wouldn't be writing a book challenging the traditional view of Hell). But this is not taught, and just the opposite is very clearly taught. We've already seen a lot of evidence to this end, and we'll see much more in Chapter 6. I'm devoting so much of this book's real estate to addressing the mortality/immortality issue because this is critical to understanding all of the "fire" passages, so we don't make the historical mistake of somehow thinking that the lost will be able to endure the consuming wrath of God and survive because they've been endowed with an "asbestos body," as many preachers claim.

If we just look at the plain language of the passage, and don't read anything into it, we'll see that the Lord doesn't say anything about eternal conscious suffering, but only that it would be better to enter into *life*, even maimed, than to be cast into the fire. That makes sense doesn't it? And He indicated in other scriptures the fire would fully destroy (*apollumi*) both the body and the soul — *death* — so again we have the contrast of life and death (and of course even here He was speaking figuratively, and likely not suggesting people sever and gouge out body parts). We'll look at some of his specific statements in the following chapter, but I've often heard traditionalist preachers, like Robert Jeffress, imply that simply losing one's life at final judgment isn't a harsh enough penalty for rejecting salvation.[26] I don't know if Jeffress realizes how offensive to God a teaching like this may be. God's wisdom is so far above ours, and His knowledge of what's in store in eternity obviously is as well, since we haven't seen it yet. Missing out on eternal life with God, and instead being destroyed out of existence, is the absolute highest and harshest punishment that could be meted out, without crossing over the line to cruel and unusual (and unnecessary) punishment, which is what tradition accuses God of.

And let's look at the word translated as "hell" in this passage. It's "Gehenna" which is a reference to the Valley of Hinnom, where a couple things have happened historically. One, God's people had gone astray in the past and were sacrificing their own children to the false god Molech there, by fire. Not good. And that's the first picture of death and destruction by fire that's associated with that valley. Secondly, from every source I've ever seen (except one who attempted to argue the point), it's claimed that in Jesus's day, that valley was used as a place to burn refuse, waste matter, and dead bodies of animals, and I suppose possibly humans as well, perhaps those who society didn't deem worthy of burial? And it's said that the fires were kept burning constantly. The traditionalist gravitates to that "burning constantly" part and tries to make a correlation there to the eternality of suffering they believe awaits the lost. But what I've noticed in life is that everything I've ever thrown in a fire eventually burned up. Fire is a picture of destruction, and only the saved survive it (like Daniel's three friends in the fiery furnace).

I've looked up pictures of that valley to see what it looks like now, and it's a lush beautiful place. In fact, on the first website I created to deal with this issue, I had a picture of that valley on my homepage, and one day my (then) 3-year-old daughter was sitting next to me while I was writing, and I asked her what that picture looked like to her. She answered back in her little 3-year-old poor grammar, "It look like Heaven." That's the last answer I was expecting, but I found it fascinating. And even that valley's current beauty, after such an ugly history, to me, is a picture of how one day evil will be gone, altogether...not still in existence and only removed from God's presence, as traditionalists claim. Now don't misunderstand.... That valley may open up again one day and become something ugly. There's some who find biblical evidence that this could even be the portal to the Lake of Fire. I'm not saying I necessarily believe this. I don't know what the Lake of Fire is...Is it like a fiery black hole? Or does the earth open up and become a lake of fire at the end of the 1000-year reign of Christ as some believe?

We are in fact getting a whole new heavens and earth at that point, so we're not going to need this place anymore. Well, I simply don't know what the Lake of Fire is, or what it takes to destroy a human or angelic soul. That's God's business. But I do appreciate the image that the Valley of Hinnom (Gehenna-Hell) offers right now, in that what was once a place of death and fire, is now a beautiful green valley. I think it's a picture of how things will one day be, after every tear has been wiped away and we are in the fullness of God's joy continuously.

Matthew 25: 41-46 "41Then he will say to those on his left, 'Depart from me, you cursed, into the eternal fire prepared for the devil and his angels. 42 For I was hungry and you gave me no food, I was thirsty and you gave me no drink, 43 I was a stranger and you did not welcome me, naked and you did not clothe me, sick and in prison and you did not visit me.' 44 Then they also will answer, saying, 'Lord, when did we see you hungry or thirsty or a stranger or naked or sick or in prison, and did not minister to you?' 45 Then he will answer them, saying, 'Truly, I say to you, as you did not do it to one of the least of these, you did not do it to me.' 46 And these will go away into eternal punishment, but the righteous into eternal life." (ESV)

We'll see in Chapter 9 that this verse, perhaps more than any other, influenced the early Church "fathers" and also later influential individuals in their belief in eternal conscious suffering. Regardless of all the language of the ultimate destruction of the lost, most have been unable to comprehend that a soul being destroyed and eliminated for all eternity is in fact an "eternal punishment." What seems so logical to a few of us, is unfortunately beyond comprehension to so many others of great influence. And why is this? It comes back to the concept that all souls are already immortal and indestructible. This misguided notion which most Christians hold to forces one to believe this "eternal punishment" must be something the lost soul will endure consciously for all eternity. There's not much more to say concerning this. Either you trust Scripture, and that it nowhere endorses the idea that all souls will always exist, or you trust tradition, and believe they will. Where you land on that decision will determine what you believe this "eternal punishment" is.

Let's also address the "eternal fire prepared for the devil and his angels" where this "eternal punishment" will occur. Fact: There was or will be an eternal fire prepared for the devil and his angels. I've thought a lot about the omniscience and foreknowledge of God, and since He knew that multitudes of human souls would also be cast into the Lake of Fire (and probably a higher percentage of humans than angels), why is it referred to as only having been "prepared for the devil and his angels" instead of for all who reject God's salvation? The best I've come up with so far, is just the time line. God knew from eternity past, that Satan would fall, and that He would work this into His plan of testing and refining humanity. And God also knew that Satan's time would be limited, so He prepared a destruction for him, so whether the eternal fire was created before, say, even humanity had been created, or whether it's only created in His mind for now and will become reality in the future, it is or was created because of the need to destroy Satan and the fallen angels after God is finished using them for His ultimate plans and purposes.

But it says it's an "eternal" fire, so the process of destruction the fire imposes must go on for all eternity, right? Not at all, actually. We covered this in the analysis of the 2 Thessalonians 1:5-10 passage, so we won't repeat that whole study again here. An eternal (aionios) fire causes a permanent condition, but does not necessarily burn for eternity. Don't forget that the fire that completely destroyed Sodom and Gomorrah was also called "eternal" in Scripture, and it's not still burning. However, it caused a permanent, everlasting condition of utter destruction and non-existence, for the city, structurally, as well as its inhabitants. We'll find even more confirming definitions of just exactly what "eternal fire" is in the next section of this chapter.

For now let's go a little deeper and address where verse 46 says the lost will go away "into" eternal punishment. The word being translated as "into," according to the *Strong's* concordance, can mean "to" or "into." They are interchangeably available to those who translate Scripture. But because the majority of Christians believe that it's a perpetual process of punishment the lost are headed for, "into" fits that more precisely, so it's what you'll find in most Bible translations. On the other hand, if the lost are headed "to" their ultimate destruction, it would sound wrong to say they are headed "into" that demise and loss of being. We should read that they "will go away to" that final and everlasting punishment. And this very passage already told us what the punishment is back in verse 41: It's eternal fire, and we know what its permanent effect is. The lost are going to their eternal punishment, which is death, caused by a fire that will eternally end their very existence.

Matthew 25:46 is just one more place in Scripture where translators and interpreters are steering people just off the path to truth, when it comes to understanding judgment most clearly. The question we've asked is: "Where did Scripture ever establish the idea that all souls will exist in some state, somewhere, for all eternity?" And the answer we've found so far: Nowhere. And it's certainly not in this verse. Universal soul immortality is a pagan idea that came from the pagan world, and we'll only briefly touch on its origin later. Others have done that research and written those books. Edward Fudge, who did much of the trailblazing of the modern fight against the traditional view of eternal conscious suffering gave some great history of the doctrine in his portion of the book *Two Views of Hell* which was co-authored with Robert Peterson, and I'd recommend it to anyone interested in this subject.

There's an Old Testament, as well as a New Testament reference to worms that "won't die" and unquenchable fire, both verses making Peterson's top ten list of eternal Hell "proofs." So we'll address them together in this last section of this chapter in the order they appear in Scripture.

> Isaiah 66:22-24 "22 For as the new heavens and the new earth which I make stand before Me, declares Jehovah, so your seed and your name shall stand. 23 And it will be, from new moon to its new moon, and from sabbath to its sabbath, all flesh shall come to worship before Me, says Jehovah. 24 And they shall go out and see the dead bodies of the men who have rebelled against Me; for their worm shall not die, nor shall their fire be put out; and they shall be an object of disgust to all flesh." (LITV)

We noted earlier that of over 23,000 verses in the Old Testament, only two are considered by traditionalists as blatant evidence of eternal suffering in Hell. The Daniel 12:1-2 passage we've already looked at, and this Isaiah 66:24 verse is the other one. Of course, it's this author's opinion that there are no verses in the Old Testament that teach eternal suffering, but for the traditionalist who believes in eternal conscious suffering, the fact that there are only two verses that even remotely could be interpreted this way is quite an accusation that God failed to properly warn people who existed before the New Testament was written, of the "true consequences" of faithlessness, even if their accusation is unintended. On the other hand, folks like myself believe that God has always given the same warning throughout Scripture, that ultimately, life and death are our choices.

Actually, while it's rare to hear the following verse claimed as evidence of eternal suffering, a third Old Testament passage did just come to mind, and this is as good a place as any to address it. It's so rare in fact, I think I may have heard this argued as an eternal Hell passage only once. But it occurred to me, so in the interest of being thorough, let's take a quick look at it.

It's in Numbers 16 where several rebels are confronting and challenging Moses' leadership, and there comes a point in verses 29 and 30 where Moses will prophesy their unusual death by the ground swallowing them up on the following day as evidence of God's hand on his leadership. And of course this happens, just as Moses said it would. And the language will vary from one Bible translation to another, but most say something like "they went down alive to the pit," or "went down alive to Sheol," and some versions may have "to the grave," and some may even say they went alive "into Hell." The actual Hebrew word for where they fell to is *Sheol*, and in the Old Testament, it always signified "the grave" or the state of being dead. That they "went there alive" means nothing more than that they were alive when they fell into this hole that opened up in the earth. It doesn't mean they remained alive, and it doesn't represent that souls are "alive" in Hell.

Moses said God was going to do something unusual as a sign of his approval of Moses' leadership, a new thing, and since people are usually dead when they are put into the ground, this was certainly unusual, and according to Moses, perhaps nothing like this had ever happened before on earth. But I actually heard it claimed that this passage means they went direct and alive to Hell where their torment would begin — that they never even physically died due to this event. Now, is it possible this event foreshadowed final judgment, when those who have rejected God's leadership must stand judgment and then be cast into the Lake of Fire? Very possible. But these men, although alive when the earth swallowed them up, then died a physical death. There's no reason to believe otherwise.

Getting back to our Isaiah 66 passage, Robert Peterson in *Two Views of Hell* indicates that he believes verse 22 gives us the time line when it refers to the new earth and new heavens,[27] which would place events in eternity, beyond time, given that the old earth revolving in front of the Sun is what created time.

But he's made a pretty big oversight. The Lord, through Isaiah, mentions the new heavens and new earth only in a metaphor that indicates how long believers will endure. Verse 22 has nothing to do with dating the passage. The time line is actually set by all of the surrounding verses in this chapter. It's speaking of the time of the tribulation when the Lord will "slay many" according to verse 16, and then the millennial reign of Christ on earth.

We know this is happening on earth for a couple of reasons. For one, there are new moons and Sabbaths. A "new moon" is a calendar event – something that happens in time...not timelessness. There aren't going to be any nights or moons in eternity when the Lord is our light, and these heavens have been consumed by fire (2 Peter 3:10 and Revelation 20:11), and it's doubtful the Jewish Sabbath will still be in practice throughout eternity, although it's possible. Certain activities God ordained are foreshadows, and some are also a "backshadow." The weekly sabbath was a look back at how God created everything in six days and rested on the seventh. And with Old and New Testament references to a day with the Lord being like a thousand years, many of us believe it was also a foreshadow of how there would be approximately six thousand years of human history prior to Christ's reign, followed by a seventh millennium when Christ is back on earth reigning as King of kings.

After this is complete and this present earth is destroyed at the end of that millennial reign and we have a new earth and heavens as we enter timeless eternity, will that foreshadow be necessary? It seems unlikely. So again, this seems to be a reference to earthly events, not eternity. Secondly, the Lord says, in verse 23, that "all flesh shall come to worship before me." The way I understand it, we're not going to be "fleshy" in heaven, after the millennial reign of Christ (1 Cor 15: 44,47,48), and we will be in the presence of the Lord continually in some fashion, and will not need to "come" to worship. Thirdly, verse 24 clearly says that these are dead bodies (not lost souls) that rebelled against God, and it says that when we go up (to Jerusalem, I presume) to worship the Lord, we will go out and see the dead bodies. Is this what we're going to be doing in eternity – looking at dead bodies? I hope not. To me, it seems most likely that these are just the dead remains of those who rebelled in the tribulation, and most likely they are visible at the beginning of the 1000-year earthly reign of Christ (when we will still have a moon), until they are consumed by worms and fire, but their souls are in Hell/Hades awaiting final judgment.

As far as the worms being undying, we're not expected to believe that God has created a species of eternal indestructible worm that will eat on these dead bodies for all time and beyond time. The worm not dying is just figurative language that indicates that some will be eaten by worms, and that the lowly worm will outlive those who rebelled against God, and also that ultimately there won't even be a physical remembrance of them. In Scripture, there are multiple places where people are commanded to do or not do some particular thing, so they will "not die." These who have rebelled against the Lord have disobeyed and instead of them not dying, it is their consuming worm that will outlive them.

Concerning the unquenchable fire, the fire that consumes these bodies will not be quenched. It's that simple. "Quenched" means "put out" or "extinguished." But the fire not being extinguished before it finishes burning whatever it is burning is a different concept entirely from a fire that would burn for all eternity. There's no such thing. These rebels will be completely consumed — some by worms, some by fire. Both of these consume wholly and completely. If anything, this image of bodily destruction is a picture of the future utter decimation and non-entity state that even the souls of these men will come to. We don't need to assume the fires never go out, although "unquenchable fire" has been twisted to mean this by many traditionalists. These are just dead bodies and they will eventually stop providing fuel for the fire when they're gone. Not only does the passage come right out and say these are "dead bodies," it tells us in verse 24 that they shall be an object of disgust to "all flesh." This is clearly an earthly event. Also, this concept of unquenchable fire appears in other places in the Bible and it never means fires that burn for eternity.

> Jeremiah 17:27 "But if you do not listen to me, to keep the Sabbath day holy, and not to bear a burden and enter by the gates of Jerusalem on the Sabbath day, then I will kindle a fire in its gates, and it shall devour the palaces of Jerusalem and shall not be quenched." (italics for emphasis — ESV)

God, through Jeremiah, just defined what happens when a fire will not be quenched: It devours.

Another is Ezekiel 20:45-48

> "45 And the word of the LORD came to me: 46 'Son of man, set your face toward the southland; preach against the south, and prophesy against the forest land in the Negeb. 47 Say to the forest of the Negeb, Hear the word of the LORD: Thus says the Lord GOD, Behold, I will kindle a fire in you, and *it shall devour* every green tree in you and every dry tree. The blazing flame shall *not be quenched*, and all faces from south to north shall be scorched by it. 48 All flesh shall see that I the LORD have kindled it; it shall *not be quenched*.'" (italics for emphasis — ESV)

If this prophecy is about something that already happened, and this is probably safe to assume, then the fire certainly "went out," but was not "put out" or "quenched." Also, it was lit for the purpose of "destruction." Unquenchable doesn't mean ever-burning. It only means that it's going to complete what God intended it to do, consume, without God or anyone else quenching it.

In the Old and New Testament, the lost are compared to chaff that will be burned with "unquenchable fire." Chaff is burned up to be gotten rid of, and I think that's why it's used figuratively to indicate the consumption and destruction of the lost, but traditionalists have used the "chaff" verses as well, to teach ever-burning flames. It's difficult to understand why. If a fire "will not be quenched (put out)" then it is going to burn up whatever is in it. That's the purpose of not quenching it.

Let's jump to the New Testament reference of worms and fire and see if we get any evidence for eternal conscious suffering in Hell, as Peterson and the traditionalists claim...

> **Mark 9:44-48** **"44 'where their worm doesn't die, and the fire is not quenched.' 45 If your foot causes you to stumble, cut it off. It is better for you to enter into life lame, rather than having your two feet to be cast into Gehenna, into the fire that will never be quenched— 46 'where their worm doesn't die, and the fire is not quenched.' 47 If your eye causes you to stumble, cast it out. It is better for you to enter into God's Kingdom with one eye, rather than having two eyes to be cast into the Gehenna of fire, 48 'where their worm doesn't die, and the fire is not quenched.'" (WEB)**

The Isaiah passage seems to be referring to an earthly event, and most likely to that final battle before the Lord begins His reign on earth. In Mark, Jesus seems to be using the same imagery of utter destruction to refer to *final* judgment. And can we first admit that perhaps we're going to find some hyperbole here? If we can't fathom this, then we would have Jesus literally recommended people amputate their limbs and gouge their eyeballs out. If someone wants to believe He was being literal, go ahead. I can't go there, personally. So in the next sentence where I see an undying worm in a fire, I have no problem taking the hyperbolic meaning. Worms will completely eat dead matter. There will be nothing left. Fire will reduce matter to nothingness. This is the point. For traditionalists to offer ideas such as this being "the worm of consciousness, forever tormenting the lost soul" is adding to Scripture and creating completely new concepts that are foreign to anything we know of these images.

This passage speaks of the same destruction Jesus always foretold for those who go down the broad path. This differs slightly though from Isaiah's use of the same images in that Isaiah was predicting literal worms and earthly fire, whereas I believe Jesus is "borrowing" the thought (as if the Word wasn't His to begin with) and using it more figuratively to describe the ultimate and total consumption of the soul in Gehenna, the Lake of Fire, the eternal punishment from which there is no return, just as something burned or eaten away cannot exist again.

A fire that is not quenched will finish its work of destruction. That's the idea here. And worms are another picture of destruction. I looked around Scripture for some examples and I thought of Jonah, who was sitting under that vine that had come up in one day, but then God sent the worm to destroy it. The ultimate point of that story was God showing Jonah that his values were out of place because the prophet was more concerned for this shade-giving plant that had grown up in a day, and then died, than he was for the many souls in Nineveh who were going to be destroyed if they didn't repent and turn from wickedness. But for our purposes here, it's a demonstration of the fact that worms destroy...even when it's just one worm.

I found something interesting in Job as well. In chapter 17 Job is announcing what he believes is his entry into death, but he's implying that his hope goes beyond Sheol (the grave, or the realm of the dead, and often translated 'Hell'). We know in hindsight that the Lord was going to raise him up again, but at this point, he's at rock bottom and preparing mentally for death, but telling his friends that his hope isn't in the grave. This is relevant to this study because he mentions the devouring worm, and after figuratively calling Corruption his father, he calls the worm "his" mother and sister. Job 17:14-15:

> "14 If I have said to corruption, 'You are my father;' to the worm, 'My mother,' and 'my sister;' 15 where then is my hope? as for my hope, who shall see it?" (WEB)

I couldn't help but notice it's singular possessive: *the* worm is *his* mother, not just "*a* worm" or all the "worms" one would expect would devour a dead carcass, just like when Jesus says "their worm" (singular possessive) in the Mark passage we're considering. It seems that while there of course wouldn't be only one single worm assigned to each dead body that ever dies, the phraseology of the Old and New Testaments in regard to this is to speak of them singularly as "their worm." The 2011 New International Version took out the possessive "their" and even altered the singularity, and changed it to read "the worms that eat them will not die" (NIV). Maybe that's the general idea of what's going on, but in the Greek, there's a possessive pronoun there and the worm is singular. So with Job we have a biblical precedent for referring to the state of bodily destruction that happens at death, as happening as a result of "his worm." Concerning Jesus's use of the same image, it's likely speaking of the destruction of the soul rather than only the body, but the same utter annihilation is implied.

As with many traditionalist arguments for eternal conscious suffering, when the proof isn't there, they resort to human reason and arguments, and instead of just letting Scripture interpret Scripture, various hypotheses are thrown out. A common one I mentioned previously, concerning this worm who will not die is that it's the "worm of consciousness" that will eternally torment the lost. That's not in the Bible. In fact, I looked up every place the word "worm" is used in Scripture and the following is everything that it ever represents: a worm, a man, mankind in general, and the House of Jacob, at least once. It's never a person's conscious thoughts.

Once again there is nothing in the verse under consideration that proves or adds any weight at all to the eternal conscious suffering model. It's just more misapplied terms and ideas, stretching far beyond the definitions which Scripture gives us.

I hope it's been helpful to review the most commonly used verses to maintain the traditional view of eternal conscious suffering which traditionalist writer Robert Peterson maintains are the "footings to the foundation" of the "house of Traditionalism." To me, if these are the footings, then the foundation is doomed, and then whatever house you build on top of that....well, I'm scared to go inside because it's coming down at some point – hopefully some point soon, because it's just plain wrong, and it turns away many people who are seeking the Lord. It also serves to confuse the believer about the merciful nature and character of God.

I think it's important for those of us who've had the traditional view of eternal conscious suffering drilled into us almost from birth, to step back and realize something. If it's true, it should be easily verifiable in Scripture, not something that has to be painfully, and against all good biblical hermeneutics, strained out. This is so important for those of us who have been in or around the Christian world all our lives to step back and realize: It's not as if there's some extra-biblical Eternal Hell reality out there that somehow, we just instinctively know is true, and thankfully we have Scripture to give us a few "descriptions of Hell." No, it's the other way around. If it's a legitimate doctrine — if there is an eternal conscious Hell reality out there, then these verses which are claimed to prove and demonstrate it should do so beyond any reasonable doubt. I hope I've shown that they do no such thing, and that many of them actually lend far more weight to a non-traditional view of final judgment which paints God in a far more merciful light.

We've also seen ample evidence of the misuse of the Garden of Eden concepts which have given us the doctrinal idea that being a "living soul" means already possessing immortality — the ability to go on existing forever. It's just not true — well, it's not in the Bible, anyway. God loves object lessons. The Bible is full of them in multiple forms, and it seems that He's given us one in our own bodies, in that what is happening on the "soul level" is being demonstrated physically right in front of us. Just as our flesh is alive, but also dying and headed for a date with death, so is our soul. We are living souls, but we are dying souls as well, headed for a date with destruction if we don't take the hand of salvation that God is reaching out to us. I pray that if you're reading this and have not yet accepted Christ as your Savior, that you'll do that right now.

Death: A Severe Punishment

"I remember the first time that my father told me, as a little boy, that someday I was going to die. Somehow the thought had just never occurred to me. But when he told me that, it filled me with terrible sadness and horror, and I just cried and cried and cried."[28] – Dr. William Lane Craig*, theologian and Christian apologist

This quote was from a man who was raised by non-believers, according to his testimony, so as a child, it was likely not the prospect of eternal Hell that grieved him so when his dad told him he was going to die. More likely it was the thought of no longer existing. Death is indeed horrible and sad, and I think a child's perspective is most interesting, and probably the least tainted by multitudes of theories and ideas about the afterlife with which adults have been inundated.

I can relate to Dr. Craig's experience. I remember one day when I was young – I don't know what age...maybe eight or nine, and I was staying at my grandmother's house for the day during the Summer as I often did, and then we got the news that the next door neighbor had been killed earlier that morning when he was electrocuted while touching his back fence. A power line had fallen on a fence a couple of houses over and there were a number of "hot" fences in the neighborhood. I suppose I should have been most upset about the man who just lost his life, but I was a child, and I had only even seen him a few

---

* By quoting Dr. Craig, in no way am I implying he holds a non-traditional view of final judgment such as what I put forward in this book. I only found the quote interesting.

times, and didn't actually know him at all.   And perhaps he wasn't all that old, but to children, all grownups seem old.   In my mind, the elderly man next door who I didn't know, and really couldn't even picture, had died.   I did feel sad about the man, but if I'm honest, what upset and struck me most was that me and a couple of other boys had been playing right next to the same network of fences that were electrified, right at the same time the man was killed.   We literally came inches away from dying that day, and as I thought about it, I became extremely distraught.   I remember crying and crying at the thought that my life had almost ended that quickly and easily, and I finally persuaded my grandmother to let me call my mother at work so I could tell her about everything.

Unlike Dr. Craig, I was raised in a Christian home, but for whatever reason, I just don't think I was paying attention in church for a number of years, and didn't come to any substantial knowledge of Christ until my teen years, and I don't consider myself to have been saved until into my 20s, although an experience with the Lord when I was 15 was highly impactful. And when I got so upset that day, I wasn't thinking that I may have gone to Hell, or that I should have been happy because I would have been in Heaven.   I was just thinking that I almost died.   My life, the only life that I could comprehend, my "eternal" life (as far as I was concerned) had almost ended.

Death is sad, and eternal death as a punishment is severe beyond measure.   .

Several years ago, early on in the writing of this book, I attended the funeral of a church friend's mother.   I didn't know her, yet I became saddened and emotional during the service. By reading entries from her diaries and recounting conversations he had with her, the pastor gave us lots of reassurance that she was in fact saved.   And although I didn't know her, I became sure of this as well – as sure as a person can be about another person.   But I was still sad – sad for the loss of her life — sad for those who knew and loved her.

It seems like God has designed us this way, even believers, such that even though we have a blessed hope, and can know that we will again see our loved ones who have put their faith in the Lord, we still feel the pain and sadness of death. It serves a purpose. The loss of this first life at the death of our flesh and the surrounding sadness is an object lesson to us of the much more grievous sadness that should be, and will be, felt for the ultimate death of a soul. If we're as sad as we are when a saved person dies, even a person that we don't know well, or a person that we know we'll see again, how much more grief should we have for those who will die ultimately and never be seen again? And shouldn't this inspire us to tell those who are headed for death about Christ? Ezekiel 33 8-9 says:

> "When I say to the wicked, O wicked one, you shall surely die; if you do not speak to warn the wicked from his way, that wicked one shall die in his iniquity; but I will require his blood at your hand. But, if you warn the wicked of his way, to turn from it; if he does not turn from his way, he shall die in his iniquity, but you have delivered your soul." (LITV)

It's an approaching death that we are to be warning people of, not eternal torment. The Bible nowhere, Old or New Testament, tells us to warn of impending eternal torment for human souls, but we *are* required to rescue those who are *perishing*. Death as a punishment is a dreaded and harsh one. You wouldn't know it to hear certain traditionalists speak of it. Non-traditionalists like myself, who choose to believe the multitude of Bible verses that predict death as the final end of those without Christ, are often portrayed as trying to create a softer image of God and His wrath than what in reality exists. But there's nothing soft about a God who destroys and brings those who reject Him to nothing.

I'll give you an idea of what I'm referring to. I've heard similar statements in different forms from a number of traditionalists, but one that struck me during the writing of this book was when nationally known pastor Robert Jeffress said in a radio sermon:

"If unbelievers are simply destroyed, that takes a little bit of the sting out of Hell, doesn't it? I mean, after all, if you're not a Christian and you're wrong, the worst that happens to you is, okay, you die, you cease to exist. It takes a little urgency out of sharing the gospel with your non-Christian friend or family member because after all, I mean, if they don't accept Christ, they won't be in heaven, but they won't be in pain forever. They just simply cease to exist."[29]

Simply? Ceasing to exist — the very loss of one's soul and being is only a "simply"? For Jeffress, a judgment of death for the wicked is just not severe enough. Apparently he believes they need to be in conscious pain forever. And he maintains that there is less urgency to share the gospel if a person's end is only death. With God's most severe form of punishment being death throughout Scripture, and with the second death of the soul being the final judgment of those who reject God's love, it's hard to believe that a line of thinking like Jeffress's isn't offensive to God. But Jeffress isn't the only one. There are many Bible teachers who state such things, all of whom I respect as it concerns their position on and their general promotion of the gospel, but whom I'm forced to disagree with on this issue. Earlier in the same broadcast Jeffress stated that the doctrine of "Annihilationism simply says that an unbeliever doesn't live forever. After the great white throne judgment, he is cast into the Lake of Fire and he's simply destroyed."[30] Yes, that is exactly what the Bible appears to say. There is no consciousness noted or predicted for humans after they've been cast into the Lake of Fire.

Also in the same broadcast, Jeffress said that the suffering which will take place in Hell defies description, but that the only way he "could possibly even describe it would be to say, it's like having your flesh on fire forever and ever and ever." He can't possibly know this since no one has come back from the Lake of Fire to report, and this is never predicted anywhere in Scripture, but Jeffress went on to say that God was too loving *not* to allow this kind of torment for all eternity. Huh? What a twisted teaching this has become in the Church. I'm sure Robert

Jeffress is a man who reveres God, as he understands Him. But he, like many others, is not accepting the plain language of the Bible, and is instead helping to perpetuate misinformation that damages people's understanding of who God really is. God is a harsh judge, but not a twisted maniac who requires the everlasting feeling of being on fire for all eternity for those who failed to accept His grace. Death is enough. It will satisfy God's wrath.

I recently found one author's take on the loss of life particularly disturbing. Dr. Clint Archer, who I'd never heard of, wrote a book entitled *A Visitor's Guide to Hell: A Manual for Temporary Entrants and Those who would prefer to avoid eternal damnation.* He implied that for the lost to experience annihilation would be blissful oblivion.[31] I couldn't believe it. Actually I could. The entire book was filled with the same arguments that are always rehashed in these sorts of books, and in my opinion Archer offered nothing to the conversation. And please know that I didn't purchase it in order to criticize it; rather, I thought it might show me something I'd missed from the traditionalist position. It didn't. It confirmed the non-traditional track I had been on for a number of years, and it was the last of six books I've purchased which attempted to prove tradition correct. There won't be a seventh.

May I state the obvious? To experience bliss, one would first have to exist. Is that fair enough? If a lost soul is annihilated at final judgment, they won't experience bliss, so the idea is complete nonsense. But it also ignores that what precedes destruction and annihilation in the Lake of Fire is a conscious judgment that the lost will endure. Where's the bliss in that? A faithless person who died rejecting Christ will one day stand judgment, and endure a mental torment that I can't even imagine, as they realize that their very existence is about to end. They're living out their last seconds, knowing it's all over. It's an absolute horror. But for Archer ...blissful oblivion.

Others have expressed similar feelings as Jeffress and Archer, regarding ceasing to exist being too light of a punishment, at least for some offenders, as if we were not all guilty before the Lord.

Sinclair Ferguson, another co-author of *Hell Under Fire*, seems to imply that only the reality of eternal Hell as traditionally understood would create the necessity of Christ's crucifixion.[32] It's poor logic, unless there is simply no value to life itself. Why would it require the reality of an eternal Hell to bring necessity to Christ's sacrifice? Death was the enemy to be conquered, according to many places in Scripture, and He accomplished that as His death now makes eternal life available for us. The Lord is not willing that any should perish (2 Peter 3:9). He takes no pleasure in the death of the wicked (Ezekiel 33:11). He did what He did so we could ultimately escape the eternal punishment of a death from which there is no return. Ferguson is correct that it would be folly if His death on the cross was unnecessary. But His sacrifice was not made necessary because of eternal conscious suffering in Hell, but so death would be defeated (2 Timothy 1:10).

> Hebrews 2:14-15 "Since therefore the children share in flesh and blood, he himself likewise partook of the same things, that through death he might destroy the one who has the power of death, that is, the devil, and deliver all those who through fear of death were subject to lifelong slavery." (ESV)

We can see from this verse that Christ took death upon Himself in order to defeat death, and the dread of impending death. And once again there is no mention that Christ saved souls from eternal suffering in Hell. It seems strange and almost silly to have to write this chapter, essentially reminding us that death is bad, and that the ultimate death of a soul is the grimmest, most sorrowful fate. But it becomes a necessary reminder when so many prominent Christians are claiming that the lost must be on fire for all eternity in order to bring value to what Christ did on the cross. And this isn't new. This thinking has been handed down since some of the early church fathers.

And as it relates to Christ taking our punishment upon Himself on the cross, if the penalty for sin isn't death, but rather endless torment for all eternity, then Christ in fact did not take our punishment upon himself, because He's not still suffering nor will He for all eternity. Now, traditionalists will come up with arguments such as, "Jesus is an infinite being, so even though His suffering was momentary, He was able to experience an eternity of suffering in those moments." Forgive me, but that's just a feeble attempt at human reasoning to make sense out of something that can't make sense. The biblical concept of a day being like a thousand years with the Lord is a far cry from a few hours being like eternity. If a lost human's fate is to suffer consciously for all eternity, and if Jesus was to take our punishment for us, then the only substitute would have been for Him to literally suffer consciously for all eternity in the place of those who put their trust in His atoning sacrifice. Fortunately for those of us who are looking forward to spending eternity with Jesus, death was the punishment He took on for us, and death is what He conquered, and eternal life with Him is what's in front of us.

The Sanctity of Life

I realize that my having no abbreviations behind my name, and otherwise no formal credentials has probably given some readers cause to doubt if they're finding reliable information in this book (although I hope I'm demonstrating that Scripture speaks for itself on this matter). And I realize that not quoting many outside sources, as so many traditionalists do when addressing these topics may further give readers some apprehension. Well now I'll probably shred any remaining credibility I may have had when I quote a line from the 1990 film *Joe Versus the Volcano*, one of Tom Hanks' lesser known movies. It was a quirky, cartoonishly fantastic movie, that, aside from a couple of choice four-letter words, I really loved, and found to be profound in its general message. I won't try to give all of the background but some is necessary.

It's the story of a man (played by Tom Hanks) who never felt well. He had been in a boring dead-end job for a number of years, had forgotten to live life, and so was dying on the inside, and it was manifesting in physical symptoms. During one of his many visits to the doctor, he's told he has a rare, incurable disease and a very brief time to live. Being a hypochondriac, he fails to get a second opinion, so believing he is at death's door, when presented with an opportunity to be a hero, though it will cost him his life, he accepts the challenge.

On his way to his destination as he crossed the ocean on a yacht that was provided by his benefactor, a storm takes the vessel down, and only he and the young lady who was captaining the boat survive. They were saved because of his over-sized waterproof luggage which they floated on for several days, her unconscious since the accident, and him neglecting his own needs and rationing the only bottle of water to her in capfuls periodically. The profound moment for me comes when after several days of scorching sun, no food, and no water, and on his way to his own death through heroism, if his own terminal disease or starvation doesn't get him first, he lifts his eyes one starry night and is struck by the beauty of an enormous moon coming up over the horizon, and speaks out with almost no strength, "Dear God, whose name I do not know, Thank you for my life." He pauses for a moment and then says slowly, "I forgot how big."[33]

And you may be wondering just exactly what my point is. It's that even this brief life, even when it is troubled, trying, discouraging, depressing, and sometimes just plain boring, is still a wonderful gift, and this man realized it as he was on the brink of losing it. And not only that, but he was thankful for what he had, even though he believed it was almost over. I'm sure this is the experience of many people near the end of their life. Even when we're not at the end of life, but are thinking back on the past, we get nostalgic and often see everything much sweeter in remembrance than we did while experiencing it. Life is so much better than we realize it is while we are living it. It's always more attractive in retrospect. Why is it that way? Is it that we're fools now for forgetting how difficult things really were in the past, or were we fools then for not appreciating every moment? Maybe it's a mix, but I tend to believe it's often the latter, and I'm certainly guilty of this. This life is a gift. We should be joining Joe and constantly saying, "Dear God (and we *do* know His name if we trust Scripture), Thank You for my life." God didn't have to create you or me, but He did. That we exist at all is really quite amazing if we'll ever just think about it. God dreamed us up, knew every wrong thing we would ever do, created us anyway, and goes to extreme lengths to draw us to Himself so we will inherit a life that will never end.

This first life is a wonderful gift, even with its troubles. But eternal life, and a tearless one at that, is then an infinitely more wonderful gift. And yet, many traditionalists don't see the eternal loss of life the unsaved face as even enough motivation for witnessing to those who are perishing. But it's obvious where this kind of thinking comes from. If one has it ingrained in their mind all their life that the lost will suffer in literal fire for all eternity, then losing their being, an extreme loss, can actually seem like a non-punishment to some. Can we see how Satan has so deluded us with the lie that "surely [we] won't die"?

> Nothingness is a horrible destiny in comparison to what's available. It won't be "blissful oblivion." It won't be anything. You won't be there for it.

I wish I could say I go around with a positive attitude all the time, but that's not always the case. Life is full of problems for all of us, whether our problems are so-called "first world problems." or if they're more dire — whether you have poor people problems or wealthy people problems. What I've noticed about problems is that they're relative, and most people believe theirs are the worst — and for them, they are. But Christians should be living in constant hope, no matter what difficulties we have. Jesus said that we'd have trouble in this life, but to take heart because He overcame the world. It's much easier to write advice like this than to live it, but it's so true. If we'd just sit and reflect on the reality that we were nothingness, and now have the opportunity to live forever in painless bliss and awe of a God beyond comprehension...life is good — because regardless of our temporary trials, it's leading somewhere good beyond compare if we persevere in faith. Existence, our very being, is a miracle — a true gift. If a person gets one day of conscious life, it's a gift, and it's one more day than we deserve by any merit of our own.

At the other end of the spectrum, but by the same token, there is nothing we can do or not do to merit an eternal existence in torment. We've already covered it sufficiently, but contrary to what is commonly taught, our *eternal* existence is not a given. It too is a gift, but unlike the gift of this first earthly life, it's given only to those who place their trust in the one true living God; and for those of us who have heard the full New Testament gospel message, eternal death can only be avoided by accepting Jesus's death as an atoning sacrifice that puts us in right standing with the Father. There is certainly nothing one can do to earn eternal suffering. There's actually nothing one can do to "earn" eternal death either. It is the natural course of all things living, including souls, to return to non-existence (death), if God does not intervene. It's the law of entropy. And he only intervenes for those who respond to His calling. Otherwise eternal death awaits, a return to the nothingness we were before God gave us this opportunity of life.

> There's nothing one can do to "earn" eternal death. It's the natural course of all things living, including souls, to return to non-existence (death), if God does not intervene. It's the law of entropy.

Nothingness is a horrible destiny in comparison to what's available. It won't be "blissful oblivion." It won't be anything. You won't be there for it. One day you won't exist if you resist the offer of salvation. The insistence by some well-meaning Bible teachers that eternal death is not a serious enough consequence for rejecting God is itself a serious challenge to the idea of the sanctity of life that we Christians claim to defend. So it's not only unbiblical to believe in eternal conscious torment, but it's a logical fallacy and gross inconsistency when out of one side of our mouths we claim how valuable even this first life is, when arguing against, for instance, abortion, but out of the other side of our mouths say that eternal death and the loss of eternal life is virtually a non-punishment. We need to take another look at our positions on these things and make sure we're being biblical and consistent.

CHAPTER 6

More Evidence Growing in the Garden

In our last visit to the Garden of Eden in Chapter 2, we noted the most apparent fact, at least regarding mortality and immortality: Eating from the Tree of Life is the action that causes one to go on living forever, and we saw that Adam and Eve simply did not eat of it, and now no humans have access to it until Jesus gives it to believers again after this life. But we also noted that this banning from the Tree of Life which resulted from Adam and Eve's willful disobedience did not condemn them to *eternal* death because God stepped in and covered their shame, and they accepted the covering. Therefore, Adam and Eve have the same sure hope for eternal life which any believer will who accepts God's covering. We observed that death became a reality, just as promised, and that it happened on the very day they ate the forbidden fruit. But God overcame death, so that only the first death will have any effect on the believer. We are safe from the second death, the death which would end our being. Death has "lost its sting" as Paul would phrase it in 1 Corinthians 15:56. But in an effort to further understand that souls without salvation are innately mortal and dying, let's go back to the Garden for more evidence.

Rather than deal only with this particular issue, we'll look at a number of common misunderstandings about the Garden of Eden. I think the reader will be surprised to find just how unbiblical many of our common teachings really are. And while a number of the issues we'll address here do not deal directly with mortality or immortality, they'll exhibit just how far we'll go to hold onto tradition, even when it cannot be supported with Scripture, and several of the issues we'll look at in this chapter will at least indirectly relate to the mortality question.

I'm going to put forward some things in this chapter that are going to be unorthodox, but I think you'll find support for everything I assert. Some of what I will claim will so go against traditional teachings however that I'm sure I will be called a blasphemer by some. But several concepts have been taught incorrectly, and what can I do but present what I see as a more Scriptural take on certain issues, and challenge people to think about some of the things we've accepted without due study?

Satan's Oldest Lie

Satan's initial lie to humanity, and really the only one noted in Scripture that I can recall, directly from Satan to humanity's ears, was that even if we sinned, death would not surely come (Genesis 3:4). And the Deceiver is so clever, that he has had Christians teaching the very same lie, and under the guise of "Biblical truth," for approximately 1800 years, in this erroneous idea that all souls are eternal. We saw in Chapter 2 where John MacArthur, Jack Graham, David Jeremiah, and Kay Arthur all claimed that we will all live forever — that we will not surely die. And while I'm aware that this is the traditional position, and it doesn't interfere with my appreciation of any of these peoples' ministries, when I hear them come right out and make statements such as, "No one will ever die" and "We will all live forever," it just really drives home, for me, just how far Satan's initial lie to humanity has inundated the body of Christ. And what's worse, not only do we deny the Biblical claim that true death, a total cessation of life, will come for those who reject God, but we further distort the biblical judgment message by claiming that those who didn't accept God's grace will exist in unbearable agony for all eternity, completely distorting our comprehension of a loving merciful Father, and turning Him more into some kind of cruel monster who actually desires and requires the unending suffering of those who failed to come to know Him, than a just Judge who requires the life of those who fail to put their trust in Him. I'm sure Satan is very pleased with himself and how he's worked his lies into our doctrines.

It's interesting to note that Paul, in 2 Corinthians 11:3, was concerned that the Corinthian believers would become deceived "as Eve was." When reading the passage we see that Paul's concern was that being deceived in this way would affect their sincere and pure devotion to Christ, and that they might be deceived if someone came along and presented another perception of God than what he had been preaching. It seems like this is exactly what has happened,

> Because the garden was the place of Satan's first lie to humanity, it's likely a stronghold area for him, where many other "lies" exist.

practically ever since Paul's time, regarding these theories of human immortality and that our merciful Creator eternally torments the lost.

So just how was Eve deceived? The only thing Eve was deceived about was that she wouldn't die. It's often erroneously taught that she was lied to by the serpent about becoming like God, knowing good from evil. God confirms about twenty verses later in the same chapter after Satan had said that, that this in fact happened when He says that Adam and Eve had become like God, knowing good and evil. (Genesis 3:22) The only lie Satan told was that, even if they disobeyed God, they wouldn't die.

I've often heard pastors say that Satan's favorite strategy is to confuse our understanding of who God is. That makes a lot of sense. If we don't know Him, we'll never love Him as we really should. This is exactly what Paul was concerned about in his second writing to the Corinthians. And it's exactly what Satan has accomplished in many of us through a false understanding of God's final judgment of unrepentant sinners. It kept me from loving God as I should for a long time, and it does the same for many others, keeping Christians from knowing God more fully, and causing many others to never accept Christ in the first place because the requirement of eternal suffering seems so out of character for a loving God who was whole before creation and certainly has no need to keep the lost in existence to be tormented without end. Therefore, many reject the entire gospel message because of the apparent lies and outrageous claims that come attached to it.

At this time, I would ask the reader to put this book on hold, and read from Genesis 1:1 to 3:24 — or at least go back to 2:15 where God places Adam in the garden, again proving that he was created outside of the garden, which we found to be an important clue back in Chapter 2. And I would ask that you not read it in a paraphrased version. As I've studied the things that transpired in Eden, and found that many of our mainstream teachings don't seem to line up well with the actual account, it's caused me to wonder if anybody is reading that portion of the Bible anymore. I confess that I avoided it often. For whatever reason, I just found it less interesting than most of the rest of Scripture. But during this study, I've found it to be rich with truth and substance that's highly relevant. But to help the reader see that I am not making up these ideas, if you're interested in an honest re-examination of the Garden, go ahead and read that portion now to get a foundation for our topics in this chapter.

The Incomplete Garden

It would seem that since the garden was the first place Satan lied to humanity, it might be sort of a stronghold area for him, where many other "lies" exist, and we can easily support this theory. As we noted earlier, the entire gospel message was laid out in the garden account, as were many other Biblical truths, so if the enemy can confuse us there, it will make understanding other concepts more difficult, and it will cause contradictions in the gospel, and we'll see just exactly how this has played out over the centuries.

I hear it taught often that the garden of Eden was the perfect environment — the perfection God always intended, that Adam and Eve were perfect and whole until they sinned by eating the forbidden fruit, and that their relationship with God was a perfect and harmonious one, and that Adam and Eve even walked and talked daily with the Lord. All of this sounds very sweet and certainly doesn't have the tone of false doctrine. But this is what's so deceptive about bad doctrine. It sounds good, or at least seems harmless enough. But we'll see how these ideas cannot be supported Biblically, and how they've lulled us away from many truths we were intended to see as foundational to the faith.

It's important these claims be addressed in this book because these common teachings contribute strongly to the traditional view that humanity was created with perfect immortal souls, and that while we lost our perfection in sin, we somehow maintained our immortality. But if we're honest, we'll discover many problems with these assumptions and teachings.

The overarching theme that should be apparent from the garden account is that God was showing humanity that, if given free will, and given commands and restrictions, we have no ability in and of ourselves to comply, and that ultimately we need the Lord. Paul, in the New Testament, confirms this when he writes in Romans 7:19, "For I do not do the good I want, but the evil I do not want is what I keep on doing." (ESV) We also find and were told that there are consequences for failing to comply: shame in the immediate, and ultimately death. Yet we see that God mercifully took it upon himself to cure both problems by apparently slaying an animal, and then making and offering Adam and Eve a proper covering as opposed to the fig leaves - their own attempts to cover their shame. This is the full gospel in primitive form.

But the first traditional notion that interferes with what appears to be a very solid theory has to do with Adam and Eve's inability to resist sin. We Christians, for the most part, are very willing to admit that we are helpless to completely resist sin, even though we're indwelt with the Holy Spirit. And we certainly maintain that non-believers cannot resist sin. We call this our sin nature, our undeniable propensity for sin. But there seems to be a general denial that Adam and Eve came into existence with this same bent toward sin.   Rather it's traditionally claimed they had perfect communion with God, knew Him fully, were perfected, and somehow against all probability, found some way to fail, and not only that, but sinned an infinitely greater sin than any other human would or could ever commit, because they sinned from the vantage point of perfect communion with God, whereas we sin as people somewhat estranged from God.

But I ask the reader this question: How could they sin at all if they had no sin nature or propensity for sin, and if they were perfected and immortal, knowing God fully? They couldn't. It wouldn't only be improbable but would be impossible. 1 John 3:2 tells us that when we see Jesus one day, we will be like him. According to traditionalists, they were seeing God daily. If this is true, why did it not perfect them, make them incorruptible, as Paul says all believers will be one day? Adam and Eve initially had no guilt of sin, and were in the very presence of God according to the common teachings, so what went wrong with the system and allowed perfected immortal beings who had a perfect relationship with Him to fail? I'm obviously being a little sarcastic. The reader will see shortly why there could not have been full communion with or knowledge of God prior to sin. And while I believe they *heard* Him numerous times, I don't believe they necessarily *saw* God prior to their "fall," but I'll come back to that thought.

If they were perfect, immortal, and sinless with no ability even to sin, then sin would not have happened. For that matter, God would not even have given a command or restriction because it would have been impossible for them to act contrary to God's will in the first place. The fact that we see commands and warnings implies that they were created with the ability to disregard God's laws. And the fact that God is omniscient, knowing the end from the beginning (Isaiah 46:10), is evidence that He knew full well that they were going to fail in obedience, yet He created them anyway.

Adam and Eve were as willing and able to sin as anyone ever would be, and God created them and all of us this way. So the question one might ask is Why? Why would God allow sin? The simple answer we most often hear is that He didn't want a race of robots, but rather wanted a people with the free will to choose or not choose to have a relationship with Him. I believe this is true, but it doesn't come close to fully answering the question of why God allowed or even intended sin to enter the creation. And this may initially sound ridiculous to imply that God intended sin to enter in, but when we look at the evidence, it will become undeniable. And as we look at this evidence which includes more facts from the garden, quotes of Jesus, Paul, and John the Revelator, we'll also go a long way toward understanding the so-called "problem of evil."

So in every way it seems that Adam and Eve had the same sin nature we have, even prior to actually sinning. And we are all personally responsible for our own sin. Ezekiel 18:20 tells us that the soul that sins, it shall die. And Romans 6:23 tells us the wages of sin is death. And the Lord through Ezekiel made the point that the son will not be condemned because of the sins of the father, but that each soul is responsible for their own actions before God.

> Ezekiel 18:20: "The soul that sinneth, it shall die. *The son shall not bear the iniquity of the father*, neither shall the father bear the iniquity of the son: the righteousness of the righteous shall be upon him, and the wickedness of the wicked shall be upon him" (KJV — italics for emphasis)

How much more then should our sin be differentiated from our ancient and first father when even a father's and son's sin are unrelated in terms of them bearing the iniquity of each others' sin?

Some might disagree though and say, "But what about original sin? What about Paul saying that 'in Adam, all die' (1 Co 15:22) Aren't we all condemned because of Adam's sin?" Yes and no. We are all condemned because we are "in Adam" before we choose to cover ourselves "in Christ." "In Adam" means that we are fleshly, mortal, sinful, and dying just as he was. And it's not as if God chose the wrong two people to begin our human race. Any of us would have failed in the exact same way. When Paul said in Romans 5:17 that through one man's sin, death overtook us all, he was certainly not condemning Adam for something that a "better" human could have avoided or resisted. He was simply saying that someone had to be the first. Adam was every man. There would be an initial sin committed by the initial humans, and all humans afterward would sin as well.

Adam's very name, in Hebrew, means "man." Some bible versions read "the man" in place of "Adam." When Paul says that in Adam, we all die, this should probably be understood to mean "in our humanity (in our 'mankindness'), all die." Please do not misunderstand. I'm not making light of sin. It's an offense to God. But with Revelation 13:8 telling us that Jesus was the lamb slain before the foundation of the world, and knowing that He was slain because of our sin problem, it is an undeniable fact that sin was a foregone conclusion in the mind of God. It was part of the overall plan of redemption before time and matter even existed, not a plan B. God anticipated sin, He was fully prepared for it, and at least in the sense that He was under no obligation to create anything yet chose to, even knowing the outcome, we can reasonably say that God intended sin to come about. This may sound blasphemous, but we'll see shortly that this is actually stated very clearly in Scripture.

God does not hold our sin nature against us. That's the state in which he brought us into being. He holds against us our unwillingness to acknowledge our sinfulness and need of salvation. He holds our pride against us. He holds the things we prioritize over Him against us. But that we are sinners — He has pity on the state we're in, and this is even the stage on which He chose to demonstrate His unimaginable love and mercy.

Here's a question to consider: Did Adam and Eve, prior to sin, know good from evil? The answer to this seems very apparent just by noting the names of the trees we learn of in Genesis. The forbidden tree that they decided to eat from was called the tree of the knowledge of good and evil. We can't legitimately claim that they had any knowledge or concept of evil or good when they haven't yet eaten from the tree that would give such knowledge, can we? We know, according to Scripture, that eating from it did in fact cause them to become like God in the sense that from that point on, they would now understand good and evil. But even with this obvious truth, the traditional teachings tell us that Adam and Eve should have "known better" than to have sinned. How? Our first parents had no point of reference for good or evil prior to sinning.

Here is John MacArthur's take on the scenario. He once said of Eve, "She believed Satan and ate, and fell, and took down the whole human race, and stained the entire universe in that one act."[34] That's a lot of blame to put on that one young lady. But after initially claiming that it was the act of eating the fruit that brought down the entire human race, MacArthur later in the same radio broadcast claims that it was actually her weak reply to Satan that constituted "the fall." He claims that it was the mistrust of God in her heart that constituted the *real* sin. While this contradicts what he initially claimed and what is traditionally taught, I think he helps make the point that I would make, that she didn't truly know God and did not have perfect communion with God, as is so often claimed.

Did Eve know God or not? Either she was in perfect communion with Him, or she wasn't and didn't fully know Him. It seems that traditionalists generally, as MacArthur has done here, seem to want both to be true, but I don't think both can. Either Adam and Eve knew God fully and in their sinless perfection could do nothing other than heed God's warnings, or they did not know Him fully, and had the ability to doubt the wisdom of His commands. And if there was mistrust in Eve's heart as MacArthur claims, it certainly preceded actual sin. And a mistrust of God doesn't paint a picture of two beings in perfect harmonious communion with Him. But what we could call "mistrust" will rather be shown to be more of an ignorance about God.

If you'll remember, the serpent asked Eve, "Did God really say you could not eat from any of the trees in the garden?" And Eve corrected him and said that they in fact could eat from all of the trees except the tree of knowledge, and that's exactly what God had said. Not only that, she went on to claim that God said that even if they touched it they would die. As far as we know, God didn't actually say that. It's not in the text at least. But MacArthur claims that Eve answered Satan's question about what trees they could or couldn't eat from in a very weak fashion by saying that they were in fact allowed to eat of any tree except the one. He goes on to claim that...

> "she should have taken a strong stand right there on what she knew to be true about God. She knew God. She knew God was true and spoke only the truth. She knew God was perfect goodness"[35]

And he then says that...

> "she should have been suspicious of anybody that caused her to question God."[36]

I think MacArthur and many other traditionalists may be missing the obvious here. We're not considering something called only the tree of the knowledge of evil. It was also the tree of the knowledge of good. There was no point of reference for good without eating of the tree of knowledge of *good* and evil, a further confirmation that there was not a complete and perfect relationship between God and man, since they did not even have a grasp on His goodness, a grasp that could not be appreciated until they experienced His mercy.

MacArthur's statements here are completely unfounded scripturally. *We* have the hindsight of knowing God is good. *We* have the Word of God. *We* know that God is perfect Goodness. But all Eve knew was that she was given a command, and then she has another voice planting doubt in her head about the motivation of the One who gave that command. She had not yet eaten of the tree of knowledge and therefore because she had no knowledge of evil *or* good, she didn't know truth, or that

God was perfect goodness, or that God only spoke truth, and she therefore had no reason to be suspicious of the Serpent, which is why she was so easily deceived.

It had nothing to do with a lack of intelligence, and some even try to claim it was her female weakness that caused her to disobey (which doesn't work either since we know that Adam was there with her, and he obviously ate also). She had a command from her Maker, and she disobeyed it. She was enticed because she saw, the text tells us, that the fruit was a source of food, and believed it was profitable for gaining knowledge. Both of these things were in fact true. And that was enough for her to ignore the commands of God. We all do the very same thing even with all of our knowledge of God's goodness and even with the indwelling of the Holy Spirit. It would seem that *we* are the ones without excuse for sin, yet we put the blame of the fall of the entire universe on Adam and Eve's shoulders, and more specifically Eve's. But that just doesn't hold up to Scripture. The fall was intended, and it was not intended by Adam or Eve, but by God. Do you doubt this? Consider this verse:

> Romans 11:32: "For God has consigned all to disobedience, that he may have mercy on all." (ESV)

That's pretty tough to argue with. The context is that Paul was telling the Romans not to get conceited in their salvation because God has temporarily blinded the minds of the Israelites so the Gentiles could be grafted in. And he is reminding them that God actually consigned all people, Jew and Gentile, to disobedience and unbelief in times past. And he did this for the express purpose of being able to show His great love and mercy to us.

Paul made a similar claim earlier in Romans 8:20-21:

> "For the creation was subjected to futility, not willingly, but because of him who subjected it, in hope that the creation itself will be set free from its bondage to corruption and obtain the freedom of the glory of the children of God" (ESV)

According to this, it was not "human will" that brought about our bondage. Verse 20 says that it was God who subjected us to this, so that we would have a place to hope from – hope for deliverance from that bondage.

One of my favorite Christian bands is The Sidewalk Prophets, and in a song called *Keep Making Me* that was released several years ago, there was a great message that goes right along with the point I'm driving at. I wish I could quote the lyrics here, but copyright rules prohibit it. The gist of the song though is that we hear a man crying out to God, asking Him to break him, but only so he can be healed, and make him empty, so he can be filled.

The wisdom in these lyrics is that when we don't have problems (or when we think we don't), we lose sight of our need for the only One who can really fill us. Our frailty and weakness is what creates our longing for God. And this is by His design, not by Adam or Eve's "mistake."

Another Bible teacher whose messages have spoken to me, probably more than any other over the years, is Beth Moore. And in a talk she did at James and Betty Robinson's Awaken Now conference, her major theme was that we, the Body of Christ, are not experiencing God in the fullest way because we are acting like we're full, instead of admitting often that we're empty, dry, and thirsty.[37] Often we try to make it seem like we have it all together, when really, we're weak and frail. Weak and frail is where God wants us. God said His strength is made perfect in our weakness, and Paul said because of this, he would then boast more in his weaknesses than his strengths. And this relates right back to how God created us from the beginning. He didn't construct Adam and Eve in a way that they "had it all together." Where would He gain glory in that? He designed them weak to sin, and physically frail, subject to death, so that they would learn to lean on Him, and love Him all the more when He shows Himself more than sufficient.

I can't help but wonder if this problem that Beth Moore and others are finding in the Church today doesn't at least partially relate back to our backward understanding of the Garden of Eden. Maybe the reason we want to pretend we have it all together is that we've never grasped onto the biblical fact that God created us weak and needy to create a platform on which to show a level of mercy and love that we couldn't comprehend if he had created us any other way. Instead, we've had it drilled into us that mankind was created perfect and immortal, but that we screwed it all up. Not only do we have trouble confessing our own sin, we often don't even want people to know when bad things have happened to us. Maybe they'll think we're being judged by God for something we did wrong. But we've read the book of Job, right? Dire circumstances and misfortune are not necessarily an indication of willful disobedience. Often, just the opposite.

And people joke about how they're gonna really let Adam have it when they see him in Heaven one day (even though his expulsion from the garden represented his eternal separation from God, according to tradition, and if they're right, he shouldn't be in heaven – sorry, I can't help but see the irony there). But we've had it ingrained in us that humanity had a real shot at everything being perfect (if it just weren't for Adam's huge screw-up) and that this current world isn't the world God intended us to be experiencing. And in eternity, it won't be. But for now, it is, and it's by design. It's a time of testing, a time that God is growing a family of faith, a time we have to trust Him when we can't see Him, and believe for more, when we're experiencing much less than we desire. And this faith-testing, faith-growing time couldn't happen in a perfect world.

If sin were not intended, and if someone else could have done a better job of resisting sin than Adam and Eve did, God could have wiped them and the earth out and created new ones in a single breath, if giving two "better" people a chance would have accomplished His purposes. But He didn't make any mistake. Any one of us, with a propensity to sin, would have sinned in that scenario. Eating of the tree of knowledge was the very act of acquisition of a conscience. Conscience means "with knowledge." They could not know the goodness of God if they did not gain a knowledge of good and evil.

So am I saying that God somehow desired them to do the very thing that he commanded them not to do - eat of the tree of knowledge? This is a question I've wrestled with. It seems that we would either have to claim this, or claim that He desired to keep humans in ignorance of evil *and* good, which would include never having any comprehension of God's love and goodness. I don't relish having to choose from either of these. And I don't think we need to. We can always rely on the fact that God is omniscient. He could have the eternal desire for full obedience from His creation, yet simultaneously have the full foreknowledge that we would fail to obey, and then even go so far as to plan our redemption. God creating man mortal and weak to temptation, and even knowing that man would sin is not the same as desiring us to sin or tempting us to sin. That He would love a creature like us is incredible, especially given the fact that He was whole and without need before creating anything. He wasn't lonely. He had no human-shaped hole in His heart that only a creature such as us could fill as is often said in reverse of our need for God. He simply is Love and He is glorious and worthy of praise, and thus created us so that He could exhibit that love and be praised for His goodness. We'll expand on this in the following section.

The Problem of Evil

We've been touching all around it, but let's now deal directly with the problem of evil. Evil is what is contrary to God. For Adam and Eve in the garden, it took committing evil, through disobedience, to even bring it into existence, at least into existence in humanity. And it wasn't that this particular tree had a certain chemical makeup that would cause it to bring about the knowledge of good and evil if eaten. Any tree that God had singled out as the one to not eat from would inherently become the tree of the knowledge of good and evil, and disobeying a command not to eat from it would therefore bring on whatever conscious awareness of sin and shame that God intended it to. But in bringing to the forefront their weakness, their inability to obey, this simultaneously brought about knowledge that God is high above them.

Just as Isaiah could not bear to look up at God, so they tried to hide themselves. When confronted with our sin, when we are convinced of our inadequacy, God's perfection is brought to light. In fact, Jesus told Paul that His strength is made perfect in our weakness (2 Corinthians 12:9), and Paul went on to say that he would therefore glory in his weaknesses rather than his strengths. I believe this is one of God's primary intentions — that we understand just how weak we are. This is when He communes with us. This is when a person becomes usable to Him. And in fact, we can't even come to salvation without this happening. The mere existence of evil isn't a problem. It's the pathway to understand all of God's attributes, and to comprehend our need for him.

The first step to accepting Christ as our Savior is realizing that we have a need for one in the first place. And there is no such thing as a close relationship with God until we are in a humbled state of neediness. And the simple fact is that Adam, until he followed through with sin, did not understand his position as it related to God. Yes, he had been told that he was dust, but what did that mean to him? What Adam knew was that he could do just about whatever he wanted to do, and he also knew that when he named something, that was its name. And he had dominion over creation. He saw that *his* words had power. It seems like a perfect breeding ground for a lot of pride. And we know from many Scriptures that God seems to hate pride over and above any other sin. Not only does pride contradict His own nature as revealed through the Lord Jesus who humbled himself to the point of death and who said that if we've seen Him, we've seen the Father (John 14:9), but it's also the one insurmountable obstacle to salvation. So He hates pride.

Even though Adam and Eve were sinless for a time, their temporary sinlessness doesn't indicate they experienced communion with God. And we certainly don't note any communion in Scripture prior to sin. In fact, although people will tell you that God walked and talked daily with them in the garden, this is simply not in the Bible at all. There is no record of *any* two-way communication between God and mankind prior to their sinning. This is why I asked the reader to read the garden account before reading this chapter. The Bible tells us that after they sinned, and after they covered themselves with fig leaves, that one day (probably the same day) in the cool of the day, they heard the sound of God walking in the garden and hid themselves (Gen 3:8). Why have we taken this fact and created the idea that God and Adam and Eve used to walk and talk together daily in the garden? I believe that at the core, it is Satanic. I know that sounds over-the-top, but this unprovable and unlikely idea that this was their daily activity completely distorts the real message that we see throughout Scripture — that communion with God happens when we acknowledge our frailty compared to His power.

This unbiblical idea implies that only "perfect" people could have communion with God and when you violate that, you're separated from God, when the very opposite is true. Only imperfect people, and people who understand their need for God can have real communion with God. And it was only after they sinned that two-way communication between God and mankind is found in Scripture. God is not impressed with sinlessness. Jesus is called a "friend of sinners" (Matthew 11:9). He communes freely with sinners, provided they understand their dependency on Him. Our right acting or our righteousness is like filthy rags to Him (Isaiah 64:6). Have you ever wondered why often non-Christians seem to think that Christians think they're "too good," or why many unbelievers think, "Well I can never be perfect, so God will never accept me"? I think that some of this thinking could be sourced back to erroneous teachings they hear about the Garden, such as what we're looking at. Now let me be careful here. I'm not going to say absolutely that they never did walk with God. I'm only saying that Scripture says no such thing, and that we have other reasons for believing that meaningful communion was not possible yet between God and man (some of those reasons we've just looked at, and some are yet to come).

There's another reason I question the common teaching that Adam and Eve walked with God. It's questionable whether we can claim they even "saw" God at all. The Bible says that no man can see God and live. When Moses asked to see God, he was denied but was only allowed to see His "hind parts," whatever that means exactly. 1 John 4:12 and John 1:18 both say that no man has seen God at any time. And remember when Paul was caught up to the third heaven. He doesn't say he saw God, but that he "heard" things that men are not allowed to speak (2 Corinthians 12:4). And the text of the Garden account clearly says that after they sinned, they "heard" the sound of the Lord walking in the Garden. And then we go on to read about their communication, none of which implies that they have a visual on God as they are speaking.

The reader might say, "But what about the appearance of Jesus, his life and ministry, and even those times in the Old Testament where He seems to have made an appearance? How can we say that no man has seen God when we believe that Jesus *was* God in flesh, and we know that many people saw Him?" We have to reconcile this if we are to trust Scripture. And while I don't have a great answer, for whatever reason, seeing God the Son in flesh just doesn't appear to be considered as "seeing God." The two passages just referenced from John and 1 John, written *after* Jesus walked on earth, say that "No man has seen God at any time." But Jesus said that if we've seen Him, we've seen the Father. So could Adam and Eve have seen Jesus, or "the Angel of the Lord"? Sure, theoretically it's possible. But the Bible doesn't say they saw Him, or had two-way communication with Him before they sinned. And these facts provide a little more evidence against the theory of pre-sin perfect communion with God — the common teaching.

It seems apparent from Scripture and from practical reality that God doesn't commune with those who don't, can't, or won't admit they need Him. And this seems to be the only position that a pre-sin Adam and Eve could have been in. They had no point of reference for good, or for evil. They didn't have any needs. They didn't lack food or water. They didn't even know they needed clothing yet. It really seems that there would be no reason for them to feel reliant on God, as we know He desires us to. So obviously Adam and Eve were without sin until the day they sinned, but I think they had a "filthy rag" sort of righteousness prior to sinning. We can't be good enough for God, even if one could somehow go about life without partaking in sin. We are still frail humanity with needs (and they were too, having not gained eternal life yet), and we could not take another breath if it were not for God allowing it. It pleases God to provide for us, provided we understand our need for Him. And he offers His highest provision for us to His own detriment ultimately in the death of His Son on the Cross. We are only considered righteous (or right with God) when we admit our need for, and accept Christ. The Bible says that we even become the righteousness of God (2 Corinthians 5:21), and this happens when we "put on Christ" (Galatians 3:27 and Romans 13:14), meaning to make the decision to accept Christ's sacrificial death as sufficient to pay our debt.

Getting back to the problem of sin and evil, as backwards as it may seem to some, apparently sin was a necessary tool to bring about a realization of our weak nature, and of God's perfections, but also a realization of His grace and mercy in that our need is the platform on which God can display His mercy. And this lines up well with other passages of Scripture. We already noted where Paul plainly told us that God consigned all to disobedience for the very purpose of being able to exhibit his mercy.

We can see from this verse, if we trust that God is unchanging, that Adam and Eve were not justified before God, even during their sinless period. No one is justified by keeping commandments. Paul said in Galatians 2:16 that "no flesh at all will be justified by works of the law." We teach this concept all the time in Christianity, that it's in reliance on God that we're saved, not in right actions, but for some reason we don't apply it to Adam and Eve. Doctrinally, they seem to be the exception to every fundamental of the faith.

A little off the subject, but one very well-known pastor once said that Adam and Eve were the only two people that ever had true free will. I found that completely ridiculous. God either intended us to have free will, or He didn't. Personally, I land on the free will side of that argument, but even if I were on the Calvinist-leaning side and believed we don't have true free will regarding whether or not we accept salvation, what a strange statement to make. It completely ignores God's omniscience, and fails to recognize He's been working out a plan from the very beginning. It implies that there was a chance for humanity to "get it right," but then Adam and Eve just messed it all up. It implies that whether we would have a world where sin is present or where all things would be perfect all hinged on the free will decision of these first two humans, and since they chose sin, now we're all doomed.   That's just not sound reasoning.

Clearly Satan has kept a hold on Eden and our doctrines that come from there. Getting back to where I was before I veered off ...They were human and needed a Savior like everyone else, even during the brief period when they were adhering to the law against eating of the tree of knowledge.

And then there's Romans 5:20 that tells us that where sin did abound, there grace did abound much more.   If God is the willing giver of grace, and if it is our sin that draws out His grace, where was the place for grace before sin entered in? Now, Paul went on to warn that this fact is not a license to go around sinning freely. I'm just making the point that it is our general fallen sinfulness that gives God the platform to display His grace and mercy, and it always has been.

Law brings about Sin Consciousness

Paul tells us in Romans 3:20 that the law brings about a knowledge of our sin. It was the same for Adam and Eve except they really only had one law (two, if we count the command to eat from all of the other trees), and even still they had no ability to obey it. Their law showed them their weakness, just as all of the later law did for everyone else. And there are many more Scriptures like this.

I'm not so bold as to claim we can understand all of the reasons God created anything at all, but one that seems apparent is that He had a desire to exhibit His grace, mercy and love outside of and beyond Himself, to creatures that have the free will to accept or reject Him. And if He had created us without the propensity for sin, which actually creates our need for grace and mercy, there could be no appreciation or even experience of it. It really all seems to come down to the concept of a point of reference. We often hear and say things like, "You can't appreciate the good days until you've had some bad days," and similar things. And this is true, and probably why there wasn't one tree that was the tree of the knowledge of good, and another that was the tree of the knowledge of evil. Evil and good are simultaneously meaningful, and meaningless without one another. And this is why I maintain that Adam and Eve did *not* know God intimately prior to sinning. They had not gained a knowledge of evil *or* good, so they had no point of reference from which to appreciate God, let alone give Him the worship He deserves. And that brings up another point.

No Worship in the Garden

There's something else missing from the garden account that you may have noticed. It's commonly taught that because Adam and Eve had not sinned yet, they could commune freely with God. But when we've been given Scriptural glimpses of what the sinless angels are doing in heaven, we see them praising God, and we certainly see ourselves, even sinners, doing that all of the time. And we know that God communes with sinners. Enoch walked with God, Moses spoke with Him as a friend, and Jacob even had a wrestling match with the Lord. And countless other people, in the Bible and outside of the Bible, have had deep and meaningful relationships with the sovereign God of the Universe. And they all have two things in common: They were all sinners, and none of them lived inside the Garden of

Eden. So if being sinless, and in the supposed presence of God in the Garden gave such an advantage to the first humans before "paradise was lost," why don't we see the pre-sin Adam and Eve worshiping God?   There is no record of two-way communication prior to sin, no record of worship prior to sin, and there is no reason to believe that we should even expect to see these.

Even after Adam had noticed that all of the other living creatures had mates, and then finally he sees Eve and states that "at last, this is bone of my bone and flesh of my flesh," even then we don't see so much as a 'thank you' expressed toward God. This first couple, prior to gaining knowledge of good and evil, simply had no point of reference that would cause them to realize that God should even be praised. They couldn't even praise Him for the beautiful garden they were in. They had no concept of ugly, so beauty is meaningless. The garden was just the garden. It probably became very beautiful to them in their nostalgia after they were driven from it, but while they were there, it's likely they didn't appreciate it.

Contrary to all traditional teaching that the garden was the perfect setting, there is actually more evidence that the pre-sin Garden was a somber time, or at least void of much emotion at all. Without the worship of, communion with, and realization of the need for God, it's more likely there was an emptiness for Adam and Eve, and God did not create them just so they could live in a pretty garden. He created them so they could know Him, and find meaning, and experience God's love through His grace and mercy. So oddly enough, evil had to enter in for this to be possible.

And regarding the grace and mercy shown, we might wonder why it took the requirement of the death of Jesus in order to show these. It might seem that something less severe could have adequately exhibited His mercy and love. This is where we get into territory that we just can't fully comprehend yet, But I think Jesus Himself gives us the greatest insight into why He had to die. Many have claimed that humanity was never intended to have been cast from the Garden and have to muddle through what can be a very trying existence sometimes, but to question this is to even question whether or not God always intended to redeem us from death or not.

We've already seen how understanding the correct order of events will create the most sound doctrine, and with that in mind, let's never forget that Jesus is called "the Lamb slain *before* the foundation of the world." With this knowledge as a starting point, we can see that even before sin, even before creation itself, God desired to sacrifice Himself to express His great love for those He would one day create, and to be worshiped because of that great love. Jesus said, "No greater love has a man than this, but that He lay his life down for his friends." He was obviously pointing to Himself and what He would do for us on the cross, and he calls us friends.

It seems that the Lord, from eternity past, intended to have a friendship relationship with us, and one much closer than what He had with Adam and Eve prior to their sin. But we nor they could really appreciate this or even fathom His great love for us if He did not suffer and die for us. The cross is His ultimate expression of love. That the eternal and only God would do this is what creates our love and appreciation for Him. If the traditional idea is correct — that the pre-sin garden setting was the world God intended for all eternity, with a sinless Adam and Eve, but also an Adam and Eve who didn't even understand good or evil, I think we could seriously question in just what way this would exhibit God's love.

It takes nothing for our infinite all-powerful God to speak creation into existence. This does not exhibit his love, but only his omnipotence. Love can only be exhibited in sacrifice, and according to Jesus, the greatest love can only be expressed in the sacrifice of life. For a sacrifice of life to be possible, the potential for death is a necessary evil. But even with death as a potential, we could not comprehend the sadness and overall awfulness of suffering and death if we never experienced it and if we had no concept of what sin run rampant has the potential to look like. And even now, as bad as the world is getting, I don't think we really know. We do still have the Holy Spirit holding back much evil.

The problem of evil doesn't really seem any more complicated than that, if we trust Scripture. I still have lots of questions about true original sin — that which originated with Satan's rebellion in heaven. And I think this may be what Paul is referring to when he used the phrase "the mystery of iniquity." So I'm not saying that God has revealed to us all the answers about evil, but at the human level at least, it seems like the answers are right there in Scripture. God desires to show His love to us, not just his omnipotence. And if God only created beautiful worlds and perfect people, we would have no comprehension of the lengths to which He would go to show us His love.

Where is Adam's faith?

Hebrews 11:6 tells us that without faith, it is impossible to please God. We could never choose Him "by faith" if we were innately perfected, complete, immortal, and "like Him" already. Clearly we are not and were not. And we could never choose Him if we did not have a choice. So the Lord created us as free will creatures, but He did this knowing from eternity past that we would first choose sin and therefore death, and that He would redeem those of us who turn from our reliance on our own merits and put our faith in Him because He loves us in spite of our sinfulness. But if Adam, as traditionally taught, had a sort of pre-sin salvation, by what means did he gain it? Exercising faith is the only way we can please God, and I just can't see where the pre-sin Adam had a platform on which to display this. Even the angels appear to have had to endure a testing, and make a choice at some point in following after Satan in his rebellion or not.

Please don't think I'm implying that God tempts any man to sin. We're told that he does not in James 1:13, but He certainly allowed the possibility, and He certainly had the foreknowledge that we would choose it, and He always knew that He would offer redemption to those who acknowledge their need for Him.

It is impossible to argue Biblically against these three facts. If God had not intended the fall of man, He would not have made Adam and Eve *able* to sin first of all, secondly wouldn't have given them a prohibition (a law or commandment), and lastly wouldn't have allowed a tempter into the garden which He knew would facilitate their breaking of that commandment. Put those three facts together with mounds of other Scriptural evidence and it's undeniable that all of that happened according to the plan and purpose of God. Sin was not some cosmic accident that God had to go into plan B mode to solve. Mankind's sin was required in order to set the stage for God to demonstrate a love that none of us deserve.

Coming back to the idea of points of references, it seems that in willingly taking on the experience of suffering and death, God Himself, who although in His omniscience could certainly know everything about how suffering and death could feel, may have created a point of reference of His own. His willingness to step out of eternity, and physically and personally experience torture and death in the course of time is mind-blowing. It's so easy to get caught up in the problems of life and forget what God Himself actually did, and forget to praise Him daily for this. I guess I'm guilty of this most every day. But as I'm writing this, what the Lord did for us is really hitting me again as if I had never heard the gospel before. It really is almost unfathomable, almost too good to be true. Eternal God, lacking nothing, willingly suffered the very opposite of His own nature, on our behalf. He is light and life, and He exhibited His highest and greatest love in experiencing the polar opposite of Himself. But this would not have been possible if there were not a polar opposite to experience. Sin and death had to enter the universe in order for God to exhibit the highest love, and for us to have any concept of who God really is, how much He really loves, and to what lengths He will go to show us His love.

> Romans 5:6-8 "6 For while we were still weak, at the right time Christ died for the ungodly. 7 For one will scarcely die for a righteous person—though perhaps for a good person one

would dare even to die— 8 but God shows his love for us in
that while we were still sinners, Christ died for us." (ESV)

So with love seeming to be the ultimate purpose in creation,
could there have been a way to express it without all of the evil
we see today, or without death entering into the equation? I
think the answer is No. We've already seen a number of
reasons for this. But when the ultimate evil, the very killing of
God in the flesh, was about to happen, Jesus prayed to the
Father to let this cup pass from Him if it was possible. The cup
didn't pass. Since it doesn't seem that the Father would deny
the Son anything, I think we can safely assume that it simply was
not possible, if God was to accomplish His plan of mercifully
and lovingly redeeming mortal man, the very exhibition of His
nature and purpose.

But the question of evil's purpose or necessity is inseparable
from the question of why God created anything. He certainly
didn't have to. He was complete and lacking nothing before
creation, so creation itself could only spring from a desire in the
heart of God, and not a need. Some would say that it was His
desire to be worshiped that caused Him to create. Let me be
very careful here again. God is absolutely worthy to be praised,
and He is good beyond measure, and I believe that He expects
praise both now and in eternity, and we will be praising Him
throughout eternity. But it doesn't appear from Scripture that
gaining worship was His chief aim or sole purpose, at least not
for His benefit, maybe for ours.

Here's the reason I say that: Jesus said that if we've seen Him,
we've seen the Father. Obviously, while one in Deity, they were
separate persons or Jesus would not pray to Him, so He was
speaking of character and all of the invisible attributes of God
the Father. And what we see in Jesus is humility and love, not
someone demanding worship. Worship comes naturally when
we understand how small and frail we are in relation to God and
when we begin to understand what He has done for us, but it
doesn't seem to be His chief objective.

Worship is for our benefit anyway. God already knows who He is. Worship of God confirms in *us* the knowledge of how great He is, and the Bible states that He even somehow inhabits the praise of His people, so in worshiping, we commune with God. But God has no needs or lacks. (I realize I keep repeating that fact, but it's foundational to sound doctrine in this area.) So even if he desires our worship (and I haven't said that He doesn't – only that it's not His *primary* aim in creation), even this is an expression of love for us, as it adds to our relationship with and knowledge of God. In fact, we see in John 17:24, Jesus desiring us to see His glory that he had before he condescended to take on flesh. It adds nothing to God's being or worth, that we recognize His worth. And it takes nothing away from His being and worth when people fail to worship. Failure to worship God is only to the detriment of those failing to worship.

Further evidencing God's humble nature, even on the day when it was foreordained prophetically that Jesus would enter Jerusalem as King, commonly called Palm Sunday, he came in humble, riding on a donkey. Everything about His earthly existence spoke of a humble heart and a loving giving spirit, humbling Himself all the way to the point of death a few days later. And remember, if we've seen Him, we've seen the Father.

Have you, like myself, ever wondered what in the world could have made a created being, who exists in the presence of God, think that he could overtake the throne of his Creator, as Scripture tells us Satan did? This has puzzled me, and it's pure speculation, but my best guess is that it could only be that God, by His sovereign will, chooses or at least chose at that time, even in heaven, to exist in a humbled state. Not only did God lead a humble life here on earth, if God were constantly showing His full potential power in Heaven, no created being, even the highest ranking angel, could possibly think they could overtake God Himself, the one who created him. Any creature would shudder at God's full infinite omnipotence; therefore He must have been expressing Himself in some kind of a humbled state for any creature to think as Satan did. So I think we have evidence of God's humility not only on earth but also in heaven.

And we wonder sometimes how the original angelic sin came about. Maybe this is a clue.

It seems likely that there was a standard for humility, a standard set by God Himself. Think about how at times in Scripture, men, when visited by angels, bowed to them, and the angels were quick to tell them to get up and not worship them. But Satan apparently desired something very different, and himself being highly exalted, and mistaking meekness in God for weakness, perhaps, somehow couldn't resist an attempt to overtake what he must have seen as an opportunity to climb the heavenly ladder of greatness. But that still leaves something unanswered. Where did Satan's first inclination to overtake God really come from? It might seem that God must have caused it, more than just simply allowing it. But I don't think we can say this. The Bible is silent on the specifics of this, but I believe we've already answered why sin in general had to come about, and we see how this happened in humanity.

While man was drawn to disobedience through the temptation of being told the attributes of eating the forbidden fruit, God tempts no man to sin, so there had to be a tempter, and God couldn't do it. So it seems that God has made use of Satan's selfish ambition, and his propensity to be jealous over God's giving Adam dominion over the earth. Satan wanted Adam dead, so he schemed to get him destroyed by tempting him to do the one thing that God had said would bring about death. But Satan didn't realize he was playing into God's hands and plan, and didn't know that God was going to come to the rescue of humanity immediately, not saving them from the death of their flesh which would violate His own promise that death would surely come, but offering a solution and a way out of the death of their souls. He couldn't go back on His word that death would become a certainty, but Adam's sin created the very problem that God would ultimately save him from.

Innocence or Ignorance?

There's another common idea about the garden that I don't think holds up to scrutiny, and it relates to what we've been looking at with consciousness and an awareness of good and evil. Genesis 2:25 reads, "And the man and his wife were naked and were not ashamed." It's commonly taught that their nudity, and their lack of shame for their nudity, was a picture of their innate innocence. But I believe we can scripturally support that it was not a picture of innocence but rather a picture of ignorance – a complete unawareness of their neediness and lack. We seem to traditionally claim that because they were in this so-called perfected state, were innocent of sin to that point, and in the presence of God, that nudity would just be expected. But Scripture shows something very different. Let's first note that Scripture doesn't say that it was good that they were not ashamed about being nude. It simply points out the fact that they were not ashamed. We find out a few verses later that the reason for the lack of shame was only because they didn't even *know* they were naked. God asked them, "Who told you that you were naked?"

So the phrase "They were naked and were not ashamed" has been framed as if it were this sweet statement of innocence. Here's another way the original text that gave us that could have been interpreted and written: *They were naked and were shameless about it.* Feels a little different doesn't it? It means the exact same thing, but now it has the connotation that we're more familiar with, and arguably the one that was more likely intended. If it were written as intended, and if you were to read that passage in an amplified modern Bible, it might read something more like "And they were shamelessly parading around naked."

There will come a day when we believers will truly be perfected and sinless, completely renewed. But if you'll remember, in John the Revelator's vision, when he looks into the future and sees people in heaven, they're not nude, but clothed in white. Consider this: When people, without any evidence for such, claim that Adam and Eve used to walk with the Lord daily in the Garden, do they picture the Lord naked as well? Sinless Adam and Eve were nude, and the Lord is sinless as well, so why would he have clothing on? I hope I've created a disturbing picture ...because this did not happen. God did not take on human form and walk around naked with Adam and Eve.

When the Lord appeared with two angels before Abraham, they were clothed...all of them. When Jesus was transfigured before the disciples, his clothes were gleaming white, but He had on clothes. If there were ever a time during the Lord's earthly existence or any of His pre-incarnate visits to earth when He would have shown Himself nude, this would have been the one, because this was Him giving the disciples a little preview of what He really is. This was the day that He made sure they knew that He was no ordinary human, but was in fact Holy God, if there was any doubt left. When Isaiah saw God in a vision, he observed the train of His robe. And when the Lord hid Moses in the cleft of a rock and showed him His "hind parts," I think it's safe to say this wasn't the pre-incarnate Christ exposing Himself, but perhaps this also is a reference to the train of His robe, or something else entirely. We really just don't know.

There is never coming a point, when even though we will have been redeemed, perfected, and made whole, that we will go about naked. Adam and Eve's nudity was the living parabolic representation that they were created with a need for a covering (even before actually sinning) and their lack of shame about it was only due to their ignorance that they needed such a covering. It was not due to an innocence that they would soon lose to the detriment of all mankind, as is so often mis-taught. The so-called "fall" was part of the plan, not something that caught God by surprise.

When Adam and Eve sinned, they didn't say, "Oh my, we've offended God." They essentially said, "Oh my, we're naked." Their weakness was exposed: They had no covering for their shame, and they suddenly had a sense that they needed one, and quickly made clothing and hid themselves. They gained a knowledge of good and evil, and it apparently wasn't good that they were naked, or else we wouldn't have seen the rush to make clothing. Our need for a covering for sin in general accomplishes the same thing. We know we are guilty, and most of us are willing to admit that we are sinners, but still so many refuse to admit a need for the salvation God offers. This is a serious problem because without that admission, salvation is impossible.

Could part of the reason for the unwillingness to confess this need be the backwards way in which we teach so many concepts from the Garden? This may seem far-fetched, but the things we hear affect us and can become ingrained in our mentalities and in our general understanding of God's intentions. The Bible plainly says and implies that God created us mortal, weak, and sinful so that He could express His unfathomable love in ways that simply placing people in a beautiful garden with no possibility for failure could have never produced. But rather than teach this, the traditional Church teaches that people, beginning with the very first people, have immortal souls, and that our maintaining a sinless state in the face of temptation was God's eternal plan A, which we quickly thwarted. This is completely contrary to Scripture, it misrepresents God's purposes, and it can only hinder our knowledge and love of God.

Nudity is always expressed as a weakness or lack in Scripture. In the Old Testament, in Jeremiah 13:26 God tells the nation of Israel that he is going to lift their skirts over their heads and expose their shame.

Here's another reference:

> Mark 14:50-52 "50 And they all left him and fled. 51 And a young man followed him, with nothing but a linen cloth about his body. And they seized him, 52 but he left the linen cloth and ran away naked." (ESV)

This is an account of when the disciples abandoned the Lord in the garden of Gethsemane. I don't believe there are any wasted words in Scripture. Everything has significance. So why tell us that this man fled naked? This passage is a little confusing, and apparently there is disagreement among commentators about who this person is. And I certainly don't know. But it seems most likely that this was not one of the original twelve disciples, but another who followed, perhaps from the house where the disciples and Jesus had eaten the Passover. But whether he was one of the twelve or not, this person, when faced with the danger of following Christ, fled like the rest. And we see that when he was seized, he fled, but that he lost his covering in the process. His shame was exposed because he abandoned the Lord.

Here's another...Read what Jesus said in Revelation 3:14-17:

> "And to the angel of the church in Laodicea write: 'The words of the Amen, the faithful and true witness, the beginning of God's creation. 15 I know your works: you are neither cold nor hot. Would that you were either cold or hot! 16 So, because you are lukewarm, and neither hot nor cold, I will spit you out of my mouth. 17 For you say, I am rich, I have prospered, and I need nothing, not realizing that you are wretched, pitiable, poor, blind, and *naked*.'" (ESV)

According to verse 17, nudity here was a representation that there was a need, but Jesus is reprimanding them for not realizing their need. It's further interesting that He also reprimands them for not being hot or cold. He says that He would even rather they be cold than lukewarm. What could a pre-sin Adam and Eve be toward God except lukewarm? If there is no knowledge of evil and good, hot and cold, ugliness and beauty, there is no perspective or points of reference at all. There is nothing except lukewarm.

Let's look at one more reference:

> 2 Corinthians 5:1-3   "1 For we know that if the earthly house of our tent is dissolved, we have a building from God, a house not made with hands, eternal, in the heavens. 2 For most certainly in this we groan, longing to be clothed with our habitation which is from heaven; 3 if so be that being clothed we will not be found naked." (WEB)

Here again nudity represents a need, a covering that we long for and without which we would die, the very covering of Christ.

In Scripture, nakedness always represents a need, a need for a covering. Why would we assume something different in the garden? Most teachers agree that the animal skin coverings were a picture of salvation from sin, but they fail to see their nudity, the very thing that was being covered by the skins, as the picture of their sinful neediness. Adam and Eve's nudity was not the beautiful innocence which is traditionally taught. They just didn't know their need yet because prior to sin and a knowledge of good or evil, they had no concept that they were frail humanity standing exposed in front of a Holy God. But this lack of knowledge of the fact doesn't diminish the reality of it. In every way their nakedness seems to express only their sinfulness, and their ignorance of their sinfulness, rather than innocence. We need to let Scripture interpret Scripture.

This is a little uncomfortable to address, but it needs to be said here. In any sort of depiction of Jesus on the cross, he's always wearing a loin cloth. And that's understandable. We don't want to turn these paintings or movies into something R-rated. But I've heard more than one pastor or Bible teacher who claimed to understand the culture of Rome say that most likely Jesus was crucified nude. We're told in Scripture that He bore our shame and that He took our place. We've seen that Adam and Eve's frailty, sinfulness, and neediness were all epitomized in their lack of clothing. For Jesus to truly "become sin for us" as we're told He did, He had to take on the very image of these first humans. He traded places with us in every way, and He is wonderful beyond description for the lengths He went to, to demonstrate love for humanity. God didn't have to do anything for us — not even make us in the first place. It's so easy to forget this. We should live in constant awe of the Lord.

While it may sound nice to say that Adam and Eve were so free and innocent that they didn't even feel shame when nude, there is not one other place in Scripture where nudity doesn't represent either shame or lack. If someone wanted to argue this, they might go to a passage in Proverbs or the two references in Song of Solomon where the man seems to be admiring the breasts of his wife. That might be a stretch to argue such, since we're not speaking of someone standing stark naked and exposed to the world, the way Adam and Eve were, the way the man who lost his cloak was, and the way ultimately Jesus, while bearing our shame on the cross, most likely was. But for the sake of argument, I'd say it's just different. Within the marriage of one man and one woman is the only place where there would not necessarily be shame in nudity, and that's because they are considered to be one flesh, no longer two, and also a picture of the future marriage of Christ to His bride.

Someone could then argue, "But Adam and Eve were married so why did they still feel shame?" Well, technically they weren't. True marriage, not modern day ceremony, actually occurs and is consummated in the coming together of the man and woman. Genesis 24:67 states: "Then Isaac brought her (Rebekah) into the tent of Sarah his mother and took Rebekah, and she became his wife." (ESV) It doesn't require much imagination to understand what occurred in the tent, and whatever occurred there was the very process of becoming man and wife, according to the verse. There's another passage earlier in Scripture that also equates sexual intercourse with marriage. In Genesis 16:3, Sarai, Abram's wife, who was barren, wanted children. This verse says that she gave her maid to Abram to "be his wife." I'm thinking she didn't throw them a big wedding ceremony. She essentially arranged for them to have sex, so that she would have a child to raise as her own, but this sex act is called "being his wife."

Scripture first notes Adam "knowing" or coming together with Eve only *after* they were banished from the Garden. They were not technically "married" yet while in the Garden, not man and wife, not "one flesh" yet, at least not in the sense that later Scripture seems to define these concepts. They therefore had every reason to feel ashamed in front of one another when they realized their nakedness. They were in what could be considered an engagement period at best.   Someone might disagree and point out that the word "wife" is used to describe Eve's relationship to Adam, even in the garden. To answer this, I would refer elsewhere in Genesis where Abraham sent his servant to find a "wife" for his son Isaac. Obviously he wasn't sent to find someone his son was already married to, but to find someone that would become his wife. And too, when God presented Eve to Adam to be his wife, this wasn't a marriage ceremony as we think of in modern times, but the beginning of an engagement. And in later Jewish culture, and most God-fearing cultures of any day, abstinence was expected during the engagement period. In the garden, Eve was only Adam's wife in the sense of being a wife-to-be, but as far as we know, they did not have a consummated marriage until after they had sinned and were banished.

Nudity has a very clear meaning throughout the Bible: lack — and most often, even an ignorance of the lack. Why would we assume it to be different in this one passage of Scripture, located in the beginning of the Word of God where we're having our foundational truths laid out? Just as we all come into the world physically naked in need of covering, so we come into the world, bent toward sin, spiritually dead, spiritually naked and exposed before God, in need for a covering for our souls, just like Adam and Eve. And God provides that in Christ.

The Perfect Garden?

It's interesting that many of the same people who claim the Garden of Eden was a perfect environment, with perfect, whole, innocent inhabitants also claim that Eve erred when she told Satan that God told them they could not even touch the forbidden fruit, lest they die. And that occurred prior to the sin of eating the fruit. Can a perfect person in perfect communion with God Himself (as traditionalists claim they had) make such a mistake? How do you reconcile this? I guess it depends on your definition of "perfect." Does it just mean sinless, or does it mean perfect in every possible way? This may be impossible to determine since the Bible never claimed they were perfect and since this concept that they and the garden were perfect is only a human construction. But most of the time when I hear it said that Adam and Eve were perfect, it seems that it's meant in every sense, because coupled with it is usually the assertion that Eden was a perfect world, the way God intended it, and that there was perfect unbroken communion between God and mankind.

God did in fact say that everything He had created was abundantly good, and this would include the garden and mankind. But as good as it was in God's sight for the time being, we've found many problems with claiming that this was the ultimate state that He intended from eternity past.

Just beginning with the most obvious as we always should, the Bible doesn't say that Adam and Eve were perfect, or that the Garden was perfect. While lots of people after the fall were either referred to as "perfect" or told to walk "perfect" before God, "perfect" meaning completeness, lacking nothing, there is no reference in the Bible to Adam, Eve, or the Garden as being perfect or complete, so this fact, combined with other evidence I'll point out shortly, and what we've already seen, shows that they were therefore not perfect or complete. In fact, we know that Satan dwelt among them before human sin occurred so this presents a problem right away for calling the garden perfect, unless we believe that Satan will always be in God's garden.

And we have the issue of Eve's "mistake" when she told Satan that God said they would die if they even touched the fruit of the tree of knowledge. I've generally heard it taught that this was a mistake and not a sin, and without giving it much thought, I believed that to be the case. But I read a commentary that brought that into question and claimed that it was neither, by pointing out that just because we're not told in Scripture that God said not to even touch the forbidden fruit, we can't assume that He did not. Then I began to think about it, and it made good sense to me to think that God probably did warn them not to even touch it. That seems to line up with New Testament teaching about even avoiding the appearance of evil, and it's also a Biblical concept that we should avoid temptation, so I began to question whether Eve made a mistake or not.

But then I read the passage again, and noticed the obvious: She flat out said that God told them that even if they touch it, they will die. God clearly said that it was the eating of it that would bring about their death, so she obviously had a "mistake in her doctrine," so to speak. It's possible that God did warn them not to touch it, and maybe even warned them to avoid it altogether, but only because these could lead to temptation, not because these things in themselves would cause death. So while I agree with most teachers that Eve made a doctrinal error, I must ask this: How can one say that Adam, Eve, or the world they inhabited was perfect when a fallen tempter was there before human sin, when Eve was clearly a fallible human, very capable of mistake even *before* the fall and their willful disobedience, and while apparently, according to Genesis 3:6, Adam stood idly by and watched the whole thing?

> Since Paul speaks of us one day becoming incorruptible, doesn't the fact that Adam and Eve were corruptible indicate that this first phase of existence was never our ultimate destination?

The point I'm driving toward is that the Garden of Eden was never intended to be humanity's final destination. And while it was beautiful I'm sure, and maybe the closest thing to heaven this earth has ever known, it and the people in it were not perfect or complete in any sense. To claim that this was what God intended is to claim that eternal life with God in Heaven is just a "plan B," and it brings God's omniscience into question regarding man's sin and His eternal plan of redemption, something that we just can't do. Believing that the original earth and the garden of Eden was meant to be our abode forever also brings into question whether or not we were meant to live in a timeless state with the Lord for all eternity, or only in a state where we mark time as we do now. And doesn't just the fact that we had the potential to be corrupted show us that this was not our eternal destiny? Will we still be corruptible after we are in heaven in eternity? 1 Corinthians 15:53 gives the answer, no. In that passage, we are told that we are corruptible, but that we will "put on incorruption." "Corruptible" means "able to be corrupted," and "perishable"—"perish *able*"—means "able to perish."

The simple fact that sin and death were possible shows that even sinless Adam and Eve were corruptible, and therefore not complete, and therefore certainly not perfect. And this should also serve as a major clue that this first earthly Eden was not to be our eternal home. Not only that, Paul tells us in 1 Corinthians 15:50 that flesh and blood cannot inherit the Kingdom of God. This seems like further Biblical evidence that they were never intended to enter the Kingdom of God in the state they were in. They were flesh and blood, so according to Paul, they weren't even able to inherit the Kingdom of God.

And concerning our final abode either being in time or outside of time, even before there was sin, God created the heavenly bodies, for one of several reasons, so man could mark time and count days and years. This is what we're told in Genesis 1:14. But we're told in Revelation 22:5 that in eternity we will have no need of created lights like the sun because God will be our light. Did God not always intend to be our light for all eternity? God's earthly creation was good, but never intended to be our eternal home. We see in 2 Peter 3:10-12, Matthew 24:35, and other places, that the current heavens and earth will pass away. And it seems highly likely that when we lose the very things created to mark time, we will be entering timelessness, and this happens at the end of the 1000-year reign of Christ, immediately following the judgment. God knew this end from the beginning. Knowing this, how could we claim that Eden was intended to be our eternal home? Again, it calls into question God's omniscience. The Garden, and the Lord there with man was only a foreshadowing in time of a future eternity when believers will forever commune with the Lord in the real and eternal "paradise of God."

Continuing on with this theory that Eden was lacking, and concerning the incompleteness of the God-to-Adam relationship in the garden, God would not have said that it is "not good" that man be alone if a full relationship with God was possible at that point. If God is complete and lacking nothing within Himself, and He is, then He would be everything Adam would ever need if their original relationship was intended to be an eternal one. And think about the word "alone" in that phrase, "It is not good that man is alone." Obviously there was not a full and complete relationship between God and even a sinless (at that point) man or he would not have been considered "alone" and it wouldn't have been considered "not good." There was already a separation.

Concerning Adam's aloneness and God's solution in providing him a completer, it wasn't that mankind's ultimate eternal goal was to be married to one another either. Marriage is a picture of a future when all believers as a whole will be the bride of Christ. This is taught all the time by many of the very same people who claim that everything was perfect, complete, and in harmonious eternal balance before Adam and Eve ate the forbidden fruit. But remember, Jesus said that in heaven there will neither be marriage nor being given in marriage (Luke 20:34-35 and other places), so we see that even the blessing of human marriage and companionship is not our ultimate end. We even have Paul, in the New Testament, advising people, if they can abstain from fleshly lust, not to get married because it can take one's focus away from the Lord.

The only marriage spoken of in eternity is our collective marriage to the Lord, and that event seems to be a pinnacle point in our life and future with the Lord. But this was never intended to happen in the garden of Eden, or the Lord would have come to Adam and Eve one day before they had sinned and told them that soon they'd be getting married to Him. And if this wasn't intended to happen there, then that first Garden wasn't what we were ultimately created for, and Adam and Eve's exit was intended and known before the Garden was ever created. But Adam was viewed as alone, and given Eve to become his wife. It doesn't line up with Scripture to say things like, "The garden of Eden was God's perfect world that He placed man into, but then we just went and messed it all up."

The Lord desires a Church to enter eternity with, a group of people who know Him and love Him, but again, how could we ever love Him if we had no real understanding of just how much He loves us? The Bible even tells us in 1 John 4:19 that "we love Him because He first loved us." We have no capacity to love God until we first believe that He exists, and then comprehend His love for us. In the same way the false teaching of eternal conscious suffering damages our understanding of who God is, this teaching that the Garden of Eden was the perfect world, "paradise lost," does much the same. It takes away from an understanding of God's omniscience and the realization that He had the plan of redemption of feeble, fallible man in His infinite mind from eternity past.

As far as we know, nothing like this experience of time will ever happen again after we enter timeless eternity, either for us or any future creation that God could endeavor in. While our intimate relationship with the Lord which we will experience one day in heaven will far exceed what we have now, this current "invisible" relationship can be very sweet as most Christians know, but can become all the more so when we throw off the lie that God is going to allow the eternal torment of billions of souls who never found Him.

We addressed a number of misconceptions and misguided teachings that source from the Garden of Eden, but none of them related directly to the immortality issue, which is the more important one, as it relates back to the entire doctrine of eternal suffering we're challenging. These peripheral Garden mistakes more or less demonstrate that we're not listening to the clear language of the account, and instead, accepting falsehood. Let's wrap up our Garden time by addressing the immortality question more directly.

I used to listen to a radio/Internet ministry called *Search the Scriptures Daily*, and it was hosted by T.A. McMahon and Dave

Hunt, who has since passed away. I really enjoyed it because they challenged false teachings that were creeping into the Church, and they didn't seem to mind confronting other Christians when necessary. I especially appreciated their willingness to stand against Calvinism. They appeared in every way to be people who are honestly searching out the truth.

Early in my research on this book, I thought I would take a look at their website (thebereancall.org) to see if they'd ever addressed the "eternal conscious suffering" or "immortality" issues. I assumed I would probably find them to be traditionalists on these matters, only because almost all Christians are, but I was holding out some hope that maybe they had already done some real research on this issue and were going against the grain on this one. I was disappointed. They had in fact addressed these issues, and far from finding solid research, what I found were some of the worst arguments for the traditional view of innate human immortality that I've seen yet.

An individual who had attended a The Berean Call event and who apparently was at least dabbling with a non-traditional view of judgment wrote in and challenged them with several verses that clearly teach that true death will be the final state for those without faith in Christ. In rebuttal and in defense of eternal conscious suffering and separation, The TBC (The Berean Call) staff responds in part:

> "What did it mean that Adam and Eve were dead, yet still living? Spiritual death brought instant separation from God the moment Adam and Eve rebelled against Him by eating of the forbidden fruit. In this earthly life, however, there is hope of that spiritual separation being ended by reconciliation with God through faith in our Lord Jesus Christ, who paid the penalty for sin and "tast[ed] death for every man (Hebrews 2:9)"[38]

The TBC representative goes on later to say that in Scripture "there is never a hint that their (the unsaved's) consciousness will ever end."[39]

But contrary to his implication that all souls will be alive and conscious somewhere for all eternity, what I can't find in Scripture is any evidence that consciousness goes on in eternity for anyone who does not "put on the incorruptible" as Paul says. And to answer his first question, "What did it mean that Adam and Eve were dead, yet still living?"[40], the Bible never says they were literally dead, even in soul. That's reading in something that isn't there. Scripture says that in the day they ate from the tree of the knowledge of good and evil, death would become sure, and it did. We covered this in Chapter 2. It's true that the unsaved are separated from God and spiritually dead in the sense that this will be their future state. But Adam and Eve's ultimate death of their souls (the second death) had not happened, and never will if they persevered in faith, which most Christians assume they did, and I would be in that camp that tends to believe they are saved.

The separation from God, if it is not reconciled, will lead to death, but one's soul cannot be *literally* alive and *literally* dead simultaneously, but is rather living and dying simultaneously, prior to salvation, just as our bodies are living, yet heading for death as well. TBC also claimed that Adam and Eve's "spiritual death brought instant separation from God the moment [they] rebelled against Him by eating of the forbidden fruit."[41] This concept has some major problems — the first being what we just noted, that contrary to common teaching, the Bible does not indicate that there was a God-and-man relationship at all before sin. There was no connection with God that could have been severed. The relationship could not be established until Adam and Eve gained a knowledge of good and evil. And contrary to TBC's response, what actually happened "instantly" after they sinned, or at least very shortly after sin was open, two-way communication, and other evidences of God's love and mercy as we've already noted. It was by the grace of God that He even allowed them to communicate (or commune) with Him. And again, this happened *after* sin occurred – not before. In considering the real implications of the banishment, this is an interesting verse:

> 2 Samuel 14:14 "We must all die; we are like water spilled on the ground, which cannot be gathered up again. But God will not take away life, and he devises means so that the banished one will not remain an outcast." (ESV)

The subject referenced here in this verse was not the banishment from the garden, but what a perfect description of what happened there. Adam and Eve were cast out, but they and every believer will one day return to the true garden of God, and not remain an outcast. And even though the subject matter in consideration in this verse was not the garden banishment, I think it's interesting and meaningful as a concept of how God interacts with and rules His people. God is unchanging, and He is a punisher, but a redeemer ultimately of all who will put their hope in Him.

As I said previously, TA McMahon and Dave Hunt are two of the more Biblically sound teachers I've listened to over the years. And as I've done with almost every Christian I've criticized in this book, I again acknowledge their ministry as being from God as far as I know. I've learned a lot from them. And I appreciate the way they stand up for the Word of God, even against other Christians, when it concerns sound doctrine. But they fall back on extremely weak arguments when it comes to Hell, immortality, and judgment. And regarding immortality specifically, in the same communication that I referenced earlier when challenged by an annihilationist with some very convincing verses, and when asked about immortal existence, TBC must go to extreme and ridiculous measures to answer the question without rocking the traditionalist boat. And just as Easley and MacArthur couldn't, neither can someone as intelligent and generally biblically-sound as the TBC spokesmen defend tradition Biblically and logically. The question was posed, "On what grounds do you define 'death' as an immortal existence?" TBC's response was:

> "Your idea of 'immortality' assumes that the lost must be immortal in order to exist eternally in hell. Not so. The word 'immortal' occurs only once in the entire Bible (1 Tm 1:17) and

is a description of God who alone is eternal, having neither beginning nor end: 'Who alone hath immortality...' (1 Tm 6:16). The immortality that God gives to man refers to the new body that can never die (1 Cor 15:53,54), received by the redeemed. Angels, demons, Satan and mankind were created, and therefore have a beginning. There is not one verse in the Bible, however, to indicate that their existence ever ends—but endless existence is never referred to as 'immortality'."[42]

There are a number of things wrong with this defense. The TBC responder first writes that the questioner's "idea of 'immortality' assumes that the lost must be immortal in order to exist eternally in hell. Not so." So what he's trying to do is redefine immortality, and create a new idea that an individual can be eternal without being immortal. And this just doesn't work. But he's forced to do it if he's going to maintain a traditionalist viewpoint, because the Bible states that immortality only belongs to God and believers to whom God grants it. So for someone to claim that the lost will exist consciously forever, they must do some mental and verbal acrobatics, and make "eternal existence" and "immortality" potentially exclusive.

There's another major problem with the response, and it may exemplify a lack of study and understanding in this area. Whoever is writing this for TBC claims that "the word 'immortal' only occurs once in the entire Bible," and then he gives a reference to 1 Timothy 1:17 as the only place it occurs. This is simply not true. Depending on what version you're reading, "immortal" and "immortality" appear quite a number of times. But even if we only look at the 1 Timothy 1:17 reference, the Greek word being translated as "immortal" there is *aphthartos*, and this exact same word is used in 6 other places in the Bible, but is often translated into the English words "incorruptible" or "imperishable." Just because it may be translated slightly different in English doesn't change the fact that the exact same God-breathed word appears in several places in Scripture. And most interestingly and most problematic for their argument, it's applied to God *and* humans.

TBC seems to miss this altogether, and is attempting to prove that there are two different types of immortality, one that only applies to God, and one that God gives to man. And he is trying to combine the fact that God existed from eternity past while humanity and angelic beings were created, with the notion that the "immortality" ascribed to God in 1 Timothy 1:17 belongs only to God, to establish his theory that one can exist for eternity yet not technically be referred to as "immortal." But this just will not work. He is correct that the verse does in fact say that immortality belongs only to God. But obviously that means that He is the only one who ever possessed it as a natural attribute of His being, because we can look at 1 Corinthians 15:52 that says: "in a moment, in the twinkling of an eye, at the last trumpet. For the trumpet will sound, and the dead will be raised imperishable (*aphthartos*/immortal), and we shall be changed." (ESV)

We can note a few things here. For one, this verse maintains that we (believers) will be changed and given the same type of immortality that God has always possessed. Never forget that we are told in Scripture that when we see Him, we will be like Him (1 John 3:2). This is in direct contradiction to what TBC is trying to establish. So not only have we shown that he is incorrect about how many times this word appears in Scripture, he also failed to prove that the immortality that only God possessed could not be granted to created beings. The Bible in fact says that it most certainly will. Next, let's look at the definition of the word. *Strong's* defines it as "undecaying," and we already saw that the English Standard Version interprets it as "imperishable." This imperishability is what God desires for all. We know from 2 Peter 3:9, that "He is not willing that any should *perish.*" And we have John 3:16: "For God so loved the world that He gave His only begotten Son, that *whosoever* believes in Him shall not *perish*, but have everlasting life." As we'll see in more detail in the following chapter, this verse draws a clear distinction between the two possibilities for all human souls: We can perish or we can become imperishable and have everlasting life. And clearly, this "everlasting life" and "imperishability" are parallels, and apply only to believers, not un-believers. We come into the world, already perishing, already dying, but this can be cured by accepting Christ and gaining the promise of one day becoming *aphthartos*, imperishable, immortal.

Next, the TBC staff wrote, "There is not one verse in the Bible, however, to indicate that their existence ever ends—but endless existence is never referred to as 'immortality'." Both of these statements are wrong. We have innumerable references in the Old and New Testaments to the full destruction of unbelievers, many of which we looked at in Chapter 3, including one verse where the enemies of God are described by a term that means "non-entity, to be no more." We wouldn't need the term if there were no one to apply it to, or if it were impossible to become a non-entity and be no more. The TBC assertion that "endless existence is never referred to as 'immortality'" is problematic as well. Consider the very passage (1 Corinthians 15:53-54) they had just referenced before he wrote that. It says:

> "53 For this corruptible must put on incorruption, and this mortal must put on immortality. 54 But when this corruptible shall put on incorruption, and this mortal shall put on immortality, then will take place the Word that has been written, "Death was swallowed up in victory." (LITV)

This "incorruption" from verse 53 is *aphtharsia* in Greek, and is virtually the same word and idea as *aphthartos*. *Strong's* defines it generally as "unending existence" and "immortality," the two very things that the TBC representative says are *never* paralleled. And not only do we have this connection within the definition, we see this "incorruption" paralleled with another Greek word, *athanasia* which is translated as "immortality" here in the same verse. And its definition is "deathlessness." And isn't it death we see "swallowed up" at the end of the passage? And this is the same death that we were all approaching before salvation and before accepting the guarantee of immortality.

Finally, even though the Bible itself is clear enough to show multiple problems with the TBC theory, let's just look at the

Merriam-Webster's Dictionary definition of "immortality": *Merriam-Webster's* defines it as "unending existence,"[43] the very thing that Mcmahon says is not meant by the word "immortality." He claims rather that one can exist and be an eternal being but not be immortal. But immortal clearly means "unending existence" according to the word of God, and the highly thought of Noah Webster. Well, someone is wrong here: Webster and Scripture, or the TBC writer. Why is it that some of the most intelligent and learned minds in Christianity are running from the simple truth of Scripture, that the lost will truly perish? It's almost as if they *desire* to believe that God will cause or allow lost souls to suffer for all eternity. I don't truly believe this, but there does seem to be some enslavement to tradition that even our best and brightest can't get free from.

No definition of any of the Greek words that get translated to "immortal" or "immortality" contains any language to indicate a blessed life in eternity with God – only deathlessness, and continual existence. And this is all the more incredible considering the fact that these terms are *never* applied to the unbelieving in Scripture, only to believers, and it therefore seems it would be acceptable to include in the definitions the concept that this is only a state believers can attain to.

Well I said it back in Chapter 2, but yes, almost everything you've been taught about the Garden of Eden was wrong. And it wasn't my intention to burst anyone's bubble. I'm sorry if I've messed up your images of God, Adam, and Eve peacefully strolling together daily in the Garden, without a care in the world. Scenarios like those are in the future for us who have put our faith in Christ. But they most likely weren't part of our past, and I hope I demonstrated many of the common Garden errors we teach and how they've contributed to false notions that damage our concept of a merciful Father.

The Intermediate State

So we've been talking about FINAL judgment, which is an event that occurs after the 1000-year reign of Christ on earth. But what happens immediately when a person physically dies?

I'm really not sure.

...okay, moving on to Chapter 8

CHAPTER 8

No Not Really

Actually, that was just my attempt at a little comic relief, while addressing a very serious topic (and a waste of a perfectly good piece of paper)   back to chapter 7...

The Intermediate State

The truth is, however, the intermediate state between the time of physical death and the time of being raised to stand judgment is more of a gray area than many want to admit. And it's also far less concerning, as it relates to the nature and character of God, which is the subject of this book. The thought of a soul being in conscious torment for potentially a few thousand years as they await final judgment is incredibly sad. But any finite period, even a lengthy one, pales in comparison to an eternity of suffering. I've used the illustration before, but it's worth repeating because it's so true: According to the traditional Christian doctrine, even after billions and billions of years (were there such a thing), a lost soul is just getting started on their journey of suffering. It literally would have no end. Their punishment will never be complete. It's absolutely the most horrific thing that we accuse God of, yet that's the routine in mainstream Christianity.

The fact is, even a few thousand years of conscious suffering is just a drop in the bucket of timeless eternity. And by saying that, I'm not implying that I necessarily believe the lost are conscious for the entire time between physical death and final judgment. It's within the realm of possibility but seems unlikely. And we'll also address in this chapter the various theories on what happens to the faithful saved during this intermediate phase between physical death and resurrection to eternal life. However, making this sub-topic a little more complicated is that what happens to saved people at the time of death probably changed after Jesus's death and resurrection. But we'll get to that.

When I said this is more of a gray area than many want to admit, I wasn't only accusing many on the traditionalist side of being overly sure of their position, but even most conditionalists who write on this topic. With some exceptions, traditionalists generally believe that at death, saved people are immediately in heaven, and lost souls go immediately to Hell where they begin "their eternity" of suffering. And at the other extreme, with a few exceptions, the more common conditionalist position is to believe that all souls, saved or lost, are in a "soul sleep" during this entire time between physical death and resurrection. I'm not going to argue strongly on either side. I've actually found evidence for both in Scripture, and I think it's likely both occur. So if I'm arguing anything, it's that a hard line position on either side, full soul sleep, or full conscious awareness is probably wrong.

I appreciate the ministry of any conditionalist who fights the good fight against the doctrine of unsaved humans suffering consciously throughout all eternity. And that's certainly the more important of the two phases of postmortem existence to address. But I believe we would serve the Church, and the unsaved better, if we admitted that the intermediate state is more mysterious than some may want to believe, rather than boldly teaching that there's no possible way there is any form of consciousness between the time of physical death and resurrection to judgment (and resurrection to life for the saved, for that matter). There is biblical evidence to this end, much of which we'll address shortly, and also numerous accounts from reputable people, including medical doctors, etc, that people are experiencing "something" during these near death (and actual death) experiences. And what's striking to me in some of these cases is not that these witnesses claim that the experiences felt real, because even dreams can do that, but that they describe it as "more real than real," and more vivid than life itself as they previously knew it. They even talk about new colors that they don't even have words to describe.

Now please don't misunderstand. I'm not saying let's buy into every single story we hear from someone making outrageous claims about some vision they've seen. I've certainly read the accounts of some who I believe are attempting to deceive, even if they believe themselves to be somehow serving Christ in the process. But we are dealing with a realm and dimension beyond this present one. And we have a God beyond comprehension Who has created a universe of which we've barely scratched the surface of understanding. So while I'm gladly in the "conditionalist" camp on this matter of final judgment, I would challenge other conditionalists to leave room for the possibility of consciousness between the time of physical death and resurrection. It seems close-minded not to.

But this chapter isn't going to be dedicated to personal accounts of near death experiences. We can't put much stock into them, and you can find those anywhere, if that's something the reader would like to research. Rather, we'll look at the biblical evidence for and against the concept that the lost or saved will experience consciousness after physical death, and before resurrection. We addressed this back in the Luke 16 section of Chapter 2. But we'll go in some different directions in this chapter and examine all of the most commonly used arguments by my fellow-conditionalists for defending soul sleep, and see that there are reasonable biblical answers to these. And we'll examine the arguments by traditionalists who believe that "Hell" begins at the moment of physical death.

The most common conditionalist take is that essentially the "soul" is not something separate from the body, but rather refers to the whole being, and that the whole being unconsciously "awaits" resurrection, from the moment of physical death. And certainly there are places in Scripture where "soul" refers to the whole person. But that doesn't negate the concept that there is an immaterial part of us that can remain conscious, and doesn't stay with this physical body when we die. Jesus seemed to make a reference to a spirit without a body in Luke 24:39 when after His death and burial, His disciples didn't believe it was Him appearing before them. He told them to look at His hands and feet and to handle Him, and then stated that a spirit doesn't have flesh and bones as they could plainly see He did.

In Genesis 35 we see Rachel naming her second child as her "soul was departing," and then parenthetically it clarifies that this happened because she was dying. Here's verses 17 and 18:

> "When she was in hard labor, the midwife said to her, 'Don't be afraid, for now you will have another son.' As her soul was departing (for she died), she named him Benoni, but his father named him Benjamin." (WEB)

Where was her soul departing to, if the soul remains with the body in the grave at physical death? This is strong evidence that soul and body are separate things and that the immaterial soul is no longer "locked into" the body at the time of physical death.

Let's begin with those who are saved — those reserved to one day receive eternal life, based on their faithfulness to the one true living God. Do they go into a soul sleep as they die, or do they become aware of a realm beyond what we can comprehend here and now?

Going to the day of the of the Lord's death, Jesus is on the cross, still alive and suffering, as were the two thieves on either side of Him. One of them is mocking Christ, and the other pleads with Him to remember him when He comes into His Kingdom. In other words, he was exhibiting his faith in who Christ was, and was asking for Him to show mercy. Jesus said to Him "Truly I say to you, today you will be with me in paradise"

Those who believe in complete soul sleep from the time of death until resurrection will say the comma is misplaced in English bibles and that it should read: "Truly I say to you today, you will be with me in paradise." In other words, in their interpretation, the only thing happening "that day" would be Christ speaking this promise that the believing thief would one day be with Him in paradise, when in reality, the thief would remain in an unconscious state until the final resurrection. It's not an unfathomable argument, but I think it has some problems.

I looked up the phrase, and of all the times Jesus used "truly I say to you," only one other time in Scripture was it followed by "today," and in that instance, it clearly meant "on that day." It was when he was telling Peter that he would betray him three times on that very day before the cock crowed. (Mark 14:30) Consider that it was always "today" any time Jesus used that phrase, but twice He added the word "today" and in one verifiable instance, He clearly meant what He predicted would happen that very day. So instead of taking it something more like "As I stand here today, truly I tell you...," it seems more likely that Jesus was claiming that on that very day, the repentant thief would be with Him in paradise. Would the man remain conscious, and maybe even perform some activity or be involved in heavenly worship for the next 2000 years until bodily resurrection? I have no idea. It sort of seems unlikely and unnecessary, and we're not told anything like this is happening, however it's not impossible either. But whether or not the thief remained conscious or eventually was laid to sleep, I believe he was consciously with Jesus in paradise that very day, as Jesus said. Another argument from the full soul sleep camp would be that it would "feel like" that same day to the man because it would be his next conscious moment. Again, that's possible – but seems less likely.

Let's now look at Stephen, the first martyr for Christ. Moments before succumbing to death by stoning, at the hands of unbelieving Jews, he looked up and saw the heavens open up and Jesus standing (not seated) at the right hand of God, presumably standing to receive Stephen (Acts 7:56). And he then in fact asks the Lord Jesus to receive his spirit. Even though it next tells us that he went to sleep, it seems far more likely this is the typical euphemism for death being used, rather than a report of what his immaterial soul was about to experience. It's difficult for me to believe, in this scenario that he then, rather than go consciously into the presence of the Lord, instead fell into a death sleep that would last almost 2000 years.

It's not impossible to believe, but it just doesn't seem to be what the text is conveying. The heavens had just opened up! He literally saw Jesus!! And then... what? Nothing? It seems far more likely that this is when he would hear, "Well done, good and faithful servant." And then after being welcomed into the Lord's arms, I'm far more open to the idea that the saved are then laid to sleep until the resurrection. Obviously I'm only speculating. But I guess I just don't know what we would do. Jesus said He was going away to prepare a place for us. Do we join in on that "construction project" as we one by one die off? Do we just play like children? (and I'm surely not against that idea) Again, it's not impossible. It just seems sort of unlikely. And something that William Tyndale wrote about this in the 1500s makes a lot of sense. He asked: "...if the souls (of saved people when they die) be in heaven, tell me why they be not in as good case as the angels be? And then what cause is there of the resurrection?"[44]

> The heavens had just opened up! Stephen literally saw Jesus!! And then... what? Nothing? He falls into a 2000 year death sleep?

Great question. If a saved person, in soul form, goes to heaven and takes on whatever "bodily form" people imagine for it, so that he or she can exist with the Lord, and do whatever tasks, recreation, or worship we imagine may be happening there, how can it get any better than that? What is the advantage, or even the purpose of a later resurrection? Yes, Paul said to be absent from the body was to be present with the Lord. And I truly believe this is the immediate experience of a saved person at the time of death. But he also referred to Christians who had died as those who "sleep in Christ." It's simply not a stretch to believe there are times of consciousness as well as times of sleep for the soul during this intermediate phase between physical death and resurrection.

There's more evidence. Jesus took Peter, James, and John by themselves one day up a mountain to pray, and was transfigured into radiant light before them, and Moses and Elijah appeared there with Him (Luke 9:28-31). Even if Moses and Elijah had been in a state of soul sleep, and I don't argue this is impossible, this verse at the very least demonstrates that one can be roused from it. Some would say that these were just visions, not really Moses and Elijah, and that these two apparitions appeared because Moses represented the law, and Elijah the prophets. It's possible. But if we go strictly with what Scripture says, it says these were Moses and Elijah, and that they even spoke with Christ. Not only that — We're even told what they talked about: Jesus's soon departure that He would accomplish in Jerusalem. So we're to believe that Jesus was just having an imaginary conversation with two magical entities who only "appeared" as Moses and Elijah? That's so unlikely. I believe this was actually Moses and Elijah, and that they were real and conscious at the time they appeared, but it's at least possible that God brought them out of a sleep for the purpose of that appearance, or they may have been already awake and aware prior to this meeting. We just don't know and shouldn't pretend we do.

Let's look at something from the Old Testament briefly. It's in 1 Samuel 28:13-20. When Saul consulted a medium to bring back Samuel from the grave, Samuel actually appeared, according to Scripture. And Samuel even asked, "Why have you disturbed me, to bring me up?" Now there's a lot of controversy about this verse. Many Christians believe this was an evil spirit which appeared and only acted like Samuel. And others believe God allowed a singular instance of some otherwise non-existent apparition to appear, only to strike fear into Saul, but that it wasn't actually the real Samuel. However, if we just trust the text of Scripture, it was Samuel, not an impostor of any sort. He also prophesied the future, which adds more weight to the idea of it being the real Samuel, and not an evil spirit or temporarily created apparition. And the question he asks about being disturbed and brought up is very interesting. It sounds like he was in a sleep state, but was awakened from it...and wasn't happy about it either.

So we've seen evidence it's highly unlikely that saved souls are locked into a sleep state. They may rest unconsciously for some of the time as they await their ultimate resurrection to eternal life, but it seems like consciousness during the intermediate state is not only possible but likely, for whatever duration and purposes the Lord determines. And this may be all we can conclude from what Scripture gives us.

Let's turn our attention now to the intermediate fate of lost souls — those who died without putting their faith in the One True Living God. A traditionalist would take you to the Luke 16 passage of Lazarus and the rich man that we looked at in Chapter 4 and say, 'Well of course the lost are conscious and tormented while in the intermediate state. See right there the man says he is tormented'. We already noted that while there is room for opinion on that story ...or parable — whatever it is, the conclusive facts we can determine are that it's not entirely literal, and it's not a picture of final judgment. But could it be some indication of consciousness at the immediate time of death? That's actually the context of the parable/story, and I think it's at least possible. And we analyzed it fairly well already.

On the other hand, a conditionalist might take a verse such as Revelation 20:5 which tells us that the lost "will not live again until the thousand years are finished," and say "See, they don't live during that 1000 years that Christ is reigning on earth, so they aren't conscious. And I think that's a fair enough argument. But does that mean they experience absolutely no time of consciousness at all? Just as I suspect that Stephen was welcomed home at the moment he physically died, but may have since been placed into a sleep state while he awaits his resurrection, I believe the lost too may have an immediate time of realization of what they've forfeited, maybe something similar to what the rich man in the Luke 16 account experienced — but then are perhaps mercifully put to sleep until the day of their dreadful judgment. This is speculation. But we do have a couple of clues. One is the Revelation 20:5 passage we just referenced. The context is the beginning of the 1000-year reign of Christ, and in verse 4 we read that the resurrected saved are going to live and reign with Christ for that thousand years. The very next verse blatantly states that "the rest of the dead" (which would be all unsaved faithless people from all ages) will "not live" during that time. Now, perhaps it just means they won't live on earth. But it doesn't say this. It doesn't say they'll be under the earth in conscious torment, having a conversation with Abraham about their desire for a drop of water for their tongues. No, it says they won't live during that time. Unconsciousness seems to be implied.

The following passage in Job offers more evidence of a holding place prior to final judgment:

> Job 21:29-30 "Have ye not asked them that go by the way? and do ye not know their tokens, That the wicked is reserved to the day of destruction? they shall be brought forth to the day of wrath." (KJV)

The word being translated as "reserved" here is the Greek word, *chasak* and among other definitions in *Strong's*, it means to restrain, refuse, preserve, hold back, and to punish. This confirms that they have been brought down, but also that they will be brought forth again, on the Day of Judgment. Notice too that the day of wrath is equivalent to the day of "destruction." This is just one more of the numerous times Scripture indicates an intermediate state for the lost after physical death, but they will ultimately be raised, judged, and destroyed, not just thrown back into another Hell as so many claim.

David Jeremiah states that when Hades is thrown into the Lake of Fire, this is transitioning from temporary Hell to permanent Hell.[45] The Bible calls the Lake of Fire the Second Death. But Jeremiah calls it permanent life in torment. I love listening to David Jeremiah and I know he's a light in a state* that desperately needs light. I used to listen to him every weekday on the radio, and if I missed, I'd catch up on an app, and I still try to catch him now and then. He's a great teacher, but he's just off on this one. And obviously not him only. This is what our seminary pastors are taught, and it's what they pass on.

---

*California. Lived there briefly, loved it, but it's not exactly the Bible belt.

Jeremiah has followed the crowd here, and what he's stating is just not lining up with Scripture. He even goes so far as to say that "if there is no permanent Hell, then there cannot be a permanent heaven, because the Bible says far more about Hell in the new testament than it does about heaven."[46] He's failing to contrast a life that will never end with a death from which there is no return, as Scripture does, and instead of using biblical ideas, is using man-made non-biblical phrases such as "Permanent Hell."

Here's an interesting passage that may shed some light on the intermediate state of the lost. It's Isaiah 14:4-27, and there are a number of interpretations of this passage. Much like Ezekiel 28 where there seems to be a dual reference to the King of Tyre and to Satan himself, that's also a possibility here, except it's the king of Babylon whose condemnation we may be seeing transition into the future condemnation of Satan. Some even say these are dual prophecies directed at the future antichrist. That's possible too, based on some of the language. Truth is, I have no idea. But for our purposes in this chapter, we don't need to figure out everything these passages refer to. We're looking for references to Sheol and Hades that may or may not indicate a time of consciousness or sleep. And I think we have that here. Please read all of the following but take special note of verses 9 and 10. And I'll add some thoughts on the other side of this passage:

> Isa 14:4-20:   "4 that you will take up this parable against the king of Babylon, and say, 'How the oppressor has ceased! The golden city has ceased!' 5 Yahweh has broken the staff of the wicked, the scepter of the rulers, 6 who struck the peoples in wrath with a continual stroke, who ruled the nations in anger, with a persecution that no one restrained. 7 The whole earth is at rest, and is quiet. They break out in song. 8 Yes, the cypress trees rejoice with you, with the cedars of Lebanon, saying, 'Since you are humbled, no lumberjack has come up against us.' 9 Sheol from beneath has moved for you to meet you at your coming. It stirs up the departed spirits for you, even all the rulers of the earth. It has raised up from their thrones all the

kings of the nations. 10 They all will answer and ask you, 'Have you also become as weak as we are? Have you become like us?' 11 Your pomp is brought down to Sheol, with the sound of your stringed instruments. Maggots are spread out under you, and worms cover you. 12 How you have fallen from heaven, shining one, son of the dawn! How you are cut down to the ground, who laid the nations low! 13 You said in your heart, 'I will ascend into heaven! I will exalt my throne above the stars of God! I will sit on the mountain of assembly, in the far north! 14 I will ascend above the heights of the clouds! I will make myself like the Most High!' 15 Yet you shall be brought down to Sheol, to the depths of the pit. 16 Those who see you will stare at you. They will ponder you, saying, 'Is this the man who made the earth to tremble, who shook kingdoms; 17 who made the world like a wilderness, and overthrew its cities; who didn't release his prisoners to their home?' 18 All the kings of the nations, sleep in glory, everyone in his own house. 19 But you are cast away from your tomb like an abominable branch, clothed with the slain, who are thrust through with the sword, who go down to the stones of the pit; like a dead body trodden under foot. 20 You will not join them in burial, because you have destroyed your land. You have killed your people. The offspring of evildoers will not be named forever." (WEB)

Whoever this is, a past king of Babylon, a future antichrist who would rule Mystery Babylon — whoever — what we want to notice is that in verse 9, souls in Sheol are "stirred up," and then they ask the question, "Have you become as weak as we are? Have you become like us?" Obviously this verse wouldn't make solid standalone evidence of either soul sleep or consciousness, because there is so much room for interpretation, and because metaphorical language is plentiful in Scripture, but when we add it to everything else we've found, I think it's valuable. The idea that these souls have been stirred up sounds like they may have been at rest, just as it seemed Samuel was at rest before Saul asked the witch at Endor to conjure him up. But then they are in fact stirred, and appear conscious as they question this one who has come to join them. If the Samuel/Saul event were something we could disregard as metaphorical, then this would have less value, but clearly that actually happened. It's Bible history.

We could go on and on with this topic. God's honest truth: My rough draft for this chapter was over 31,000 words. That's a small book in itself. The problem was that a good 20,000 of them were sheer speculation. It's difficult to watch your own words and study hit the "cutting room floor," but I've said it over and over – This intermediate state is a mystery, so even if there might have been a few thought gems in there (and it's just as likely there weren't), I've decided to spare the reader some time, and spare this book the additional weight of pages of all my random thoughts on the matter. Before we close though, let's look at two more aspects of judgment. One is getting a clearer understanding of the various words all being translated into the English word "hell," and the other is considering the possible necessity or value in there being an intermediate state of conscious judgment for the lost. We'll take the latter first.

Most traditionalists may find my interpretation of Hades, and judgment in general, to be soft compared to the traditional teaching that the lost will literally be on fire there in Hades and for all eternity after final judgment. On the other hand, many non-traditionalists/conditionalists who believe in full soul sleep might find my conclusions about Hades to be overly harsh. Some of these would argue that God subjecting the lost to *any* measure of suffering in this intermediate state would have no ultimate purpose and would only be cruelty. They might argue that there's no value in God subjecting those who are destined for destruction anyway, to endure any time of torment, short or long. In one sense I would agree. Their stay there will not rehabilitate them, and it will not purge them of their guilt and sin, nor gain them salvation. But I think it serves a purpose nevertheless — The idea of even a finite time of conscious regret and agony in the afterlife could serve as a deterrent to continuing in unbelief in this life. This is speculation, but I think it's within reason. A traditionalist might read this and say, "Well exactly...That's why we teach eternal hell...so people will be scared of that and seek God." I get that. But that traditional position on hell can't be backed up soundly, and so its effect can be short-lived, or can even backfire. However, it's far easier to defend the idea biblically that there could be at least some time of conscious suffering, even in the interim and prior to final judgment.

My theory is that, even as awful as extinction of the soul is, many, even if they believed this was their destiny, would trade seventy years of trying to have it their own way here on earth, for eternity with their maker, if the only consequence was a painless slip into non-existence. Even among Christians we can become overly caught up in the highlights and lowlights of this brief life, with little focus on eternity at times. This is possibly why God has enabled or created an intermediate state for the lost and foretells in Scripture how they will be raised to stand judgment, rather than simply annihilating them immediately upon physical death. It serves as a deterrent to continuing on leading a Godless life. We know from 2 Peter 3:9 that the Lord is not willing that any should perish (does that make the 8th time I've made that reference? Well, you'll never forget it), and from Ezekiel 33:11 that He takes no pleasure in the death of the wicked (Don't forget that either). So it seems reasonable that God would make every attempt to create a motivation to avoid ultimate death. And this is likely what we have here in Hades.

Death is incredibly sad, and the thought of going out of existence is quite depressing. But for many people, that is simply just not enough motivation to seek the Lord. Think of all the people who already go about their lives with the belief that they are simply going to cease to exist after this life. Many aren't seeking the Lord. They're living for this vapor of a life. If there weren't the looming possibility of conscious punishment, in the intermediate state and on judgment day, many might rather choose death, the very thing the Lord does not want. Unfortunately, this very real Hell that precedes a real extinction for the lost is not what is commonly taught. Instead the common teaching is that lost souls will go to the first Hell, then be judged, and then cast into a different Hell where they will spend "their eternity." Because this eternal conscious suffering is in such stark contrast to the merciful character of God that we tell people of, and also seems most useless to a God who was complete and lacking nothing before creation, because it cannot rehabilitate the lost, and because it cannot be strongly supported Scripturally, this concept which should seem scarier, is actually counterproductive with many hearers. If we simply taught what the Bible says, we might be surprised at how effective it would be.

We can't reasonably claim that the Lord causes unnecessary suffering, but allows what He must in order to move people toward Him. It also seems that the principle of varying degrees of suffering is plainly laid out in scripture, and likely applies at the time of judgment, as well as during any time of consciousness in the intermediate state.

Jesus taught that punishment is commensurate to knowledge. In Matthew 11:21-22, He was denouncing the cities where He had performed great miracles and yet they didn't repent. And He said that it would be more tolerable for Tyre and Sidon on judgment day than for Chorazin and Bethsaida, because Tyre and Sidon didn't experience anything like what these latter cities did. In John 15:22 Jesus is warning the disciples that they're going to be persecuted just as He will. But He adds that if He had not come and spoken to them (the lost who would reject the gospel message), they would not have been found guilty. Luke 12:47-48 also seem to confirm varying levels of punishment based on knowledge:

> "That servant, who knew his lord's will, and didn't prepare, nor do what he wanted, will be beaten with many stripes, 48 but he who didn't know, and did things worthy of stripes, will be beaten with few stripes. To whomever much is given, of him will much be required; and to whom much was entrusted, of him more will be asked." (WEB)

So the torment experienced at final judgment, and also during any conscious time in Hades prior to final judgment is by nature going to be far more severe for those who had more access to truth and the knowledge of God.

That's my speculation on why conscious suffering in Hell/Hades is necessary. Fear is a major motivator, and according to the Bible, it is the beginning of wisdom and knowledge. And while a painless death is horrible in its own way, I don't think it alone creates the kind of fear that's needed to motivate some to seek an alternative. I believe the Lord uses potential punishments in the same way, as a deterrent to sin, and ultimately against the deadly sin of unbelief.

This is a book about final judgment...about "Hell" in a sense. So let's now address that word and concept.

What did Jesus really say about "Hell"?

It's often said that Jesus spoke more of Hell than He did of Heaven, and because of this, it seems we're expected to trust in whatever version of "Hell" the Bible teacher has advanced. But we need to examine what Christ actually said. I've never counted the Lord's references to Heaven, and so I've never compared the counts, but I don't doubt the statement at all that He spoke more about Hell, in one form or another, than Heaven. It makes sense that He would give many warnings about perishing or being destroyed since He doesn't want this to happen to us. And we'll see that in fact, this is exactly what He did. While Jesus seems to have given a clear warning about the intermediate state at times, He more often spoke of the ultimate destruction of souls. So, part of delving into the study of the intermediate state of Hell, is first establishing that there are two very different words and ideas which are unfortunately both translated into the same concept and English word Hell.

Keep in mind that Jesus did not speak in English. There's some disagreement – of course – but most scholars believe that He spoke in Aramaic, and that His words were originally recorded in Greek. So Jesus never actually said "hell." The two different Greek words being translated in English as "hell" that Jesus spoke are so very different, and the contexts in which they are spoken of are so very different, it's impossible to deny that these are two very different ideas. This causes lots of confusion for people who don't look beyond English translations because both are translated as "hell."

There are sixteen times in Scripture where Jesus is recorded as uttering a word that is translated as "hell." Five of these sixteen times, Jesus used the Greek word *hades*, and eleven times He used the word *Gehenna* which is a combination of two Hebrew words meaning "valley" and "Hinnom," and we'll come back shortly and discuss this word, but we've already noted in previous chapters why it is such a perfect description of final judgment, and how it confirms the teachings that death and full destruction await the lost.

Hades is the place of departed souls, and equivalent to Sheol in the Old Testament (translated as hell, pit, and grave). At the time that Christ spoke of Hades, there was no essential difference in Hades and Sheol. Hades is the Greek word and Sheol the Hebrew word for the same place or state. Here's a great evidence of this: The *Strong's* concordance primary definition of "Sheol" is actually "Hades." Here's what *Strong's* has for the definition of Sheol: "hades or the world of the dead (as if a subterranean retreat), including its accessories and inmates." And *Strong's* primary definition of Hades is: "unseen" and "the place of departed souls." (not only lost souls, you will notice — although now, since Christ's resurrection, it's probably only the place of lost souls).[†]

Hades has changed now that Christ, through His death on the cross, has entered the Holy of Holies once for all and has ascended to the Father. Now, souls of saved people, whether they're asleep or awake, most likely go to be with Him there, whereas before, all souls, believers or unbelievers, went to Hell (Hades). Believers didn't suffer there however, but were rather comforted, whereas the lost likely suffer for part or all of the time there until they are resurrected for judgment at the end of the 1000-year reign of Christ on earth (Revelation 20:5 and 13).

[†] That second parenthetical was mine — not *Strong's*.

But there's every indication that this is more of a mental suffering than physical as we noted in Chapter 4.

Let's now look in a little more detail at why we can say that believers prior to Christ's death on the cross went to Hell (Hades), and why they now go to heaven. Paul implied in 2 Corinthians 5:8 that to be absent from the body is to be present with the Lord, and while he can say this now, after Christ's sacrifice and resurrection, this was never claimed before. It wasn't even possible for the saved to go to the Father in Heaven prior to Jesus's death because He had not done the cleansing with His own blood that was represented in the Old Testament yearly by the Israelite high priest entering the Holy of Holies with the blood.

Once a year, according to God's exacting specifications, the lone Israelite high priest would enter into the Holy of Holies portion of the Temple with a blood sacrifice, that we now know represented what Christ would one day do by taking on flesh and losing His life for us. In Mark 15:38, we see that at the very moment Jesus died, the veil to the Holy of Holies in the temple was torn in two. This represented the fact that now there is access to heaven that was previously denied. The veil had not represented a blocked access to God generally. We know this because many people are recorded in the Old Testament as having communicated with God. Rather, the veil covering the Holiest place literally represented a blocked access to where the Father resides in Heaven. Jesus is called "the lamb who was slain before the foundation of the world" as we've previously seen; and certainly it was because His sacrifice was sure to happen and known in His own omniscience that Old Testament believers could be reserved for salvation. But before the actual death of Christ, the covering for sin was only a sure promise for the future. Until the ultimate sacrifice actually occurred in the course of time, believing sinners could not literally "put on Christ" and have their sinfulness covered from God the Father. This is why believing individuals such as Job asked God to hide them in Sheol (hell) until His wrath was past. We'll look at that verse shortly.

Furthermore, Jesus confirms that none had ascended to heaven yet in John 3:13 where he says that only the Son of Man has ascended to heaven.

> "No one has ascended into heaven except he who descended from heaven, the Son of Man." (ESV)

I've read where people try to claim that this is not what Jesus literally meant here, and they reference Enoch and Elijah as examples of people who went to heaven upon their disappearance. It's true that neither of these died a normal human death. But it's also true that they did not go to heaven before Jesus died on the cross. Let's examine these.

While a few versions of the Bible, in Hebrews 11:5, say that Enoch went to heaven, the Greek text doesn't actually say that, but only indicates that he was translated in such a way that even his flesh did not see death, and most believe this was done as a singular example and foreshadowing of the future bodily rapture of Christians, and this thinking is probably correct. In Hebrews chapter 11, commonly called the "hall of faith," Enoch is mentioned in a long list of people who were justified by faith before God. But then the writer of Hebrews concludes that none of these (which would include Enoch) had yet attained the promise, as though they would be perfected before Christ's death (Hebrews 11:39,40).

As far as Elijah being taken up in a whirlwind into heaven (2 Kings 2:1), this does not mean he went into the presence of the Father. Even in the story of Lazarus and the rich man that we looked at, Lazarus is said to have been carried away by the angels. But he was carried to a place of comfort commonly called Abraham's Bosom by the Jews. He did not ascend to the presence of God the Father. Nor was He yet with the Lord Jesus. Jesus was the One telling the story, and He had not died on the cross or created that access to heaven yet. And concerning Elijah being seen going "into heaven," the Hebrew word being translated as "heaven" is *shameh*, and it can mean where the Father resides or simply "the sky."

The first time the word appears in Scripture is during Creation when God creates "the *shameh* and the earth," and then a few verses later we are told that it is the firmament that God named the *shameh* . It appears that generally in the Bible this word is used to describe the physical first heavens — the sky. And it was in fact the physical heavens that Elisha witnessed Elijah going up into, not that he saw him enter the presence of God in the third Heaven. What God did with Elijah's and Enoch's bodies, I couldn't say. But we cannot deny that Jesus said that the only one who has ascended into heaven was the one who had descended *from* heaven, meaning Himself. And we can't deny that prior to Jesus's death, the veil was still whole in the temple, symbolically denying Heavenly access to any sinner, even God's prophet who is as much a sinner as anyone else. All of this is enough evidence for me to believe that neither Elijah nor Enoch entered the eternal heaven, or what Paul called the third heaven, until after Jesus opened access to it through His death.

Let's now look at why we can say that even faithful believing people went to Hell (Sheol/Hades) in the Old Testament. Job talks about going to Hell, and David does too. This is Job speaking:

> Job 14:11-14 "11 As the waters fail from the sea, and the river wastes and dries up, 12 so man lies down and doesn't rise. Until the heavens are no more, they shall not awake, nor be roused out of their sleep. 13 "Oh that you would hide me in Sheol, that you would keep me secret, until your wrath is past, that you would appoint me a set time, and remember me! 14 If a man dies, shall he live again? All the days of my warfare would I wait, until my release should come." (WEB)

This is an incredible passage. The book of Job is said by scholars to be the first penned book of the Bible, yet Job already has knowledge of several things that are confirmed later in Scripture. First, he knows that Hell (Sheol/Hades) is a place of safety for those who know God. And notice how verse 13 was translated in the 1889 *Darby Bible*:

"Who will grant me this, that thou mayst *protect me in hell*, and hide me till thy wrath pass, and appoint me a time when thou wilt remember me?" (italics for emphasis)

Hidden and protected in Hell until wrath is over. That's not a concept you'll hear taught often today. It nevertheless is exactly what happened prior to Christ's sacrifice. Second, he knows that there is a day of renewal coming for those in Hell who know God. And third, he is aware that his renewal will come after God's wrath occurs. But while it appears that Job believed that his renewal would not come until God's final wrath against sin happened, with that being the destruction of the heavens and the earth (v.12), we have a fuller revelation than he did at the time, and we know that His wrath toward sinners of faith was ended when Jesus took our punishment on the cross.

Job understood that this present heavens was temporary and would be destroyed. But Scripture actually teaches that the bodily resurrection of the saved happens *before* the millennial reign of Christ on earth, whereas the destruction of this present heavens and earth will occur *after* the millennium, but Job didn't have the full picture of end times events yet. It's still incredible that he had as much understanding as he did. This destruction of the heavens that Job speaks of is referred to in 2 Peter 3:7 where we read, "But the present heavens and the present earth are, by the command of the same God, kept stored up, reserved for fire in preparation for a day of judgment and of destruction for the ungodly." And we also see the resurrection and the destruction referenced in the book of Revelation.

Let's look at what David said about Hell. When he, the man after God's own heart, said that the Lord's presence would be with him in Hell (Psalm 139:8), he did not mean a Hell of Judgment, if by some chance he failed in faith and ended up in a tormenting Hell. David knew he was saved, and that even in Hell (Sheol), the Lord's presence would be with him, just as it always had been. Just like Job, he knew that he would be safe in Hell, comforted by the Lord.

"If I ascend into heaven, thou art there: if I descend into hell, thou art present." (1899 *Douay-Rheims Bible*)

It almost seems as if he's implying consciousness while in that intermediate state. The word *Sheol* is used in at least two different ways in the Psalms, and one can usually tell from context or surrounding language which one is intended. Sometimes it is used to simply refer to death itself or the grave, and it is often translated "grave." But at least three times it is referring to the place of departed souls and Psalm 139 is one of them. But there are two reasons I don't believe the psalmist is referring to a negative place of judgment. One, he knows God and is not in fear of eternal judgment. After all, it is his very faith in God's protection of him that is pleasing to God. Two, there are at least two other passages from the Psalms that speak of redemption from Sheol (Hell).

Psalm 49:16 (Sons of Korah) "But God will redeem (ransom) my soul from the hand of hell, when he shall receive me." (1889 *Darby Bible*) [Notice it reads, "his soul," not just a body in the grave. This has the same tone as some of Job's sayings.]

Psalm 86:13 (from David) "For thy mercy is great towards me: and thou hast delivered my soul out of the lower hell." (1899 *Douay-Rheims Bible*)

He's likely speaking of what God would one day do in the future. Some view this differently and believe this means that he is "delivered" in the sense of not having to go there, but it says "out of," and the Psalm 49:16 reference above says "ransom my soul *from* the hand of hell." We could compare this to Paul saying that nothing could take us out of the hand of God, whereas we see here that it is possible for God to take someone out of the "hand" of Hell, but the implication is that one must first be in the hand in order to be taken out of it. It doesn't seem we could support that David feared God's judgment after this life. He seems to always be praising God for His salvation.

We also couldn't support that anyone ascended to heaven before Christ's death. Jesus plainly said that none had done this. And the Old Testament Holy of Holies atonement practice confirms it, representing that prior to Christ death, there was blocked access to God, and this foreshadowing practice was not fulfilled until the crucifixion of Christ, when He, as our high priest entered once for all into the true Holy of Holies (Hebrews 9:12).

Even though believing individuals were protected in Hell, going there was still part of the process of death, and not God's ultimate best, in comparison to what would one day be available for believers after the sacrifice of Christ. We already looked at where Paul said to be absent from the body was to be present with the Lord. Let's now look at where Christ essentially claimed the same thing. In Matthew 16:18 Jesus said that he would build His church and the gates of Hell would not prevail against it. I often hear this preached as if it is simply a statement of victory, indicating that believers will not be condemned, generally. And certainly it is a statement of victory. But it's more specific.

Jesus didn't say "the gates of Gehenna," and He didn't say "No believer will ever be cast into the Lake of Fire" (although that's true). Rather he said, "The gates of Hades will not prevail against" his Church. We looked at how prior to Christ's death even the saved went to Hades. This provides the grounds for understanding the significance of the statement. If we never differentiate between the words that Jesus used that are being translated as "hell," then we'll probably miss this, but when Jesus said this, He was speaking to Jews who knew that even faithful believers such as David and Job and all others were being taken to Hades, even though they had a hope for renewal.

We see the same thinking in the New Testament. In John 11:21-25 Jesus's friend Martha acknowledged that she believed in a renewal from death, but that it would be at "the resurrection." But remember what Jesus told her: "I am the resurrection." So His death and resurrection are going to change the process of death. In Matthew 16:18 Jesus was probably literally saying that when believers lose their physical lives now, they will literally no longer pass through the gates of Hades.

Death has lost its sting, as Paul said, quoting an Old Testament reference. And it's reasonable to believe that the souls of those who had believed in the one true God prior to Christ would likewise no longer be held in by the gates of Hades. Consider Matthew 27:52-53 which states that when Jesus was resurrected "the tombs were opened, and many bodies of the saints who had fallen asleep were raised. And coming forth out of the tombs after His resurrection, they entered into the holy city and were revealed to many." (LITV)

This is where there's some room for disagreement. Did *all* believing souls resurrect and come out or did only some? Did some souls stay in Hades? We don't know for sure, but I personally believe that all believing souls left Hades/Sheol and went to be with the Lord from then on, but that only some of those souls were raised bodily to appear to others as a sign and evidence of what had just happened, that death had truly been conquered. Please note that I'm not claiming that leaving Hades and going to be with the Lord implies that they are now conscious somewhere from that point forward.   As I've indicated throughout, that's a gray area, and both consciousness and unconscious sleep seem to be possible during the time before final resurrection to life. But whatever state they're in, conscious or unconscious, the souls of the faithful saved seem to have been vacated from Sheol at the time of Christ's death and going forward, and when believers die now, we don't go to Sheol/Hades.

Yes, death has clearly changed now, for believers.   Paul confirms this when he said that it would be better for him to die and be with Christ (Philippians 1:23). No longer will the gates of Hades prevail over the faithful, but their souls will now go directly, in some form, into the presence of the Lord. Jesus seems to confirm this idea that now the saved will have direct access to Heaven rather than waiting in comfort in Hades when in Matthew 16:19 He says that He now gives the "keys to Heaven" to His church. No Old Testament believer was ever told that they would be given the keys to Heaven. So this was far more than just a statement that believers would not be condemned. It was another confirmation that those saved prior to His resurrection were subject to Hades, but now they aren't. And it's another confirmation that Hades and Gehenna are very different ideas in Scripture. Had the Lord said "gates of Gehenna," then we could assume that he was in fact only saying that believers would not be condemned, but that's not the language He used. But while no other believers who die after Christ's resurrection will go to Hades, He in fact did. We see this in this passage:

> Acts 2:31-32 "He (David) seeing this before spake of the resurrection of Christ, that his soul was not left in hell, neither his flesh did see corruption. This Jesus hath God raised up, whereof we all are witnesses." (KJV)

Verse 31 makes a distinction between His soul, and His flesh. And while the flesh was in a tomb for three days, it was the soul that went into Hell (Hades/Sheol) where even saved people were at that time (in Abraham's Bosom (a Hebraism for paradise), according to Jesus in Luke 16).

Hell/Gehenna

We've touched on this already, so we'll only briefly review while we're addressing various words that unfortunately are all translated into the English word "Hell." Hell (Gehenna) is a completely different concept from Hell (Sheol/Hades). Gehenna is a transliteration of "Valley of Hinnom," a valley just outside of Jerusalem that it is said served as a trash dump where fires were kept burning to consume their waste, and even sometimes dead bodies of people and animals. So when Jesus spoke of the detriment of being cast into Hell (Gehenna), given all of the massive amounts of language about the ultimate destruction of the wicked elsewhere in the Bible, it seems clear that He was using Gehenna figuratively to warn of full destruction/eternal death, not eternal conscious torment. What was cast into the Valley of Hinnom burned up, and the people Jesus was speaking to understood the object lesson, I'm sure. And to any familiar with the prophet Jeremiah, the valley of Hinnom had a further connection with death and destruction because it had been the place where disobedient Jews had built high places and offered their own children as sacrifices to the false god Molech (Jeremiah 32:35).

We looked at the word "eternal" (in Greek, *aionios*) and how it can mean permanent, or causing a permanent condition. This is Gehenna, the eternal fire, the second death, causing the permanent condition of extinction of soul from which there is no return.

David said in Psalm 37:20 that the wicked "consume away like smoke," and as we've already seen, there is good evidence from surrounding verses that he was speaking of eternal judgment and not something that would only happen bodily to the enemies of the Lord. But even if he was speaking of earthly demise only, the foreshadowing is significant. There are numerous other references to the total destruction of the wicked in the Old Testament, and I think all of it prefigures what ultimately happens to souls after they are judged as well. And God is often referred to as a consuming fire in the Bible. We've listed most of these earlier in previous chapters but here are just a few verses that indicate full destruction for the unbelieving:

> "'For, behold, the day comes, it burns as a furnace; and all the proud, and all who work wickedness, will be stubble; and the day that comes will burn them up,' says Yahweh of Armies, 'that it shall leave them neither root nor branch...'" (Malachi 4:1) (WEB)

> "As wax melts before the fire, so let the wicked perish at the presence of God." (Psalm 68:2,) (WEB)

> "For yet a little while, and the wicked will be no more." (Psalm 37:10) (WEB)

> "But the wicked will perish; the enemies of the LORD are like the glory of the pastures; they vanish—like smoke they vanish away." (Psalm 37:20) (ESV)

> "How suddenly are they destroyed, perished and horribly consumed" (Psalm 73:19) (*Geneva Bible* 1587)

"But transgressors shall be altogether destroyed; the future of the wicked shall be cut off." (Psalm 37:38) (ESV)

"...He will burn up the chaff with unquenchable fire" (Matthew 3:12) (LITV)

"For God so loved the world, that he gave his only Son, that whoever believes in him should not perish (*apolummi* – be fully destroyed) but have eternal life." (John 3:16) (ESV)

And do any of these verses sound like a prediction of an eternity of conscious torment? This is the consistent theme of how the Lord ultimately deals with the faithless, and what will happen to His enemies. There is never even so much as a foreshadowing of endless torment for God's enemies, much less does the Lord or any inspired writer ever come right out and state such a thing.

Finally, straight from Jesus's mouth: "And fear not them which kill the body, but are not able to kill the soul: but rather fear him which is able to destroy both soul and body in Hell (Gehenna)." (Matthew 10:28) (KJV) We looked at it a number of times, but it's so important to not ignore what the meanings of the original words of Scripture are. The Greek word being translated as "destroy" here is *apollumi*, and it means "destroy completely" according to Greek lexicons. It also looks a lot like the English word "abolish," and has essentially the meaning. *Apollumi* is also used in John 3:16 and translated as "perish." Traditionalists claim that this destruction doesn't really mean full destruction but that we are indestructible, able to endure the wrath of God for all eternity, and that we will never truly perish either. But this is never taught in the Bible. And you'll also notice when you study it, concerning the use of Hades and Gehenna, Hell (Hades) is the only one ever mentioned in conjunction with human torment; And Hell (Gehenna) is always used in conjunction with either death or destruction. Hades and Gehenna are clearly two different concepts.

And further, if Hades were full of literal fire and torment as is often claimed, and if the Lake of Fire is also full of literal fire and torment, as is also often claimed, what then is the purpose of raising those in Hades up for judgment, only to then cast them into another Hell virtually identical to what they were already in? It really makes no sense at all. It not only lines up with what Scripture teaches, but it makes far more sense to understand that Hades and Gehenna accomplish two very different things in the process of God's judgment. One is a holding place, once a holding place for all souls, and now a "death row" for those who've rejected salvation, and the other is the place of destruction, a place where the sentence is carried out, the second death, as the Bible calls it.

To recap, there's substantial evidence that at the very least, there's some period of consciousness after physical death and before final judgment. But does this imply that all the verses about those who "sleep in the dust," "sleep with their ancestors," or "sleep in Christ" mean nothing, or at least mean something far different than what they appear to mean? I don't find it hard to believe that after a period of consciousness, the Lord may then lay souls into a sleep until resurrection. And I mean this for the lost as well as for the saved. Let me be clear. I don't find in Scripture any passage that singly comes right out and makes this claim, but with so many good arguments on both sides, isn't it more likely that both happen — that sleep as well as consciousness are possible during the intermediate state? It's certainly not unbiblical or heretical to believe in this possibility, with so much evidence on both sides of the matter. However, I'm not claiming this theory is flawless, but only that it's a valid possibility.

Regarding the lost, it seems the potential for the torment of the immediate afterlife, however long or short it is, is one more of the deterrents to unbelief which God has put in place. He doesn't desire anyone to perish, so He takes various measures throughout our lives to drive us to Him, and the possibility of a conscious time of regret and torment in Hades after death is just one more measure. But does the Bible claim this torment lasts until resurrection for final judgment? If it does, I haven't found that verse. I couldn't tell you how long God lets the time of torment go on. Maybe it's different for every lost soul. Or perhaps it does in fact go on until judgment day. But let's not forget that our God is Merciful. And He's sovereign. He's not obligated to shorten suffering for anyone. But consider this. After a lost person has died physically, their ultimate fate is decided, even though eternity has not yet begun until the end of time after Jesus's 1000-year reign on earth. So if the promise of torment in Hades was not enough to deter one from unbelief, then after death, there's no possibility of rehabilitation, and just as I don't believe the Lord desires or requires the eternal torment of the lost, I personally no more believe that He desires or requires thousands of years of suffering while waiting for judgment. Is it possible that He does? It's possible. But given His merciful nature as revealed in Scripture, and given the verses that speak of sleeping after death, a deep soul sleep following temporary torment in Hades seems more likely. This is my personal opinion after studying it out, but not anything I'd state as fact.

Regarding believers, I'll concede to the arguments of more scholarly Christians than myself such as William Tyndale who asked (and I'm paraphrasing), "What then is the great reward and expectation of resurrection if we have already been existing with the Lord?"[47] It's hard to argue with this. Paul speaks a great deal about the hope of resurrection, but if we have died physically and been intimately united with Jesus for say hundreds of years, what's so grand about resurrection? If however, there is a brief time of consciousness, perhaps even some glimpsing of the Glory of God, or at least, the comfort of knowing we have persevered, have put our faith in the right God, and will, after an unconscious sleep, be with our Lord forever, then resurrection still holds all of the intrigue that it should. Maybe it's like Christmas Eve for a child. We have to go to sleep so when we wake up, we can receive our gifts.

This is Not Universalism

Sometimes all doctrinal concepts that stand against a mainline tradition can be carelessly lumped together. Conditionalism and Universalism both portray God as far more merciful than tradition would have us believe. But make no mistake — This is not Universalism that I'm putting forward in this book. But could the universalists be correct? It's highly doubtful. It far over-stretches what logically works with many scriptures and themes in Scripture. But the truth is, it's at least remotely possible, at least some versions of it, so we'll take a look at it. What I'm calling "Universalism" goes by different names such as Universal Salvation, Universal Reconciliation, and Christian Universalism (CU), among others. I'm referring to those who would consider themselves Christians, but who believe that ultimately *all* mankind will be saved and live eternally with their Maker, even those who rejected Christ in this life, rather than there being a judgment which would result in either eternal torment (the traditional view), or eternal death and loss of being (the non-traditional view I hold and promote).

This wasn't a topic I initially planned on addressing in this book – not more than a brief mention anyway, even after reading Rob Bell's *Love Wins* that promoted a version of the doctrine several years ago. I didn't think his arguments warranted much of a response. But a couple years after I read Bell's book, I came across another Universalism-promoting book by Julie Ferwerda entitled *Raising Hell.* And it was such a well-written and well thought out attempt, that if I had not already researched this subject extensively, I might have jumped on the bandwagon with her myself, being a person seeking an alternative to the traditional view of judgment, and one certainly hoping to find a more merciful God than what tradition has given us. However, at the end of the day, I find that she didn't address many Scriptures that would negate her claims. And I think she stretched too far in other places, such as suggesting that there's really no concept of eternity in Scripture, at least not in relation to judgment.

Although Universalism isn't new, and while some of what I'll address in this brief chapter will be the general teachings of this doctrine, I'll focus as much on some of Ferwerda's specific positions, since hers is the most recent work I've read on the matter, and one that I'm concerned could sway many people. I don't know Ferwerda personally, and I've only read one of her books. But based on what I'm reading, my belief is that she's probably a saved Christian who believes that it's only by Christ's death and resurrection that any can be saved. I don't believe she's a heretic, at least not in the sense of being a person setting out to intentionally destroy the work or Word of God. Nevertheless, I believe she's wrong in her ultimate conclusion that everyone will eventually be saved from eternal judgment, however you want to define it.

There's a theme that runs through the entire Bible, and it's the necessity of faith. It's what God grants in some measure to all, and it's what He requires the exercise of in order to be made right with Him. There is no thematic evidence in Scripture that all people will be saved. Just the opposite. Jesus said that most would go down the broad road that leads to destruction, and watching the faithless and rebellious go down, is something one can do in almost every book of the Bible.

There are a handful of verses that, if not considered in light of all Scripture, and if taken out of the context they were given in, can be surface-interpreted to mean that all people will ultimately be saved. And these verses, combined with a strong desire to reject the unmerciful traditional view of a God who would torment billions of souls for all eternity, are the basis for

Universalism. But just as the traditional doctrine of eternal suffering is based on too little Scripture, and those verses taken out of context or misunderstood, so too is the other extreme, represented by the doctrine of Universal Salvation. If we would accept that God is merciful in that His grace extends to all, and in that those who reject it will not be saved, but at the same time will not be made to suffer into eternity, we wouldn't need to hyper-extend into a doctrine which negates God's requirement of faith for salvation.

Most likely the truth on judgment is somewhere in the middle ground. It's in between those who believe that a loving God can bring billions into existence, with the full foreknowledge that they would reject Him, with that rejection resulting in an eternity of suffering in a literal or non-literal lake of fire, and then those who believe God would still save those who rejected Him in faithlessness and instead loved this world. God is merciful, yes. But it is only by faith that we can please Him according to Scripture. Does this mean He won't save some that don't please Him? Arguments can, have, and will be made for the potential salvation of some who didn't know better, and who never received a full revelation of Christ. And there definitely seems to be a theme in Scripture that personal responsibility is in proportion to personal revelation, but that goes beyond what I want to address here. I'll touch on it briefly at the end of the chapter. But for those who outright reject the revelation that God gives them...Will they be saved? I think we would find little evidence for this, and much evidence that those who reject God will in turn be rejected.

What we'll do in this chapter is first see why the universalist doctrine *almost* works. We'll take a look at some of the proof texts that universalists are relying on. Then we'll see where it breaks down. Sometimes we'll be looking at things Ferwerda specifically stated, since she, in my opinion, has made the best modern attempt at defending Universalism. But may I give a challenge to universalists to consider? If you're a universalist, and are 100% convinced you are right, then go with your heart, I suppose. But if you believe there's even a small chance you're wrong, can you see how potentially dangerous it is to tell people that all souls will be saved one day, no matter the decisions they make in regard to the Lord? Wouldn't many who are feeling the pull of God on their hearts more likely take the path of least resistance and remain in unbelief if they've been made to believe there are no permanent consequences for faithlessness?

Julie Ferwerda begins her defense of Universal Salvation by analysis of three parables in Luke chapter 15 which she considers to be a series.[48] They are the parables of the lost sheep, the lost coin, and the prodigal son. If I understand her correctly, she maintains that the fact that the sheep couldn't "find" itself, but that the shepherd went looking for it is evidence that all mankind will be saved — same for the lost coin. And she sees the father's waiting and watching, even while the prodigal was in rebellion, as evidence of the same. I love these parables, but simply can't come away with the same conclusion. A shepherd looking for the lost one is a picture of what God does. He seeks the lost. And Jesus said that those who are His will know His voice. This implies that a person who would be saved is looking and listening for their Shepherd. And the prodigal came to the end of himself, and repented. He had to take this action in order to be restored. Ferwerda seems to see the prodigal as representing one who went into judgment after this life, but then saw the error of his ways, and essentially "left Hell," so to speak. The traditional view of Hell and universal immortality is partially to blame here. The widely accepted traditional idea that a human soul is able to survive the second death in the Lake of Fire is the foundation for the universalist error that one could then exit such a judgment, and by their own will. And indeed Ferwerda believes there is some form of judgment after this life but that a soul can repent and confess and be saved from it. Sounds very Purgatory-like to me.

These parables were a response to some Pharisees and scribes griping that Jesus receives and eats with "sinners." In the middle of telling these parables, Jesus stated that there is more rejoicing in heaven over one sinner who repents than over many who need no repentance. It seems that He was condemning the pharisees, in their arrogance, not seeing themselves as needy. And it also seems that he was or had recently been in the act of "eating with sinners," the very thing that prompted the parables, and so Jesus was doing what the parables teach. He was seeking the lost. And people were in turn repenting and following him – now – in *this* life. There doesn't seem to be any evidence that this is about something that can happen after this first earthly life. And the best evidence may be Jesus's very statement about the rejoicing in heaven over those who realize their need, because he contrasts these with those who don't see themselves as needing salvation. Who, in the Lake of Fire, (were it possible to survive it) would not see their need to then repent? It just doesn't work. These parables are not about exiting final judgment to enter eternity. They're about God seeking us out to save us *from* final judgment in the first place.

Next, after personal testimony on how she left her traditional belief in Hell, Ferwerda began, somewhat flippantly it seemed, naming all of the classes or types of people who are going to end up in Hell, if the place truly exists, and if Scripture is to be interpreted literally,[49] as if Scripture doesn't maintain salvation is offered to all, of any class and type. And I sense that she is using this growing number of peoples as an evidence that this simply couldn't be, at least not if their end will be eternal torment. But concerning the sheer numbers of those who will face final judgment, is this not exactly what Jesus predicted when He said that wide is the gate and broad the road that leads to destruction and many there will be who take that path? She names off the wise and learned, the Jews, the Gentiles, the Calvinists, the Armenians, among others. Even just naming the Jews and Gentiles essentially included everyone. As I've made clear throughout this volume, I of course reject the doctrine of eternal conscious torment. But I completely accept Scripture's statement on final punishment, in that it ends with destruction. And what she seems unable to accept (the idea that such a large majority are headed for final judgment) is exactly what Jesus said. The road is broad and the gate wide that leads to destruction, and many are going down that road. And He went on to state that few are on the narrow path that leads to life.

Rob Bell, Julie Ferwerda, and many other universalist writers and teachers do not deny that there is some time of judgment for those who rejected God in this life. This is one reason why I say their doctrine *almost* works. In *Love Wins* Bell seems to imply that those in Hell can at any time confess Christ and be taken out of judgment. It's up to them — our human freedom is not stifled (except temporarily) by being cast into Hell.

Universalist Proof Texts

In John 12:32 Jesus said that when He would be lifted up, He would draw all men to Himself. And universalists go on to point out that the Greek word being translated as "draw" in this verse can actually mean "drag." They use this as evidence to demonstrate that He will pull people "from Hell" at some point. If God is not trying to grow a family of faithful followers who love Him, as Scripture seems to indicate, but is rather ultimately saving everyone, this leaves me to wonder what the last 2000 years have been about, and why be missional in sharing the gospel? And why choose God in this life? Ferwerda makes attempts at demonstrating that these still have value, but I remain unconvinced. If our choices in faith or faithlessness have no ultimate consequences regarding whether we gain eternal life or not, then I don't see the point. Even a lengthy earthly life in pain, or lengthy time of trial and testing after this life are less than nothing compared to timeless eternity.

Ultimately, this life, our decisions for or against God, and anything of lesser importance are of no ultimate consequence and have no bearing whatsoever on our eternal state, if the universalist doctrine is correct. If Christ's being lifted up (which was a reference to His death on the cross) was the thing that literally saved/dragged every soul to Him, and if with Him is where we'll be for all eternity, regardless of our actions, thoughts, and pursuits now, our ministries, etc., then just what are we doing? Nothing of any ultimate value, I would think.

Back in Chapter Five I mentioned Robert Jeffress's thought that if Hell isn't eternal torment, it takes some of the urgency out of witnessing. Best I could tell, he was stating this as an argument against Conditionalism, not Universalism. While that logic doesn't apply well in relation to conditionalist ideas, since the consequences for faithlessness are still quite dire in the conditionalist model, it actually applies very well to Universalism. What exactly is the point of witnessing to anyone, if all will be saved regardless? And according to some universalists who still believe there is a place of burning torment, they maintain that those who go there don't have to be there any longer than they want to be. After physical death, when the faithless ones find themselves in a raging inferno, all they have to do is humbly admit they were wrong to not believe, and they're free to go. If that were how it works, I'd say most would stay there about .1 seconds, and that would then lead me to the question: Why create that place? But that's not what Scripture teaches. There would not be the call to faith throughout Scripture if it were not critically important, and if all wrongs of faithlessness were correctable after this life.

It's far more likely that the verse is making it clear that salvation would be *available* to "all men," and that the Holy Spirit, the Spirit of truth would be working on the hearts of "all men," pushing, pulling, dragging, whatever it takes. The Lord isn't willing that any should perish, and therefore He has gone to monumental lengths to demonstrate His love toward us. But that level of His will is over-ridden by the requirement of placing faith in Him to be saved. Again, to take it as the universalists do would negate hundreds of verses, and actually make all forms of ministry, outreach, or any attempts at living for Christ of no ultimate value, if everyone's end is the same, regardless of how we believed or lived in this life.

Scripture tells us that God isn't willing that any should perish. Universalists go on to claim that God's will cannot be thwarted, so, it is reasoned that ultimately none must perish. But it is clear from Scripture, that "God's will" is often thwarted, leaving mankind in detrimental circumstances. God can "will" that Cain do right and be accepted. But when Cain followed up his first disobedience with the murder of his brother, God can (and did) banish him from his presence. This doesn't mean that he wanted him to kill Abel. God can "will" that mankind spread out over the whole earth, but when we congregated to build the tower of Babel, God can (and did) come down and confuse languages so that we were forced to spread out. I could literally go on and on with examples of God's will thwarted. So God can certainly be willing that none perish, and so make a provision in Christ by which we will not perish, yet when we reject the provision, there are dire consequences.

God has an ultimate will to save all those, and only those, who will place their faith in Him. He is building a family of faith. This ultimate will overrides his general will that none perish. Jesus did *not* say that one day he would tell some who mistakenly believed they had been doing His work: "Depart from me, I never knew you...oh, but hey, I'll catch up with you on the other side of your correction in the Lake of Fire." No, that last part isn't actually in Scripture.

In her book, Ferwerda creates a typical conversation between her and an orthodox Christian[50] where she "wins" the argument by ultimately quoting James 2:13 which states that "Mercy triumphs over judgment." This is a great example of how universalists, like traditionalist Christians (as relates to eternal conscious suffering), pluck verses out of context and use them as proof texts to back their views. She didn't mention the previous sentence in the verse that stated that judgment would be harsh for those not showing mercy. And apparently she fails to see in the following verse that James is ultimately teaching on faith, and that faith without works is dead. Why is teaching on faith so important if faith in this life isn't even necessary for eternal salvation? Compared to eternity, time-wise, this life is less than a grain of sand in comparison to every beach on earth. Why are James, and God (through James) and so many writers of Scripture spending all this time on the matter of faith? Because it is of eternal importance. Those who prevail in faith are those who will spend eternity with God.

Let's look at another text that Ferwerda believes states that salvation will be given to all. It's Acts 17:30-31.

> "Truly, then, God overlooking the times of ignorance, now strictly commands all men everywhere to repent, because He set a day in which "He is going to judge the habitable world in righteousness," by a Man whom He appointed; having given proof to all *by* raising Him from *the* dead." (LITV)

She claims that the Greek word *pistis* that's being translated as "proof" is a mistranslation.[51] *Strong's* concordance gives several ways to translate it, such as "persuasion," "moral conviction," etc. And the King James version translates it as "assurance." Ferwerda points out that the word *pistis* is often translated as "faith" and "belief" in other places where it's used, but she doesn't seem to recognize the context and statement of this verse. It blatantly states that God "strictly commands all men everywhere to repent" because He "is going to judge the habitable world." Why the strong warning to repent, if the actual point of the verse is to give assurance that everyone is going to be saved? It just doesn't work. The last part of verse 31 is stating that it is the raising of Christ from the dead that gives us the "grounds for" faith and belief – the "assurance" that the promises of God are real and true. But His resurrection doesn't automatically save everyone. Only those who act in faith on the "persuasion" that His resurrection was in fact substitutionary on our parts for saving us from the penalty for sin.

Ferwerda believes there's a verse in the Old Testament book of Daniel that prefigured a false teaching about Hell. I found this to be one of the more odd arguments in her book. You may be familiar with the story of Shadrach, Meshach, and Abed-nego. These were three Jewish young men who were exiled to Babylon during one of Israel's rebellions, yet they remained faithful to God, refusing to bow down to the image that Nebuchadnezzar had erected. Because of this refusal, they were cast into the fiery furnace that had been heated up seven times hotter than normal, just for them. But they were unharmed. Ferwerda seems to believe that these men in a fire, yet not being burned by it, is a metaphorical prophecy that one day there would be a false doctrine about Hell, but just as these men were unharmed, so will any who might have been in danger of Hell, by traditional standards, be ultimately unharmed...since it's not even real.

This is an odd take on Hell because these three Jews were faithful to God and not even in danger of His judgment. Ferwerda using these as a foreshadowing that no one will ultimately be in danger of fiery judgment is to ignore the very thing that set them apart to begin with — their faithfulness to God. The claim of Scripture is that the faithful will be saved from the second death that happens when the lost are cast into the Lake of Fire, and if anything was foreshadowed here it's the salvation and survival of these three men *because of* their faith. Notable too is that Ferwerda attempts to disregard the fact that the men who cast Shadrach, Meshach, and Abed-nego into the fire were themselves killed while doing it because the fire was so hot. Her method for avoiding this was to include a footnote claiming that the captors' death is not in the Septuagint version. But the Septuagint is a Greek translation of the original Hebrew Scriptures. If those who translated it left something out, that's no evidence that it didn't happen. It was still in the original Hebrew.

Ferwerda voices her concerns about the Lake of Fire being interpreted as something literal, when so much of the book of Revelation is figurative. Her point is fair enough. But with the likely correlation between the Lake of Fire and what Jesus called the "eternal fire, prepared for the devil and his angels," to me it sounds like this is a real thing that has been or will be literally prepared. And even if it isn't, the Bible states what it is. It is the second death. The first death is the death of the body, and the second is that of the whole person: the soul and whatever manifestation of body that God gives to stand judgment in. And whether the Lake of Fire is a literal lake of fire, or is symbolic for something beyond our comprehension, perhaps something extra-dimensional even, it doesn't matter.

What matters is that it is stated to be the place and/or process of final death and destruction. And while I reject the traditional notion that it's a place where the lost will be able to exist and suffer for eternity, I can't deny that it's real in some form, and appears to be much more than some sort of correctional or refining fire. And yes, there are those sorts of terms in Scripture, and we Christians are told that we will endure "fiery darts" and "fiery trials," and certainly, these are not literally fiery darts (although some Christian martyrs of other ages did literally endure fiery trials). Ferwerda makes much of the fact that fire in Scripture can be for purifying and refining. But I'm just gonna put it in kindergarten language: Fire burns stuff up. We know this from experience, and from Scripture, such as Sodom and Gomorrah being destroyed by fire, and this being said to be a foreshadowing of the final end of the lost. Fire is God's means of destroying those who reject him. Consider John 5:24. Jesus says:

> "I tell you the truth, whoever hears my word and believes him who sent me *has eternal life* and *will not* be condemned; he *has* crossed over from death to life." (italics for emphasis — ESV)

The logical conclusion is that if one will *not* hear His word and believe, they will *not* gain eternal life, they will be condemned, and they will *not* cross over, but rather stay on a course with death.

Jesus said that blaspheming the Holy Spirit would not be forgivable. What do universalists do with this unpardonable sin? Do they simply say "Well, unforgivable at the time of judgment, but of course, later, all will be overlooked"? I just don't see it. Furthermore, If Christ's suffering death atoned for the sins of all, regardless of whether active faith is placed in Him, then why do those who are ultimately saved still have to suffer *any* time of judgment, as many universalists believe they will? What's the purpose? Is God saying, "Well, you failed to put your trust in me, and I'm going to save you anyway, even though you denied me in faith. But first you have to go through this punishment"? Seems that either Christ took their punishment or He didn't. They don't both need to suffer. What the Bible teaches instead is that either we're going to suffer the eternal punishment of death, for sins uncovered, or we're accepting Christ's death on the cross as our covering from God's ultimate wrath.

To be fair, there are more verses that universalists believe add to their theory than the ones I've addressed. But I don't want this chapter to turn into a stand-alone book. I hope that answering the sampling I chose demonstrated the issues with trying to bend these verses to mean something they don't. And truthfully, there's not that many more. If there were just hundreds and hundreds of verses like these few that have been used to create the universalist doctrine, and only a handful of other statements that made it sound like judgment was final, then I, and I'm sure most Christians, would accept this as truth. But that's just not the case. And when a handful of verses *can* be surface-interpreted to mean something, but if that something is in direct opposition to too much other Scripture, it needs to be questioned. The same thing applies to the traditional Hell and immortality doctrine. Both are built on too few verses that conflict with the major statement on judgment in Scripture.

Nevertheless, there's a big part of me that hopes I'm wrong and universalists like Ferwerda are correct. It's no problem to me if at the end of all of this, God relents on final judgment and saves us all. But then, I'm not a Holy God with righteous requirements who has stated consistently that it is only by faith that I can be pleased. I'm just a sinner who needs God's grace and mercy. So, what I want is of no consequence. And I'm just never going to get beyond Jesus telling us that there will come a time when He says to many: "Depart from me. I never knew you." God stating that He will send one to "restore all things" is simply not the same thing as Him saying that ultimately he will save every soul He ever created. He so blatantly stated just the opposite in many places as we've already seen.

I wrote this book to demonstrate that God is more merciful than traditional Christianity has led us to believe. I have that one thing in common with the universalists. But they take the concept of a merciful God far beyond what Scripture will allow. Not only does their doctrine deny the permanence of all the warnings of coming judgment, Universalism negates all of the foreshadowing of judgment, such as Noah and his small group of faithful being saved from the destruction that fell on the many, and Lot being saved out of Sodom before destruction fell on it. The Bible is so consistent on this. But it has no significance outside of the events themselves if all are ultimately saved. We know these stories do have significance however because we have two other books of the Bible claiming that the utter annihilation of Sodom and Gomorrah were a picture of what will ultimately happen to unbelievers, and that "as it was in the days of Noah, so will it be at the coming of the Son of Man." It's stated very plainly, and there's never a hint in those passages that there is restoration after this destruction.

Who then can be saved?

The universalist doctrine is tempting to latch onto because, were it true, it would help answer some difficult questions about who can be saved. One question that many have asked is: "What about those who were never reached with the gospel? How can it be fair that they should suffer for all eternity just because God put the great commission in human hands, and then human missions attempts failed those unreached people?" The reader already knows my answer to at least part of that question. No one is going to suffer for all eternity, even those who reject Christ, much less those who never even heard the name. But can these who never received the details of the gospel be saved? The universalist answer is simple: Yes, *everyone* is going to be saved eventually.

My answer is a little more complicated – first, because I'm still not omniscient and can't claim absolute knowledge. But here's a few things to consider: Rahab, the non-Jew, pre-Christ-era harlot made the New Testament list commonly called the "Hall of Faith," found in the eleventh chapter of the book of Hebrews. And she likely knew very little of God, and likely nothing of a promise of a Messiah. She acted in faith on the little she knew, and she is counted among the faithful according to the writer of Hebrews. For that matter, *none* of the Old Testament faithful, Jew or non-Jew, had much of the details of what exactly Christ would one day do. The gospel is called a mystery. Yet many were faithful to what they knew of God, and will be saved.

Further, it's almost universally accepted among Christians that children who have died in the womb, very young children who pass away, and those of any age who die without the mental capacity to grasp the concepts of the gospel and salvation, are going to be saved. And we give those in these categories "a pass" so to speak. And I'm not arguing that we shouldn't. I'm in agreement. But I'm only asking: *Why* are we giving them a pass? Best I can tell, the criteria is that they don't know any better. So how is a person who likewise doesn't know better, any more responsible, simply because they've grown to be an older child or an adult? I know what some readers are thinking – "Age of Accountability." But let's be reasonable. It's knowledge and revelation that makes us accountable...not time and date.

We're responsible to act in faith on what we know of the one true God. The one difference is that an older child, or an adult, even one who hasn't heard the full gospel, has begun getting some revelation of God. I believe that God is always (and always has been) attempting to draw all mankind to Himself. Paul asks in Romans 10:14 how one can believe without a preacher. He goes on to claim in verse 18 that *all* have heard "the preaching" as he makes reference to Psalm 19 which states that the creation itself is the first "preacher" telling us who God is. What's generally taught is that if we respond in faith to the little revelation we have, God will send more revelation, ultimately sending full revelation of Christ, which can be accepted or rejected. Others believe that a response in faith to whatever you know of God will produce salvation. I'm not going to act like I know the absolute answer. But I do believe that one or the other of these is true, because God isn't willing that any should perish. (Does that make twelve times I've said this now? It's still true)

However I don't believe we can put our faith in just anything, and therefore be saved "by faith." When God stated that it is only by faith that we can please Him, I don't think He meant faith, just for the sake of faith. It's been stated often that it takes more "faith" to be an atheist these days, with all of the evidence of a Creator. But God isn't going to save a person who lives and dies as a faithful atheist. Scripture is clear enough on this. So it's not just faith, but faith in what we know of God, the real God...not some false version or concept of God.

I believe God is moving on all people and is making Himself known to everyone, on some level, in a way that if they respond in faith, it will either save them, or bring further revelation which they will be able to respond to in faith and be saved. The only other possibility, if in fact God is not willing that any should perish, is if He truly did look over the "times of ignorance." Something like this is stated a couple of times in Scripture, and there are different interpretations of what it means; some believe that in various times in history God did not reveal Himself, and that the people who weren't exposed to knowledge of God were used by God for a particular role in history. And the thinking would be that this is not their fault, but was God's plan, so we would take the couple of verses in Scripture that seem to say that these will be overlooked, and trust that God knows what He's doing.

Would He save these who had zero knowledge of Him, if in fact anyone has ever existed who had zero knowledge of Him? First, it's difficult to believe that any have existed in this state, with creation screaming that there's a Creator. But ultimately, I've got to admit that His ways are higher than my ways, and I'm just going to trust that He has made a provision whereby any and all can be saved. In the end, my point is this: There are a number of ways to interpret Scripture that don't violate it, yet do not maintain that God is rejecting people who lacked revelation. We don't need to resort to Universalism to be able to handle this question.

If someone grows up in a country that has kept Christianity out, and they are going about the motions of their religion, let's say for instance, a religion that believes in multiple gods, but are then impressed that "this is wrong," and there must only be one God, and they respond to these promptings in the best way they can in their position, it's hard for me to believe that this isn't faith in action, even if a full revelation of Christ isn't available.

By the same token, if a person is involved in that same religion that denies the one true living God of Scripture, and they're being impressed that it's wrong, presumably by the Holy Spirit, yet they reject those promptings to perhaps challenge tradition, etc., and simply continue on, it's impossible for me to believe they'll be saved. But I've gone a little off topic. All of that was just to say that there are ways to understand that God is merciful in our various levels of revelation that we'll receive, depending on where we live, when we live, etc. So the real question is less about how God could save one who appears to have not received the full gospel (With God, all things are possible), but more like "Will God save those who reject the revelation He gives and never seek deeper or repent from faithless living in this life?" And I just don't see the affirmative 'yes' answer to this question in Scripture that the universalists see.

Ultimately, let's not get hung up on questions about "what happens to the aborigine who never got the gospel?" since it's just as likely that none have ever existed that didn't receive at least some revelation of the one true God that they could either respond to in faith and be saved, or respond to in faith, and be granted further revelation that could lead to saving faith. But please do not think I'm negating the importance of outreach and missions. God wants people to know Him as fully as possible in this life. I don't believe He's content with partial revelation. But because the great commission of spreading the gospel to the nations has been given to a bunch of sinners who fail miserably at this most of the time, it's difficult for me to believe that He automatically outright rejects those who do not get the *full* gospel of Christ.

Well, I don't claim authority on this matter of who can be saved. I have some questions of my own. I only went on a little there to demonstrate that there are plenty of ways to be at peace with God on the matter, without resorting to the false conclusion that "God must save everyone, or else He is unjust."

Ferwerda makes much of those from whom God "hid" truth in parables. She seems to imply that if she's wrong about her universalist position and everyone one day being eternally saved, that we have literal proof that Jesus rejoiced that God was sending many to an eternal Hell.[52] My first issue with this is that she juxtaposes all of her positions against what I already believe is a wrong position in the idea of eternal conscious torment, and she completely ignored the conditionalist position except for a single end note that acknowledged that Conditionalism maintains that death is eternal. But secondly, everywhere in Scripture where I see God hardening someone or hiding information from someone, the someone had already hardened themselves to God first, and the hardening has a purpose. It's not random or unmerciful. We saw a great example of that with Pharaoh and the exodus back in Chapter 1.

When it's all said and done, any individual, group, or sect can take Bible verses and turn them to what they believe -- or want to believe. And I've certainly been accused of this over the course of this discovery, and the writing out of this book, and I'm sure more opposition is headed my way. But I'm asking the reader to seek which interpretation is the most biblically linear, the most logical, and most lines up with the nature and character of God, as revealed in Scripture.

The traditionalist can take a handful of verses and turn them to mean that the lost will suffer consciously for all eternity, even though doing so violates many other concepts, forces the redefinition of common terms and ideas, and contorts possibly the most consistent theme in Scripture, painting a picture of a very unmerciful God. The universalists, at the other extreme, have taken another small handful of verses and created a god that would negate all the emphasis on the importance of faith, another theme which is highly important to Scripture, because Universalism would tell us that ultimately it doesn't matter if you demonstrated faith in this life or not — You will be saved, and with the Lord for all eternity. It sounds good, but ultimately it raises more questions than it answers, and it's overly hopeful, beyond what Scripture allows.

The answer is in the middle ground. God is a righteous judge, and at the same time a Merciful Father. His grace extends to all, but His salvation belongs only to those who accept the gift. There are wonderful blessings awaiting those whose faith is in Him. And there is judgment and death awaiting those who reject the moving and prompting of the Holy Spirit on their hearts and minds.

We all have our explanations of the verses that we use to forward our beliefs. But we can't all be correct. Of the traditional, conditional, and universalist takes on this matter of judgment, either none of us are correct, or one of us is correct. At least two of us are wrong. But if asking "Why do I believe what I believe?" is an important question, and it is, then the answer to that question being sound and solid is even more important. And I don't find the traditionalist or universalist defenses of their positions sound and solid. Let's rather ask, "Does why I believe what I believe make the most Scriptural sense, in light of all the evidence?"

In *Raising Hell*, Ferwerda recounts the story of a man named Kent whose family was murdered, but who felt strongly that God was telling him to forgive.[53] Ferwerda is using this as evidence that God wouldn't ask us to do something that He doesn't also do (forgive one that didn't ask for forgiveness). She seems to ignore that this prompting of God could more likely have been to demonstrate God's love so that the murderer would come to faith in Him (because coming by faith to God happens to be of critical importance in this life, as Scripture makes clear), and she only sees it as something that proves her points.

Universalist proponents, and Julie Ferwerda is no exception, have a very one-sided way of viewing things. They see all people as "God's children" when clearly the Bible states that we all begin as enemies of God, capable of being adopted as sons and daughters of the King through faith. She however believes that we as parents, who love our children unconditionally, are the ultimate evidence that God will not destroy those who reject Him. The way I'd view it, I can love a rebellious child all I want, but if they've left me and will not return, we don't have a relationship...end of story.

And I can't state fervently enough that the Bible makes it clear that we are counted as righteous, only by faith in God. This is where the comparison between us as parents, and God as the "parent" of all people sort of breaks down. We don't require "faith" in us (at least not in any sense like God requires) to have a relationship with us. We're not "blood relatives" until we've put ourselves under the blood of Christ. All people are not God's children.

As earthly parents, we are a dim likeness of the heavenly father. We just can't metaphorically equate every aspect of our parenthood directly with God's Fatherhood and come to the conclusion that because we are commanded to love our children, and all people for that matter, God will not ultimately reject those who reject Him. It just doesn't work. And her theory that no loving parent would ever let their child go doesn't match up with reality.

I wouldn't be shocked to find out many universalists are "Calvinist rejects." Or it might be more correctly stated that they are those who for their soul's sake, were forced to reject Calvinism. Just a quick two-sentence reminder/summary of what I use the generalizing term "Calvinism" for, in case the reader missed or forgot what I wrote in Chapter 1 about the doctrine: Essentially, it's the belief that we do not have free will, and that God predestined most of His human creation for eternal conscious punishment because He chose not to give them the ability to respond to the Holy Spirit. It's a sickening doctrine, and it took me into the depths of despair more than once before I dug into it and found the logical problems with it, and some great answers to it. Prior to my research in that area, because scholarly, "respectable" people who write lots of "Christian" books are teaching such things, and because there are a couple of Bible passages that on the surface seem to support the concept, for a time there, I was feeling forced to accept it, and the unmerciful God that it creates was more than I could bear.

I've found many people on Calvinist forums who have felt the same way, but who have yet to reject it, and now that I've educated myself more about it, I've often peppered them with questions that should bring their belief into serious question. Generally, the response I get is "I'm gonna to get back to you on that. I'll write a lengthy explanation that..." Well I'm still waiting for those responses. Bottom line: Selective mercy isn't merciful. I'm just gonna say it. And if I'm wrong, then I'll answer to God for it one day. But I'll never fathom how some can believe God is merciful when they also believe that He brings us all into existence as sinners, none of us able to ask for life or existence, then sets a requirement of faith in Him for salvation from judgment for our sin, but only gives the ability to respond by faith to the relative few. That's quite monstrous to ask the impossible, and then when unavoidable failure happens, to then punish with the most detrimental of punishments — to suffer consciously, not for a billion years only, but for timeless eternity.

Thankfully, there are wonderful scriptural defenses against Calvinism, and other ways to comprehend its proof texts, and we only touched on a few of those back in Chapter 1. But Ferwerda, it seems, was never able to get beyond some of the concepts that comprise the Calvinist doctrine. She seems to scoff at those who believe we have free will to choose for or against God. So in turn, she just dumps the "eternal" part of judgment, and in that way, finds a merciful God.

Ferwerda, in defending the idea that we have nothing to do with initiating our salvation goes to the exodus from Egypt, and God stating that He would bring them out. She points out that they had absolutely nothing to do with this, and believes this is a picture of all of us having nothing to do with our "rescue."[54] There's some problems with this. First, the Bible states clearly in

Exodus 3:7 that the people who had become enslaved in Egypt were crying out to God for deliverance. So they were certainly seeing their need, and calling out to the only One who could do anything about it.

But secondly, although God brought them all out, most of them ultimately proved to be faithless, and perished in the desert. And then, when you take in this last fact, you see that more likely this symbolizes what those of us who believe in free will would claim, which is that God of course makes the first move in deliverance. None could be saved if first He had not offered Christ's sacrifice to us, and secondly if He did not endow us all with a measure of faith to be able to believe in Him. But then we can exercise this God-given faith toward God, or put our hope in other things such as our own "goodness" or the pursuit of the riches of this life, etc. And the exodus and later results are a perfect picture of this. God heard their cry and saw their need, and made the first saving move. But He required faith and trust to enter into the Promised Land, and ultimately most forfeited it, just as Jesus stated of all mankind, that "many" would go down the broad road that leads to destruction, and that "few" would take the narrow path that leads to life.

Free Will

Ferwerda seems to mock those who believe in free will. And her method is to imply those who think we have the free will to make a decision for the one true God, must also believe we have free will over every aspect of our lives. Clearly we don't. There are multiple forces, good and evil, that are constantly infringing on our will – not to mention multiple places in Scripture that indicate that God steps in whenever He so chooses, to direct humanity. And yes...he even hardens some people toward what would otherwise appear to be His will that they do or believe. But we already noted that this only seems to happen in cases where the person or people group has already rejected Him. But believing we have the free will to make a faith decision for or against the Lord, is different from believing that God is hands-off or that we have perfect control over all aspects of our lives.

God clearly uses those who are unrighteous for His purposes, just as He uses those who do believe, trust, and hope in Him for His purposes as well. But none of this interferes with my belief that God is intentionally building a family of faith, and that the members of this family become members by their own free will. I'm not denying obvious Scriptures that indicate that no one seeks after God in the natural and that it is only by divine intervention that *anyone* seeks after Him. But we do this with the faith that He has granted us. He draws all men. Some will respond and some won't. It likewise doesn't infringe on His sovereignty for us to have free will because He has sovereignly determined to give us the ability to reject or accept Him. And by His omniscience, His foreknowledge of every single future human decision, He can, and does, play all of that into His own moves. And His purposes cannot be thwarted because His purpose is to save those who will by faith receive Him. If that's one person, or one billion people, His purpose is fulfilled.

> We're not "blood relatives" until we've put ourselves under the blood of Christ. All people are not God's children.

In Ferwerda's version of Universalism, she seems to accept the Calvinistic position of Sovereign Election, but then rejects the idea that those not elected in this first life will actually be lost, rather seeing them needing further correction in the Lake of Fire which she believes is figurative for a purifying learning process.[55]

As I've done in most every other chapter in this book, I've pulled much of the original material out for the sake of space. There's certainly much more that can be said in addressing the issues within Universalism. But I hope this at least demonstrated some of the weaknesses of the universalist doctrine that all humanity will one day be saved. This idea is a serious hindrance to spreading the gospel of Christ, with an accompanying warning of potential judgment.

CHAPTER 9

The Broad Road to Traditionalism

Humans are fallible. I don't need to look any further than my own life to know this beyond any doubt. I've been around the spiritual block in my journey back to faith in Christ after briefly detouring as far off the path as atheism and new age beliefs in my 20s. And even with my feet back firm on the foundation which is Jesus Christ, I've had my own thinking challenged in several areas of doctrine as a believer, and have been forced to alter my views to where the most evidence points. Because this is the case, when I began discovering and leaning heavily toward a non-traditional view of final judgment, I went out of my way to make sure I had heard everything the traditional side had to say on the matter. Maybe I had missed something. So I've read several books written to promote the traditional view of Hell.

Numerous Christian authors and pastors will make a few comments about judgment in their various works, reinforcing their belief in eternal conscious torment. But only a few have gone out of their way to write full books addressing the matter and defending the traditional position. In our modern time, one man, Robert Peterson, has been the most prolific writer to take a stand for tradition, authoring or co-authoring several books and numerous articles on the topic. We already met him back in Chapter 4 where we examined the ten verses of Scripture he believed were the foundation for the traditional position. In this chapter we'll take a look at his other main line of defense — the long list of human writers and thinkers who fill the echo chamber of the traditional position. The pull of the pack is quite strong, and there's a tendency to let tradition be more influential than it should. The apostle Paul and Jesus both warned against falling into the traditions of men. Nevertheless, when some of the most verbal and published defenders of the traditional view of Hell begin their defense, they lean back into the arms of all the "big names" in the faith who have thought the same way they do, and this is the first "strength" of their arguments. If the defense of your theological position requires you to rely heavily on the writings of other humans' opinions *about* Scripture, rather than primarily on Scripture itself, that speaks volumes. Point to what Scripture says — not to everyone else in the world's statements about what Scripture says.

I've already mentioned one traditionalist book I read during my study. It was *Hell Under Fire,* co-authored by nine writers, including Robert Peterson, who was also one of the editors. It was difficult to push through because it was so light on serious biblical analysis, and loaded with attempts at philosophical reasoning that didn't line up with Scripture, and countless references either to statements made by the other authors of the book, or to other traditionalist writers and thinkers, from modern time or the distant past. I probably dog-eared the corners of half the pages and I marked it up like no other book I've ever read with notes on things I'd like to address. It was lacking in substance and filled with errors, and I couldn't help jotting down all the questions I'd ask these authors if they were sitting in front of me. My notes and comments on that book could fill another entire book.

In *Two Views of Hell* Robert Peterson divided his case for tradition into three parts, the first being History itself, notably placed before Scripture and Theology — and I don't mean Bible history. I mean a list of men who have lived since the Bible was penned and have shared their opinions about it. Peterson calls his argument from history "The Road to Traditionalism"[56] and gives excerpts from the writings of eleven different prominent Christians. He chose seven from church history: Tertullian, Augustine, Thomas Aquinas, Martin Luther, John Calvin,

Jonathan Edwards, and John Wesley, and four more modern thinkers or writers: Francis Pieper, Louis Berkhof, Lewis Sperry Chafer, and Millard Erickson. I agree with Peterson that all of these have had a large influence on the acceptance of the traditional view. Only, I think that's not necessarily a good thing. We'll take a brief look at them in the order Peterson gave them, which was the order of history itself.

Tertullian

Tertullian was a theologian who lived in the late second and early third centuries. Around the year A.D.208 he wrote *On the Resurrection of the Flesh,* and in his comments on Matthew 10:28 where Jesus speaks of the destruction of the body and soul in Gehenna, Peterson seems to believe Tertullian has found great evidence for eternal conscious suffering. The excerpt Peterson chose was the following:

> "If, therefore, any one shall violently suppose that the destruction of the soul and the flesh in hell amounts to a final annihilation of the two substances, and not to their penal treatment (as if they were to be consumed, not punished), let him recollect that the fire of hell is eternal – expressly announced as an everlasting penalty; and let him then admit that it is from this circumstance that this never-ending 'killing' is more formidable than a merely human murder, which is only temporal."[57]

I don't know why being consumed by fire at the hand of God isn't considered "penal treatment," when it could easily be considered the very highest form of penal treatment. Scripture says the wicked will consume away as smoke. Tertullian's statement implies that being consumed, having your very soul ended, isn't even a punishment. We've noted a number of times in this volume that for a penalty to be everlasting, this doesn't require the recipient to be conscious into eternity. In fact, the very stated penalty of death negates that they even *could* be conscious, yet it is an eternal and everlasting punishment because there is no return from the second death, the death of the soul. He then goes on to create new verbiage and concepts that aren't in the Bible, with "never-ending killing." Tertullian's choice to define eternal punishment as "never-ending killing" should have no effect on one whose interest is sticking to biblical concepts. But Peterson seems to find it valuable in defining his own view of judgment. I won't go on and on. His is a ridiculous statement, completely contrary to Scripture.

Augustine

Robert Peterson acknowledges Augustine's great influence on the Church,[58] and I would agree. It's true that his impact on the church has been monumental...unfortunately. This area of final judgment isn't the only one which Augustine has negatively influenced. After digging into some of his writings personally, I found a great deal of poor Scriptural logic, and I've been relieved to hear a number of modern pastors confess that Augustine's teachings led them astray as well. This let me know that it's not just me. Much of it is simply dark ages thinking. He was a product of his day and time to some degree. And Satan worked his way into our doctrines early on. And as he continues to into our own day, he often works through well-meaning people. I'm not calling Augustine a heretic. I'm just calling him wrong on certain matters. Back in Chapter 2 we made reference to his concept of the "spark of divinity" which he believes all humans possess — remember? ...that little piece of God that He surely wouldn't destroy, according to Michael Easley.

In *Two Views of Hell* Peterson focused on Augustine's analysis of Matthew 25 where "eternal fire" and "everlasting punishment" are mentioned. I won't rehash in detail everything already written about these in Chapter 4, but I'll give you the quote that Peterson used, and make a few comments on it. As it relates to Jesus saying the lost will go away to eternal punishment, and the righteous to everlasting life, here's Augustine's thoughts:

> "If both are 'eternal', it follows necessarily that either both are to be taken as long-lasting but finite, or both as endless and perpetual. The phrases 'eternal punishment' and 'eternal life'

are parallel and it would be absurd to use them in one and the
same sentence to mean: 'Eternal life will be infinite, while
eternal punishment will have an end.' Hence, because the
eternal life of the saints will be endless, the eternal punishment
also, for those condemned to it, will assuredly have no end."[59]

Augustine seems blinded to the idea that the punishment of a
death from which there is no return, the loss of one's soul and
being for all eternity, is not only an eternal punishment, but
actually the highest form
of it. And he's blind to
this because he bought
into the unbiblical pagan
idea that all souls are
immortal. He actually
wrote specifically about
this, and even credited

> Augustine compared a Christian's
> claiming of the pagan doctrine of
> immortality to the Israelites plun-
> dering the gold of Egypt. But
> what was the first thing they did
> with that gold? Make a false idol.

Plato with the immortal soul concept which he believed
Christians should grasp onto. Consider the following quote
from Augustine:

"Moreover, if those who are called philosophers, and especially
the Platonists, have said (that which) is true and in harmony
with our faith, we are not only not to shrink from it, but to
claim it for our own use from those who have unlawful
possession of it. For, as the Egyptians had not only the idols
and heavy burdens which the people of Israel hated and fled
from, but also vessels and ornaments of gold and silver, and
garments, which the same people when going out of Egypt
appropriated to themselves, designing them for a better use,
not doing this on their own authority, but by the command of
God, the Egyptians themselves, in their ignorance, providing
them with things which they themselves were not making a
good use of..."[60] (parenthetical clarification mine)

Here, Augustine compares our taking of pagan concepts, if we
find them valuable to our doctrines, and using them for our own
"good" purposes, to when the Israelites were liberated from
Egypt and plundered the Egyptians' gold and silver. I find that
so interesting, because the very first thing the Israelites did with

all that plundered gold was form it into a false idol and worship it. Remember the golden calf incident? Now, of course later they did use the gold to make articles of worship that God commanded them. But it's notable that the first use was misuse. So actually, I think Augustine's comparison may be perfect, although it's not what he intended I'm sure. We've taken this pagan idea that all souls are immortal and with it, in a sense reshaped God into something He's not. If we're immortal and truly indestructible, then the Lake of Fire, instead of destroying the lost as Scripture predicts and promises throughout, would in fact torment them for all eternity, thereby making God into more of a monster who will only annex evil, than a merciful Creator who desires to one day rid the universe of all pain, suffering, and evil.

Thomas Aquinas

Peterson calls Aquinas the greatest Christian theologian and philosopher of the medieval period. The first quote used from Aquinas is "We set aside the error of those who say that the punishments of the wicked are to be ended at some time."[61]

We're going to run into this over and over in this chapter, and I apologize up front for the coming repetition. But there is a literal blindspot — a total inability among traditionalists to recognize that death is the punishment for faithlessness, and it will never end. So most certainly, conditionalists like myself also believe in an eternal punishment. We simply do not redefine it, but leave it as stated in Scripture. And no conditionalist claims this second death will ever end at some time. There is no return from this death. The Bible plainly says theirs is an everlasting punishment. But we are never told that the punishment for unrepentant humans is eternal conscious torment. If Aquinas was implying that the death of a soul is an end of punishment, which seems likely, he like so many others just couldn't comprehend the horror of standing judgment before God and losing one's life and the potential to live throughout all eternity.

The next Aquinas quote Peterson uses is:

"The duration of a punishment does not match the duration of the act of sin but of its stain; as long as this lasts a debt of punishment remains. The severity of the punishment matches the seriousness of the sin."[62]

This is an interesting theory, but unfortunately for the traditionalist who relies on church history over God's Word, the concept isn't found in the Bible. It's constructed from his imagination.

Peterson quotes Aquinas once more:

"Further, the magnitude of the punishment matches the magnitude of the sin. ...Now a sin that is against God is infinite; the higher the person against whom it is committed, the graver the sin — it is more criminal to strike a head of state than a private citizen — and God is of infinite greatness. Therefore an infinite punishment is deserved for a sin committed against him."[63]

So now we see where this particular defense of Traditionalism possibly started. Again, we have an interesting theory, but it cannot be supported with Scripture. What does it even mean to say that "a sin that is against God is infinite"? It sounds somewhat legitimate, but it has no scriptural basis. This is just a case of using some human philosophy to try to justify unending agony administered by God. God is sovereign and all-powerful. If He desired to keep the wicked alive so they would suffer for all eternity, He could certainly do it without Aquinas' attempt to justify it for Him. But with an undeniable track record of giving fair warning to those who are going in the wrong direction and describing the punishment for continuing in sin, the Lord would have made such a thing abundantly clear, first in ancient times through the writings that became the Old Testament, then in the New Testament. But the traditional doctrine of Hell is not clear at all. It's just not there.

In *Hell Under Fire*, Christopher Morgan did something similar to Aquinas with the "infinite God" idea. He implies that because all sin is against God who is infinite in perfection, punishment must go on for infinite time as well. Strangely he goes on from that, to encourage his reader then to not see Hell as a "horror," but rather to view it as accomplishing an ultimate justice in a "universe once marred by sin."[64] Once again, attempts through human reasoning to explain away something that we deep down know would be an unmerciful treatment of feeble mankind simply do not work. How does Morgan not see that if there is a place where billions of sinning souls are in conscious agony for all eternity, the universe would *still* be marred by sin? The problem of sin would not have been fixed – only annexed. The non-traditional, but more biblical position that one day the lost will be taken out of existence altogether actually rids the universe of sin.

Also in Christopher Morgan's section of *Hell Under Fire* was another of the least workable statements from the eternal conscious suffering side that I've ever heard, and really, it's another argument for the conditionalist position, as was the above. Sometimes while reading the Morgan section, I wondered "Which side of the issue is this guy on?" At one point Morgan implies that while an eternity of conscious punishment is the closest thing to true justice that's possible, even this will never fully satisfy God's wrath because there would never come a point when it ends.[65] To me, that's a great argument for the conditionalist side. Isn't that why it's far more likely that God does destroy the lost (as His Word says over and over)?

Doesn't Morgan's own realization that an unending punishment can never be called complete give evidence that this is very likely then NOT how the process of final judgment occurs? Otherwise, we're to believe that God would set up a system of punishment where not only are billions of souls who are beyond help and rehabilitation suffering needlessly for eternity, but His own requirements of justice won't even be satisfied? That's lumping an accusation of failure on top of an already outrageous accusation of unmerciful treatment. Can we just stop and let the Bible tell us what happens to those who reject God? And can we trust that Scripture has said that it's death, destruction, and non-entity which await those who have rejected their Maker's offer of hope and salvation? What's notable about that entire book, *Hell Under Fire*, is that it amounts to little more than a lot of men trying to give reasons why it's "okay" for God to punish people consciously for all eternity. Rather than going on and on trying to make their reader feel better about the idea of an eternal conscious hell through a variety of philosophical arguments, why not first demonstrate conclusively that their version of hell, or the concept of innate soul immortality are even in Scripture? Start there. Prove that. Then make me feel better about billions of souls writhing in agony for all eternity.

Martin Luther

I don't want to take anything away from Martin Luther's courageous stand against the Roman Catholic church which began the protestant reformation. He corrected a lot of what was wrong with organized Christianity of his own day. But any honest pastor who knows church history would tell you he didn't get it all corrected — nor should any one man be expected to. What he did was incredible and he should be respected for that. But if I'm judging his stance on eternal conscious suffering by his quotes which Peterson chose, it's obvious that he was still taking the broad road on that issue, although he thankfully veered off the broad road of so many evil beliefs and practices that had come into the Church of his day.

An immediate problem I notice with his teaching is that he claims that "the Day of Judgment will not last for a moment only but will stand throughout eternity and will thereafter never come to an end."[66] It's unprecedented to believe that "Day" refers to eternity when the Bible refers to a day of judgment. Another quote from Luther that Peterson uses is, "Not as though the ungodly see God and His appearance as the godly will see Him; but they will feel the power of His presence, which they will not be able to bear, and yet will be forced to bear."[67] There are a couple of problems with this. First of all, it contains some assumptions that aren't biblical, but instead are what Luther imagines Hell to be like. The idea that one will not be able to bear something, yet they will be forced to, is actually nonsense. Either one can bear something, or they can't.

Another place in Scripture asked something to the effect of "Who can dwell with a consuming fire?" Most likely that was a rhetorical question that meant, no one can. You cannot be consumed and yet dwell, and you cannot bear something that you cannot bear. The other real problem is claiming that God will be present in Hell for all eternity, in any form. The traditionalist tries their best to deal with this by claiming that they are referring to God's general presence but without any of the blessings associated with His presence. But where are they getting this? It's just "not Bible." Also, Revelation 14:10 says that they "will be tormented by fire and brimstone in the presence of the holy angels and the Lamb." Is this just the general presence of the holy angels and the Lamb, too? Surely not. This is the Lamb, Jesus, and the holy angels witnessing the punishment of those who accepted the mark of the beast. And it's just not reasonable to assume that this is what they'll be doing throughout eternity.

John Calvin

John Calvin lived in the 1500s and did untold damage to our concept of a merciful God through his doctrinal positions which would later become known as Calvinism. I've touched on it a couple times in this book, and that's all I'll do here as well, but it implies that God not only foreknew who would and would not ultimately be saved, but that He even predetermined it.

The fallout from that has been far-reaching because as we noted in the introduction, the same people who follow the Calvinist line of thinking also believe in eternal conscious punishment, so you end up with a god (small 'g' intended) who brought billions into existence who would have no legitimate opportunity to be saved from the consequences of their sin nature, and those consequences are to suffer for all eternity. This is a monster of a god, and I'm sure Satan is proud of his confusing and distorting work through this man. But Robert Peterson apparently finds great value in Calvin's writings. As evidence that there will be no relief for the wicked, Peterson points to Calvin's statement: "What and how great is this, to be eternally and unceasingly besieged by him?"[68] (the "him" being God)   Please note that I too agree that the lost will not experience conscious relief. The time of judgment is going to be excruciating as they realize they've forfeited eternal life through faithlessness — and they will feel this torment for every moment that God allows them consciousness up until the time they are destroyed in the Lake of Fire. So while I agree there will not be a time of "relief," their suffering does come to an end, as their very soul comes to an end. But there's no excuse for statements that go far outside of Scripture such as implying the lost are "eternally and unceasingly besieged by him." This is what God's going to be involved in during eternity? Seriously? And He's going to do that without even being present? Amazing.   Well, here's a portion of another statement of Calvin's that Peterson highlights:

> "The perpetual duration of this death is proved from the fact that its opposite is the glory of Christ. This is eternal and has no end.   Hence the violent nature of that death will never cease"[69]

We've seen this line of poor logic before and we'll see it again. It's a total blindness to the eternal life Christ offers being the true opposite of eternal death. Life and death are contrasted throughout Scripture — NOT eternal life in bliss and eternal life in torment as the new and improved definition of "death" would offer us. And while I agree that the nature of the death of the lost will be violent in a sense, as they are cast into the lake of fire, this idea that the "violent" aspect of it cannot or will not cease is completely fictitious and foreign to Scripture. I've maintained throughout this book that the second death — the final death of the lost person's soul is in fact an "eternal punishment" because it's not something that can be undone. But this is all we can get out of Scripture unless we plug in our own ideas, or others' ideas.

Jonathan Edwards

Peterson jumps forward a couple centuries to Jonathan Edwards, who is famous for traveling throughout the colonies of the Eastern Seaboard in the 1700s with his message of "sinners in the hands of an angry God." The stories go that people often screamed and fainted when they heard his words from the pulpit. Scripture tells us that the fear of God is the beginning of wisdom (Psalm 111:10 and other places), and Jesus said not to fear man who can only kill the body, but to instead fear God who can destroy both body and soul in Gehenna (Matthew 10:28). We already noted that Jesus did *not* say to fear God who can or will torment a soul for all eternity, but who can destroy it. We also already looked at the word being translated as "destroyed" and noted it means "to fully destroy" and bring to nothing.

Clearly it's appropriate and necessary to have a healthy fear of the One who made us and can "un-make" us, if I can phrase it that way. But while fear may be the beginning of wisdom, love, not fear, is where the story begins. Fearing for your life and turning to the One who can determine its fate or duration is entirely sensible, but turning to Him out of fear only, without a balance of love for Him, because He first loved us and demonstrated an unimaginable love, is going nowhere good. In spite of this Peterson views Edwards as "America's greatest philosopher-theologian."[70] I haven't read a lot of Edwards' works. Maybe in the works he's not so famous for he expounds more on God's love. So I realize I may be in a poor position to judge his "theological abilities," but I'm so thankful for the day and age we live in, in terms of the preaching and teaching that's available to us now. Give me Jonathan Cahn, Steven Furtick, Perry Stone, Mark Batterson, Beth Moore, Mark Biltz, James MacDonald or probably forty others I could name from our own day for theology and scriptural clarity. And don't misunderstand — All of these I listed would probably disagree with me on the eternal suffering doctrine, and they each have very different styles, but they all dig in and open up God's Word and explain it. And while none of these preachers and teachers completely avoid the topic of judgment, it's not their primary focus.

They focus on loving God by knowing Him more, and that's accomplished by digging into and expounding on His Word — not beating people to oblivion with fear of an angry God who we're made to think would almost rather us burn for all eternity than live. I do realize that comparing preachers from the 1700s with those from our day isn't completely fair, but wow, am I thankful for how far Bible teaching has come and how much more we're always learning from God's Word. Peterson then quotes Edwards as saying,

> "the bodies of wicked men as well as their souls will be punished forever"[71]

And...

> "This doctrine is indeed awful and dreadful. It is dreadful to think of it, but yet 'tis what God the eternal God who made us and who has us soul and body in his hands has abundantly declared to us, so that so sure as God is true there will absolutely be no end to the misery of hell."[72]

I sure would be more convinced if Paul the apostle had said that...or better yet, Jesus. I'd believe it if they said it. For that matter, we take some of our doctrines from even questionable people in Scripture. Job's friends, while clearly in error in certain areas, are sometimes quoted and their doctrinal ideas adopted. Nebuchadnezzar, evil as he had been, after being humbled by God, later made statements we declare as doctrinal truth...and maybe we should. But in the Bible, we don't even have a peripheral character saying anything like "the misery of hell will have no end" — much less the Lord or one of His apostles. But we have "America's greatest theologian" telling us that. For most people unfortunately, that's enough. For me, I'm trusting Scripture, which paints a picture of a harsh, but merciful God, who doesn't play with sin, and who destroys His enemies, but who will not and would not see them tormented throughout eternity. They gave up life and gained death, and that death will not end. It is an eternal punishment, but conscious suffering ends.

John Wesley

Wesley lived in the 1700s and I've only ever heard positive things about his life and story. I don't relish being critical of him or most all of the people who I challenge on this doctrinal issue. And actually I won't much.   While I feel that most of the traditionalists who have molded and shaped this doctrine are missing the forest for the trees, my issue in this chapter is more with Peterson who seems to believe that well-known people simply re-expressing the doctrine adds validity to it. And in his section on Wesley, one of his statements really exemplifies this. He posed a question about how Hell should best be described, and then tells his reader that Wesley's answer appealed to a distinction that dates back to Augustine.[73] And that may be the problem right there: If he appealed to something that only goes back to Augustine, then he stopped about 400 years short of Scripture.   It doesn't matter what Augustine said if it doesn't match well to what can be validated in the Bible.

From there, Peterson seemed to be paraphrasing Wesley's thoughts instead of quoting him, so because I've chosen not to quote any printed copyrighted material in this book which isn't now in the public domain, I'm forced to refrain from sharing it, but can only summarize what I believe his message was. He indicates that it's Wesley's, and I suppose Augustine's, opinion that Hell involves a two-fold punishment — that of loss, and that of sense. The punishment of loss is that of being removed from God's good presence, and the punishment of sense is the torment which he believes is indicated by the worm and fire images.

We addressed the worms and fire in Chapter 4, and found that these are not agents or methods of eternal torment. The idea of removal from God's good presence likely goes back to the 2 Thessalonians 1:5-10 passage we looked at where the wicked are destroyed *apo* the presence of God, with *apo* more clearly taking its "because of" meaning in this case rather than its potential "away from" meaning (both are offered as ways to interpret this Greek word in the *Strong's* concordance).   Or the reference could be going all the way back to the supposed banishment of Adam and Eve from God's presence when they were made to leave the garden. And while they were in fact banished from the Garden (and we saw exactly why they were), we noted that they were given a little going away present, the gift of a covering that signified their reservation to eternal life, and God was certainly with them and countless others, outside of the garden. But we don't know what Wesley based his ideas on and can only speculate because Peterson didn't include that information, if it exists. Peterson closes his section on John Wesley with this Wesley quote:

> "...I believe that, as the unjust shall after their resurrection be tormented in hell forever, so the just shall enjoy inconceivable happiness in the presence of God to all eternity."[74]

Maybe elsewhere Wesley has given an explanation of his view and position, but Peterson didn't offer it if that's the case. Because John Wesley is a "big name" in the Christian world, I suppose we should just trust his judgment on this issue. At least that's what I take away from Peterson giving us so many of these quotes where the traditional view is re-stated by someone the believing community respects, but without Scriptural evidence or a demonstrated logical process for why they believe as they do.

Francis Pieper

Peterson next jumps forward to the 19th and 20th centuries and Francis Pieper. After offering us Pieper's "pedigree papers" as evidence of the value of his thoughts on Scriptural matters, Peterson quotes Pieper as saying:

> "But all objections (to everlasting punishment) are based on the false principle that it is proper and reasonable to make our human sentiments and judgments the measure of God's essence and activity."[75]

I'm sorry for being so repetitive with the following, but it's necessary because every argument from the traditionalist seems to go here. I'm not arguing, nor is any other conditionalist, that

290 The Broad Road to Traditionalism

there isn't an everlasting punishment for the sin of faithlessness. The lost being subjected to an eternal punishment is a biblical fact. But the traditionalist refuses to accept that a death from which there is no return is in fact that punishment, no matter how many times Scripture stated it. In the quote, Pieper implies that it is human sentiment and human judgments that are informing our non-traditional doctrine that God is far more merciful than tradition would tell us. I would say the opposite is true. Within Christianity, it is the great majority, in their unmerciful human sentiments, who deny the mercy God will extend the lost by ending their torment, and who believe something more cruel is the only thing that will atone for their sin. We are far less merciful than God. I think we saw this in statements like those Robert Jeffress made back in Chapter 5.

Louis Berkhof

I'll keep this one short and sweet, because there's nothing to say that I haven't already. Here again Peterson chooses someone else with a long theological pedigree, and then quotes their re-statement of the traditional view — again with no logical arguments...just statements. And I suppose we should just accept it.

Lewis Sperry Chafer

Here we have the first president of the often admired Dallas Theological Seminary. Peterson chose the following quote from Chafer:

> "It (eternal suffering)...is as clearly set forth in the Scriptures as it is possible for language to serve in the expression of ideas."[76] (parenthetical statement added)

The ellipses are Peterson's, so I don't actually know what was left out of that quote. I'm quoting a quote, so I'm limited. But if this is accurately portraying everything Chafer meant in this statement, this may be the most out of place assertion I've heard in all the arguments in favor of the traditional position. A lot can be said on the traditionalist side of the court. There are certainly verses, as we saw, that can be stretched into evidence for the traditional idea of eternal suffering. But one thing that cannot be truthfully stated is that the idea of eternal conscious suffering is stated in Scripture as clearly as language allows. Really? Here's just one very clear way it could have been stated: 'If anyone chooses to reject God's offer of salvation through His Son Jesus Christ, the punishment for such will not be to merely suffer death or the loss of your soul and being, but to be forever in conscious torment, forever regretting your decision, throughout all eternity.' Now, to be clear, I just made that up. And there's countless other ways the same could have been clearly expressed by any of God's authors of Scripture. But you won't find any clear statement like that anywhere in Scripture, and that's one of my arguments against the whole idea.   If eternal suffering, rather than death, was in fact the punishment for faithless unbelief, then Scripture certainly failed to state this as clearly as language allows. But I don't believe Scripture, or God, failed us in any way. It is traditional misinterpretation which is failing us.

Millard Erickson

I've never even heard of this person, but maybe it's appropriate Peterson concluded the way he did because it truly exemplifies what I've been trying to say — that we put more stock in man than in God's word. Perhaps Millard Erickson has argued convincingly against the idea that souls are ultimately annihilated, but if he has, Peterson failed to include it. In fact, he included no process of logic at all that Erickson conducted to come to his conclusions. All Peterson did was re-state Millard Erickson's traditional broad-road opinion that "the doctrine of everlasting punishment...is clearly taught in Scripture."[77] Is it? Where? Peterson made reference to Millard's statement that annihilation contradicts the teaching of the Bible. Does it? Why do you think so? What makes you come to that conclusion? The strongest argument Peterson offers for Erickson's position is that he summarized that Isaiah 66:24 and Mark 9:43-48 "make it clear that the punishment is unending." Again, I would ask — In what way? We already looked at those passages and found a more clear way to view them that doesn't violate any themes in Scripture and yet also doesn't indicate eternal conscious suffering. But Peterson, while grabbing another person from history who he believes is foundational in Christianity as a witness to Scripture's statement on eternal suffering, offered zero evidence. Again, perhaps Erickson has given excellent statements as to why he comes to the conclusions he does, but if so, wouldn't that be what Peterson would include ...in a book which is intended to sway people to maintain or adopt the traditional position on eternal suffering in Hell?

This is really the core of the problem. We want to feel the support of those around us. We don't want to rock the boat. We typically like to move with the herd, so we won't get run over. And all of that is understandable. I've struggled with the same feelings the entire time this book has been a concept. But in the end, truth is truth, Scripture is Scripture, and God is Merciful.

Wrapping Up

Did we make the case for a more merciful God? Or will those who failed to find and accept salvation somehow attain immortality, subvert the perishing that is predicted for them, and remain alive for all eternity in conscious suffering?

There's certainly much more that can be said on the topic, and this isn't the only book in town that addresses this issue. Others have come at it from their own angles and points of view, but I hope I've offered something new to the conversation — other ways to consider the debate, and I certainly hope you've seen that there are many flaws in the traditional view of eternal conscious suffering and at the very least have been given a lot to think about. Many of us who are passionate about a particular topic wish we could just transplant our comprehension of a subject into everyone's head. But it doesn't work that way. So we plead our case however we find to do it, and I've attempted to do it in book form, which was made very difficult, because I'm not a writer, and don't claim to be one. And that fact may have been evident throughout. And if I were a writer by trade, this might have been finished a decade or more ago.

Instead it's been a long battle to get this information out. I've battled my own mind, my schedule and obligations and the challenges of prioritizing. I've battled fear — of offending people, of being called a blasphemer or a heretic, and if I'm honest, the fear of being wrong. Even in the face of all the evidence for the view of judgment I've put forward, it's incredibly difficult to challenge tradition and challenge individuals you respect. And for me personally it was difficult to believe that I'd found truth on such an important doctrinal matter, when so many more formally educated Christians seem to be upholding something completely different. This, more than anything I've ever found in Scripture, has at times caused me to doubt my conclusions. I'm as much a victim of tradition as anyone else — but I'm recovering from it. In the end, Scripture seems to speak for itself, and I hope I've pointed the way through it accurately on this topic.

Unfortunately, I can't change anyone else's mind, but can only put the evidence in front of them. If the reader wants to believe we're all immortal beings, beginning with Adam and Eve, even though they didn't do the one thing Scripture said could make them go on living forever, go ahead. If a traditionalist insists on rejecting the plain language of destruction and non-entity that awaits those who deny God's salvation, all I can do is point you to the verses that seem to prove it — Do with them what you will. When studying judgment passages, if the reader wants to believe that worms, which in any other instance would be seen as devouring and consuming, are instead the "worms of consciousness" that will forever torment their conscious victim, that's your prerogative.

If Scripture blatantly telling us the complete destruction, obliteration, and extinction of Sodom and Gomorrah was a foreshadowing type of what will happen to all the un-Godly one day is just not enough for you, that's your choice to believe as you wish. If we can find multiple places where *eternal* and *everlasting* clearly mean "permanent in effect" rather than "perpetually in process," and apply that understanding to final judgment (and we did), and if the reader wants to deny this, I've done all I can. If we are given the phrase "eternal fire" right there in Scripture, and then even shown specifically that what it did was forever destroy something, NOT burn something for timeless eternity, and if you want to reject the clarity Scripture offers, so be it. If the reader insists on believing a lot of created concepts about what was happening in the Garden of Eden, rather than just trust the narrative the Bible gives us, who am I to stop you?

Well, I won't go on. I'm not going to re-hash every argument I've made. But to me, the evidence is overwhelming, and the only strength I find in the traditional position on eternal conscious suffering is tradition itself. There's a multitude of people who will assure you you're correct if that's the doctrine you want to hold onto. And if people want to put more trust in the opinions and traditions of man than in the plain words of Scripture, again, that's their choice. But we're going to have to answer one day for what we did with God's Word. I don't want to hear something like: "You told people what?!? ...that I was going to allow most of my creation to suffer intensely in fire for all eternity? Why would you do that? I never said that."

Now maybe my imagination is getting away with me in picturing that conversation. It's been said that all of our doctrinal issues and mistakes are going to be fixed in a moment and of no consequence at that point. Maybe the glory of God overwhelms all of what may seem so important now, and our doctrinal errors won't even be addressed after this life. On the other hand, Scripture says we'll answer for the things done in the body. And much of the New Testament was a warning about false doctrine and advising to try to right it and avoid it. So I don't know. But why take a chance? Go with the bulk of biblical evidence in matters of doctrinal controversy. And on this topic of final judgment, the overwhelming evidence appears to be on the non-traditional side.

We addressed how foreshadowing is a major method of God communicating to mankind. The Bible is filled with precursor events that are a "picture" of something that happens on a greater scale at a later time. We also looked at the biblical evidence that there's a distinction between our physical body and our immaterial soul. It seems logical then to view our living, yet aging dying bodies as a picture or object lesson of what's happening at the soul level. Our soul is alive, yet headed toward death, just as our body is. That's the miracle of the offer of salvation that would save us from that soul death — that second death. And just as a foreshadowing event in Scripture is only a small scale sample of the more important event it predicts, so would the death event of our souls be so very much more tragic than the death of our body. But nothing about this object lesson God has given us in our own body gives any hint that the death of the soul is somehow something that could go on experientially for all eternity, as tradition has told us — just the opposite.

While one reason for writing this book was to bring relief to any believer in Christ who was struggling with the ramifications of the traditional view of eternal suffering, it was also my hope that this book would find the hands of those who have not yet gone to Christ for salvation - especially if it was the traditional doctrine of Hell that in any way held them back from embracing the Lord. If that's you, I don't know how much time you have left to make that decision. It's a great time to get to know the God of the Bible, and put all your trust and hope in the forgiveness He provided through Jesus's death on the cross. There's no hope anywhere else. I'm wrapping up this book in mid-2018. I don't know what year you're reading it in. Perhaps world events have settled down, and a great many years or decades have passed since this book was written. But from where I'm sitting right now, I'm looking around at a world that seems to be right in the middle of the birth pang events that Jesus prophesied would happen shortly before the end of this current age: the Church Age. Particular political alignments of nations that were prophesied hundreds of years ago in Scripture seem to be occurring now. And there have been so many significant prophetic dates related to the nation of Israel in this year of 2018.

There are world leaders that seem determined to create a peace deal in the Middle East in the very near future, and while the idea of reaching peace is a noble pursuit, Scripture predicts no legitimate or lasting peace in that area until the Lord is back on earth. To the contrary, we're told that when "peace and security" are declared, sudden destruction will happen. If you keep up with current events, you may have heard the "peace and security" mantra which is all over the place lately.

The earth itself is going crazy lately and the number and intensity of earthquakes, water displacement events, sink holes, flooding, and other strange phenomena of "biblical proportion" is off the charts. There are strange and unusual things happening in our skies and outer space as well lately. Pilots, who have at times been under orders of silence, are now allowed to talk about unexplainable things they're seeing, and open talk of this has come to mainstream news in 2017 and 2018. All of these sorts of things were prophesied as end times events. And there's deception in the political world on a scale which most people who think their big problem is the "right" or the "left" couldn't even imagine. What looks good often isn't, and that's all I'll say on that topic in this book. And this was Jesus's first warning in Matthew 24 when asked what the signs of the end of the age would be: Don't be deceived. No one knows when the end will be, but time may be very short.

But even if it's not... Let's say this is all just a bump in the prophetic road and it only "looks like" end times events are upon us, and maybe there's still centuries out in front of us before the Lord returns. Time is still short. No one knows when it's their last day in this life. And even if you get a really long life, it goes by really quick, I'm noticing. I'm finishing this up around my 48th birthday. I still feel like I was a kid just yesterday (and I asked for a skateboard for my birthday this year, if that tells you anything).

Time flies, and putting a lot of stock in the things of this world is a waste. I'm not discouraging anyone from pursuing their passions or dreams. I have kids of my own, and would never tell them to stop moving forward, just because it looks like we may be nearing the tip end of this age. Live your life. Go for it. Work out, stay in shape, go to school, get your degree, go to work, build, plan, do, and all that good stuff. We're supposed to take care of what we have while we have it, and God didn't put us here to just sit, waste away, and watch the clock, even the prophetic clock. We occupy until the Lord returns. Stay excited about your life and future. But don't be blind to the signs of the times either.

Or if you're not excited about your life, then get excited about Jesus coming back because even if it isn't as close as it seems some days, it's still going to happen. That's what all history is pointing toward. But ultimately, don't trade anything this life offers you for your soul. Jesus asked "What does it profit a man to gain the whole world, and lose his soul?" It doesn't. It profits zero. The Lord made you, lived for you, died for you, and wants to know you intimately for all eternity. And I hope you'll make the decision of faith to follow Him from here on out. And if the traditional doctrine that God is going to burn people for all eternity was causing you any hesitation in faith, for whatever reason, it's my hope that this book has settled your mind on that issue. God does not look the other way when we sin, and it's only by placing our faith and hope in Him that we can gain eternal life. He will regretfully destroy all who offend in the matter of faithlessness. But He will not torment souls throughout eternity, and I hope this truth has helped draw you a little closer to the One who has always loved you and has always been calling you home.

Are you at the other extreme? Have you denied all the language of judgment in Scripture and decided that God is just going to save everyone eventually? I hope this book has helped you see that while God is merciful in judgment, He nevertheless still judges, and it's only by faith in Him that we can go on living forever. There's some middle ground in between "God saves everyone" and "Billions will be in torment for all eternity," and if it was the latter idea that made you run to the former, I hope these pages have brought clarity to the matter.

To those whose hope was already in Christ, and who reluctantly held the traditional position on Hell because you just didn't realize there was a biblical alternative way to view judgment, I hope the evidence that tradition gave us a false doctrine to begin with has brought you the same relief it brought me when I first began discovering it. And I hope it helps draw you even closer to the God who loves you. I also hope you will continue in your own study on this matter because I have certainly not exhausted the subject.

Even in the face of all the evidence we've seen, staunch traditionalists will still insist I'm wrong and that I'm misunderstanding many concepts. So be it. I can only offer what I've personally found when I prayed for answers, dug in and studied, and I found a more merciful God.

References

Archer, Clint. *A Visitor's Guide to Hell*. New York: Sterling Ethos, 2014.

Bell, Rob. *Love Wins: A Book About Heaven, Hell, and the Fate of Every Person That Ever Lived*. New York: HarperOne, 2011.

Craig, William Lane. *Let My People Think*. n.d. radio. <https://www.oneplace.com/ministries/let-my-people-think/>.

Easley, Michael. *Moody Presents*. n.d. radio. ca.2007. <https://www.moodyradio.org/programs/moody-presents/>.

Ferwerda, Julie A. *Raising Hell: Christianity's Most Controversial Doctrine Put Under Fire*. Kindle. Vagabond Group, 2011.

Gill, John. *Exposition of the Entire Bible*. 1748-1763, 1809.

Graham, Jack. *Powerpoint*. n.d. radio. <https://www.oneplace.com/ministries/powerpoint/>.

Jeffress, Robert. *Pathway To Victory*. n.d. <https://www.oneplace.com/ministries/pathway-to-victory/>.

Jeremiah, David. *Turning Point*. rebroadcast on OnePlace.com, n.d. <https://www.oneplace.com/ministries/turning-point/>.

Joe Versus the Volcano. Dir. John Patrick Shanley. 1990.

MacArthur, John. *Grace To You*. n.d. <https://www.oneplace.com/ministries/grace-to-you/>.

Merriam-Webster. n.d. <https://www.merriam-webster.com/>.

Moore, Beth. "Awaken Now Conference." 2013.

Morgan, Christopher W. and Robert A. Peterson. *Hell under Fire*. Grand Rapids: Zondervan, 2004.

Moulton, James Hope and George Milligan. *The Vocabulary of the Greek New Testament*. Grand Rapids: The Vocabulary of the Greek New Testament, 1930;1974.

Peterson, Robert A and Edward William Fudge. *Two Views of Hell*. Madison: InterVarsity Press, 2000.

Sidewalk Prophets. "Keep Making Me." 2012.

St. Augustine of Hippo. *On Christian Doctrine*. Vol. Book II. 397.

Strong, James. *The New Strong's Exhaustive Concordance of the Bible*. Nashville: Thomas Nelson Publishers, 1990.

Thayer, Joseph H. *Thayer's Greek-English Lexicon of the New Testament*. Peabody: Hendrickson Publishers, Inc., 2005.

The Berean Call Staff. March 2002. <https://www.thebereancall.org/content/march-2002-q-and-a-2>.

The New English Bible with Apocrypha. Oxford University Press Cambridge University Press, 1961;1970.

Tyndale, William. *An Answer to Sir Thomas More's Dialogue*. Vol. Parker's 1850 reprint bk.4. ca.1530.

End Notes References

[1] This quote is from Kay Arthur's *Precepts for Life* program that is rebroadcast on One-Place.com. I believe it to be from the May 18th 2007 program, but I'm not 100% sure of that. However, I stand behind it being an accurate word-for-word quote, regardless of the exact date

[2] From Jack Graham's *Powerpoint* program rebroadcast on OnePlace.com on March 21, 2014

[3] From David Jeremiah's *Turning Point* program ca.2014 which is rebroadcast on One-Place.com. I regret that I don't have more precise date information, but I stand behind it being an accurate quote of David Jeremiah's

[4] *John Gill's Exposition of the Entire Bible* published 1748-1763, 1809 Public Domain

[5] From *Moody Presents*, Michael Easley, ca.2007 radio broadcast. I regret that I don't have more accurate date information of this broadcast, but I stand behind the accuracy of the quote

[6] Ibid.

[7] From John Macarthur's *Grace to You* radio program which was rebroadcast on One-Place.com ca.2009. I regret that I don't have more accurate date information, and I may even have the year incorrect, but I stand behind the accuracy of the quote

[8] Ibid.

[9] Ibid.

[10] Ibid.

[11] Ibid.

[12] Ibid.

[13] Ibid.

[14] Ibid.

[15] Ibid.

[16] Ibid.

[17] Ibid.

[18] Ibid.

[19] Ibid.

[20] Ibid.

[21] Robert Peterson *Two Views of Hell* 153

[22] *Crossway English Standard Version* compact thinline edition, 2003, p.989

[23] Robert Peterson *Two Views of Hell*,157

[24] Peterson *Two Views of Hell* 158

[25] *John Gill's Exposition of the Entire Bible.* Published 1748-1763, 1809. Public Domain

[26] From Robert Jeffress's *Pathway to Victory* program which is rebroadcast on One-Place.com ca. 2009

[27] Robert Peterson *Two Views of Hell* 130

[28] I originally heard this quote on Ravi Zacharias's *Let My People Think* program that was rebroadcast on OnePlace.com ca. 2007. As I remember, it was something said during a question and answer period that Dr. Craig and Ravi Zacharias participated in at a college. I regret that I don't have more accurate date information for this reference, but I stand by the accuracy of the quote itself.

[29] Robert Jeffress *Pathway to Victory* radio program rebroadcast on OnePlace.com ca.2009 I regret that I don't have more accurate date information, but I stand behind the accuracy of the quote.

[30] Ibid.

[31] Archer *A Visitor's Guide to Hell* 42

[32] Ferguson *Hell Under Fire* 226

[33] *Joe Versus the Volcano* 1990

[34] From *Grace to You*, John MacArthur's radio program ca.2010. I regret that I cannot offer the exact date of the broadcast. That information was lost over the years I've been studying this and collecting quotes, but I stand behind the accuracy of the quote.

[35] Ibid.

[36] Ibid.

[37] Beth More *Awaken Now Conference.* 2013.

[38] The Berean Call staff https://www.thebereancall.org/content/march-2002-q-and-a-2

[39] Ibid.

[40] Ibid.

[41] Ibid.

[42] Ibid.

[43] https://www.merriam-webster.com/dictionary/immortality

[44] William Tyndale, *An Answer to Sir Thomas More's Dialogue* (Parker's 1850 reprint), bk. 4, ch. 4, pp. 180, 181

[45] David Jeremiah, February 5th 2014 broadcast of *Turning Point*

[46] Ibid.

[47] William Tyndale, *An Answer to Sir Thomas More's Dialogue* (Parker's 1850 reprint), bk. 4, ch. 4, pp. 180, 181

[48] Ferwerda, *Raising Hell*, 14

[49] Ibid., p.30

[50] Ibid., p.74

[51] Ibid., p.35

[52] Ibid., p.28

[53] Ibid., p.73

[54] Ibid., p.208

[55] Ibid., p.64

[56] Peterson, *Two Views of Hell*, 117

[57] Peterson, *Two Views of Hell*, 119, ref. Tertullian, *On the Resurrection of the Flesh*, in *The Ante-Nicene Fathers*, ed. Alexander Roberts and James Donaldson, 10 vols. (Grand Rapids, Mih.: Eerdmans, 1973), 3:570.

[58] Peterson, *Two Views of Hell*, 119.

[59] Peterson, *Two Views of Hell*, 120, ref. Augustine *The City of God* (trans. Bettenson) 21.23

[60] St. Augustine, *On Christian Doctrine*, Book II, 40.60

[61] Peterson, *Two Views of Hell*, 121, ref. Thomas Aquinas *Summa contra Gentiles* (trans. Bourke) 144.8.

[62] Peterson, *Two Views of Hell*, 121, ref. Thomas Aquinas *Summa Theologine* (Blackfriars ed.) 1a2ae.87.5.

[63] Ibid., 1a2ae.87.4.

[64] Morgan, *Hell Under Fire*, 210

[65] Ibid., 212

[66] Peterson, *Two Views of Hell*, 122, ref. Ewald M. Plass, *What Luther Says*, 3 vols. (St. Louis: Concordia, 1959), 2:627.

[67] Ibid., 2:626-27.

[68] Peterson, *Two Views of Hell*, 123, ref. John Calvin *Institutes of the Christian Religion* (trans. Battles) 3.25.12.

[69] Peterson, *Two Views of Hell*, 123, ref. John Calvin, *The Epistles of Paul the Apostle to the Romans and to the Thessalonians*, Calvin's Commentaries, ed. D.W. Torrance and T.F. Torrance, trans. R. Mackenzie (Grand Rapids, Mich.: Eerdmans, 1961),p.392.

[70] Robert Peterson *Two Views of Hell* 123

[71] Peterson *Two Views of Hell*, 123, ref John H. Gerstner, *Jonathan Edwards on Heaven and Hell* (Grand Rapids, Mich.: Baker, 1980) 55

[72] Peterson *Two Views of Hell*, 123-4, ref John H. Gerstner, *Jonathan Edwards on Heaven and Hell* (Grand Rapids, Mich.: Baker, 1980) 74

[73] Peterson, *Two Views of Hell*, 124

[74] Peterson, *Two Views of Hell*, 125 ref. John Wesley, "Letter to a Roman Catholic," cited in Oden, *John Wesley's Scriptural Christianity*, p. 357 n. 102.

[75] Peterson *Two Views of Hell* 125 ref. Francis Pieper, *Christian Dogmatics*, trans. J.t. Mueller (St. Louis: Concordia, 1953), 3:545.
[76] Peterson *Two Views of Hell* 126 ref. Lewis Sperry Chafer, *Systematic Theology*, 8 vols. (Dallas: Dallas Seminary Press, 1948), 4:430.
[77] Peterson *Two Views of Hell* 126

ABOUT THE AUTHOR

Scott McAliley has served as a deacon, elder, Sunday School teacher, and regular Sunday morning musician at various times over the course of his Christian life. He boasts no theological degrees, and makes no apologies for the missing letters behind his name, believing Scripture, and its honest in-depth study to be sufficient for coming to sound doctrinal conclusions. Born into the mainstream Christian church, and part of it for almost five decades now, he loves the Church more than ever, but considers himself a "recovering traditionalist," as it regards the doctrine of final judgment. After years of being taught concepts about God that didn't seem to line up with His merciful nature, and only halfheartedly believing these doctrines, he delved into a study to find out for himself. In this volume he hopes to reveal Biblical truths rarely pursued, to any who are willing to admit that perhaps they've accepted and held onto some old traditions in error. In so doing, it's his hope that the reader will come to know God more intimately, and therefore love Him more than ever.

Printed in Great Britain
by Amazon

48565579R00180